THREE REMARKABLE WOMEN

Works by Harold Balyoz:

Signs of Christ
Three Remarkable Women

THREE REMARKABLE WOMEN

by

HAROLD BALYOZ

ALTAI PUBLISHERS
P.O. Box 1972
Flagstaff, Arizona 86002

Acknowledgements

The following people have my undying gratitude for their enthusiastic assistance, advice, and labor in producing this book:

Susan Howell for her beautiful cover composition,

Paul Albert Balyoz for his expert typography,

Shirley Morgan Balyoz and William Brewster Balyoz for their careful proofreading and editing,

Thomas Paul Withey for his very able computer assistance and positive support throughout this whole project, and

Cynthia Tait for her topflight typing skills, helpful comments, and enthusiasm for this work from the very beginning.

Contents

Illustrations

Introduction

"There is no religion higher than truth"—H.P.B.

The development of Western science in the nineteenth and twentieth centuries had nearly overshadowed the existence of the far older, more profound and complete Eastern, or spiritual, science until the latter was brought to the attention of the west by three remarkable women.

This Eastern science includes philosophy, religion, history, psychology, practical rules for living, and many other things because it does not limit itself to the materialistic science we are used to thinking of as the only science. It is concerned basically with uncovering the laws of nature and learning how to live in harmony with these laws. It deals with future visions because it knows the past and can see the glorious future ahead for mankind, a future that everyone can have if mankind strives to reach that future. It is a future that sees the human race, man and women both, as divinely originated beings heading again to their former home of divinity. This teaching says that God did not make a robot or a slave and call it "Man". It says man is destined to be a co-worker in the divine plan and will be if he only works hard to do it. Christ told us this when he said, "The least of you will do greater miracles than you see here." And what are miracles? They are nothing more than the understanding and utilizing of the higher laws of nature, of God, to speed up the evolution of man and of all nature back to our Father's home according to His plan.

At no time in the eighteen million year history of the evolution of man on this planet was it possible previously for this teaching to be given out to more than a very few people at one time. The lifting of the veil of secrecy from this very advanced teaching and the response to it by humanity is due to the enormous increase in human consciousness in the last several hundred years. And who has given us this teaching and is still doing so? It is none other than the Christ, the head of the Spiritual Hierarchy of the Masters of Wisdom![1] The name Christ is the name of the office, the Head of the Spiritual Hierarchy. Under His guidance are His disciples, the Masters of Wisdom, the Lords of Compassion, and They include all the avatars who founded all of our great religions. The Christ is not just the Christ of Christians, but the Head of all departments of life: politics, education, philosophy, art, science, religion and economics. Under His jurisdiction, His disciples, the various Masters of Wisdom, work in all countries, with people of all religions in all political and economic areas in a manner suitable to the peoples needs and level of understanding.[2] The time is growing closer when it will be revealed that all of our various religious beliefs came from one source and all the great religious teachers: Jesus, Buddha, Moses, Krishna, Hermes, Zoroaster, Mohammed, etc., all came from this same one source. They were the ones who gave us the preliminary training to enable us eventually to live together harmoniously under one God, with one universal religion and with equal rights, equal opportunities for spiritual growth and in freedom and peace, with complete equality regardless of religious, racial or political beliefs or national and sexual differences. It will be possible to recognize the unity of divinity and at the same time accept all the different ways of worship and contact with that divine unity which the human race has developed over the ages and in different religions.

Since 1949 many millions the world over, whose ranks are rapidly growing, have been studying this teaching and attempting to penetrate into its essence, compare known scientific facts to it and to find in its principles the causal reasons for their own thoughts and subjective experiences in the spiritual

---

[1]The Masters of wisdom are called masters by their disciples and all who know them as a sign of the great respect they generate. A master is one who has mastered life, who has conquered the physical, emotional, and mental planes; i.e. the personality, and life no longer forces him to reincarnate. Masters have learned all their lessons; i.e. mastered the lower worlds, and now stand ready to help all who are ready to achieve their same high state.

[2]see: Signs of Christ by Harold Balyoz

realms. Their very real penetration into this realm has led to an ever-increasing grasp of the laws of our planet and solar system by people in both the East and the West.

It is interesting to note that the three great persons who have brought this teaching to our attention were all women. Why is this so? It is so because women, by their very nature, are more intuitive than men and the intuitional plane, being one step higher than the mental plane, is more in harmony with the higher laws of nature than the plane of mind.

It is clear that the wisdom they presented had a common purpose. This purpose was to end separation, create brotherhood in humanity, and help achieve the freedom necessary to pursue spiritual goals in order to learn the necessary techniques needed to communicate with the Higher Forces in the cosmos.

Each of these three remarkable women gave us facets of this great ocean of wisdom. Can we really compare them? No! As one great sage replied when he was asked which was the brightest star in the sky: "Who can say, we can only be enraptured by their radiance."

<u>Keynote</u>:

The Secret Doctrine teaches that in order to become a divine, fully conscious God—aye, even the highest—the Spiritual, Primeval Intelligences must pass through the human stage.

When we say human, this does not apply merely to our terrestrial humanity but to the mortals that inhabit any world, i.e. to those intelligences that have reached the appropriate equilibrium between matter and spirit, as we have now ... Each entity must have won for himself the right of becoming divine, through self-experience.

Chapter 1

Helene P. Blavatsky

Helene P. Blavatsky was born Helene Petrovna von Hahn on August 12, 1831 (new-style calendar), in Ekaterinoslav, now Dnepropetrovsk, Russia. Her father, Peter von Hahn, a captain in the horse artillery of the Russian army, was a direct descendent of Count von Rottenstern-Hahn of Mecklenburg, Germany, who had emigrated to Russia in the previous century.

Her mother, Helena Andreyevna von Hahn, was a highly regarded novelist. She wrote under the pen name of Zenaide R. or Zeneide R-Va and was called the George Sand of Russia by Belinsky and other literary critics who regarded her as one of the principal founders of the women's liberation movement. Helena Andreyevna was a direct descendent of a still older and more aristocratic family than her husband's—the Dolgurokovs of Russia.

The Dolgurokovs were of a fiery, independent nature and brooked no interference in their personal freedom from any quarter. Their ancestry has been traced back to Rurik in ninth century Russia. Even then they were known to be distinguished by an extreme courage, a daring equal to every emergency, a passionate love of personal independence, and a fearlessness of any consequences in the carrying out of their wishes. The name Dolgurokov means "the long-armed one." Interestingly enough, the quality of having long arms, with hands reaching even to the knees, has been considered one of the thirty-two signs of divine origin since ancient times.

From 1606 to 1608, the Dolgurokov Prince Gregory defended the convent of Saint Sergius against a massed attack of Poles and Cossacks led by some of the most able military leaders of the time. In 1624 a Dolgurokov princess married Michael Romanoff, thus founding the Romanoff dynasty which lasted for nearly three hundred years. There were many other

2

Dolgurokovs in Russian history who had the fiery, courageous, independent spirit inherited by little Helene Petrovna.

In 1842 Helena Andreyevna died when she was only twenty-seven years old, but with her literary reputation already well established. She realized early how rebellious, how courageous and brilliant her eleven-year old daughter was. On her deathbed she stated that perhaps it was just as well that she was dying for she would be spared seeing what befell little Helene. "Of one thing I am certain," she was quoted as saying. "Her life will not be as that of other women, and she will have much to suffer." Her words proved all too prophetic.

After her mother's death, little Helene went to live with her maternal grandparents, the Fadeefs, first in Saratoff and later in Tiflis. Madame Nadejda Fadeef, the aunt whom Helene deeply loved, wrote about her in later years:

"We who know Mme. Blavatsky ... can speak of her with authority ... From her earliest childhood, she was unlike any other person. Very lively and highly gifted,[1] full of humor, and of most remarkable daring; she struck everyone with astonishment by her self-willed and determined actions ... It was a fatal mistake to regard and treat her as they would any other child. Her restlessness and very nervous temperament, one that led her into the most unheard of, ungirlish mischief ... Her passionate love and curiosity for everything unknown and mysterious, wierd and fantastical, and foremost of all, her craving for independence and freedom of action—a craving that nothing and nobody could control; all this combined with an exuberance of imagination and wonderful sensitiveness...

"Left alone with no one near her to impede her liberty of action, no hand to chain her down or stop her natural impulses, and thus arouse to fury her inherent combativeness, she would spend hours and days quietly whispering, as people thought, to herself and narrating, with no one near her, in some dark corner, marvelous tales of travels in bright stars and other worlds...

[1]Note: She was an accomplished pianist and artist. —H.B.

"It was enough to forbid her doing a thing to make her do it, come what may. Her nurse, as indeed other members of the family, sincerely believed the child possessed by 'the seven spirits of rebellion.' Her governesses were martyrs to their task and never succeeded in bending her resolute will, or influencing by anything but kindness her indomitable, obstinate, and fearless nature.

"Spoilt in her childhood by the adulation of dependents and the devoted affection of relatives who forgave all to the 'poor, motherless child.' Later on, in her girlhood, her self-willed temper made her rebel openly against the exigencies of society. She would submit to no sham respect for or fear of public opinion. She <u>would</u> ride at fifteen, as she had at ten, any Cossack horse on a man's saddle! She would bow to no one as she would recede before no prejudice or established conventionality. She defied all and everyone."

She was, however, capable of restraining her passionate nature and making amends when the necessity of it was firmly pointed out to her by her maternal grandmother who was quite as strong-willed as herself. Colonel Olcott mentioned one incident in his book, <u>Old Diary Leaves</u>.

"I will now tell a story which I had from her own lips, and the incidents of which had a most lasting effect upon her through life. In childhood her temper was practically unrestrained, her noble father petting and idolizing her after the loss of his wife. When, in her eleventh year, the time came for her to leave his regiment and pass under the management of her maternal grandmother (the wife of General Fadeef, born Princess Dolgurokov), she was warned that such unrestrained liberty would no longer be allowed her, and she was more or less awed by the dignified character of her relative.

"But on one occasion, in a fit of temper at her nurse, a faithful old serf who had been brought up in the family, she struck her a blow in the face. This coming to her grandmother's knowledge, the child was summoned, questioned, and confessed her fault. The grandmother at once had the castle bell rung to call all of the servants of the household, of whom there were scores, and when they were assembled in the great hall,

4

she told her grand-daughter that she acted as no lady should, in unjustly striking a helpless serf who would not dare defend herself; as she ordered her to beg pardon and kiss her hand in token of sincerity.

"The child at first, crimson with shame, was disposed to rebel; but the old lady told her that if she did not instantly obey, she would send her from her house in disgrace. She added that no real noble lady would refuse to make amends for a wrong to a servant, especially one who by a lifetime of faithful service had earned the confidence and love of her superiors. Naturally generous and kind-hearted towards the people of the lower classes, the impetuous child burst into tears, kneeled before the old nurse, kissed her hand, and asked to be forgiven. Needless to say that she was thenceforth fairly worshipped by the retainers of the family. She told me that that lesson was worth everything to her, and had taught her the principle of doing justice to those whose social rank made them incapable of compelling aggressors to do rightly towards them."

Very little is known of her youth, but she herself told of one incident:

"I hated 'society' and the so-called 'world' as I hated hypocrisy in whatever form it showed itself; ergo, I ran amuck against society and the established proprieties. I hate dress, finery, and civilized society; I despise a ball room, and how much I despise it will be proved to you by the following fact. When hardly sixteen, I was being forced one day to go to a dancing party, a great ball at the Viceroy's. My protests were not listened to by my parents, who told me that they would have me dressed up—or rather, according to fashion, undressed—for the ball by servants by force, if I did not go willingly. I then deliberately plunged my foot and leg into a kettle of boiling water, and held it there until nearly boiled raw. Of course, I scalded it horribly, and remained at home for six months. I tell you, there is nothing of the woman in me. When I was young, if a young man had dared to speak to me of love, I would have shot him like a dog who bit me. Till nine years of age, in my father's regiment, the only nurses I knew were artillery soldiers and Buddhist Calmucks."

When nearly seventeen, she married General N. V. Blavatsky who admitted to being fifty but was more probably close to seventy.

"Details about my marriage?" She wrote:

"Well, now they say that I wanted to marry the old whistlebreeches <u>myself</u>. Let it be. My father was four thousand miles off. My grandmother was too ill. It was as I told you. I had engaged myself to spite the governess, never thinking I could no longer <u>disengage</u> myself. Well, Karma followed my sin. It is <u>impossible</u> to say truth without incriminating people that I would not accuse for the world, now that they are dead and gone. Rest it all on my back. There was a row already between my sister and aunt—the former accusing me of having slandered my dead relatives in the question of my marriage, and that my aunt had signed their and her own condemnation. Let this alone."

In three weeks time she fled this unconsummated marriage, abandoned Russia, and spent ten years in Central Asia, India, South America, Africa, and Eastern Europe. Years later in an interview in the <u>New York Star</u> she said, "I am a widow, a blessed widow, and I thank God. I wouldn't be a slave to God Himself, let alone man." This was, of course, her personality talking. In her Soul, she knew she was an initiate of the sacred mysteries and a disciple of the Masters of Wisdom.

She had always seen the form of a tall Hindu man near her, helping her whenever she was in danger, and in London she saw Him in person for the first time. Countess Wachtmeister wrote in her <u>Reminiscenses of H. P. Blavatsky</u>:

"When she was in London, in 1851, with her father, Colonel Hahn, she was one day out walking when, to her astonishment, she saw a tall Hindu in the street with some Indian princes. She recognized him as the very same tall, commanding figure she had seen often as a child.

"Her first impulse was to rush forward and speak to Him, but He made her a sign not to move, and she stood as if spellbound while He passed on. The next day she went to Hyde Park for a stroll... alone... Looking up, she saw the same form approaching her, and then her Master told her that He had come to London with the Indian princes on an important mission, and He was desirous of meeting her personally, and He required her cooperation in work He was about to undertake. He then told her how the Theosophical Society was to be formed, and that He wished her to be the founder. He gave her a slight sketch of all the troubles she would have to undergo, and also told her that she would have to spend three years in Tibet to prepare her for her most important task.

"After three days serious consideration and consultation with her father, H.P.B. decided to accept the offer made to her, and shortly afterwards left London for India."

Although she reached Tibet earlier, it was not until 1864 that she was able to stay long enough to receive the necessary training from Him: Master Morya.

Finally, after many more exciting visits to several countries (including Italy where she fought in, and was wounded at the battle of Mentana in 1868), she set out for America to bring the teaching of the Ancient Wisdom to the world once again.

In Le Havre, as she was about to board the steamer to New York, she saw a poor, bitterly weeping woman with two children by her side. H.P.B. asked her why she was crying. The woman replied that her husband had sent her just enough money to buy steerage tickets for herself and her two little ones. She had bought the tickets from a charlatan, and they had turned out to be worthless counterfeits.

"Come with me," Blavatsky replied, her Dolgurokov spirit aroused. They found the real ticket agent, and Blavatsky had no problem convincing him to exchange her own first class ticket for steerage tickets for herself, the poor woman, and her two children! So in July, 1873, an avatar carrying the Ancient Wisdom in her heart and mind arrived in America herded in steerage class, a living example of the sacrifices all avatars, major and minor, have made for the liberation of humanity since the beginning of the race.

In 1874, she met Colonel Henry Steele Olcott, and it was with his collaboration that the marvelous philosophy of the

Ancient Wisdom began to be published. Isis Unveiled appeared in the fall of 1877 in New York. H.P.B. received her United States citizenship in 1878. In 1880, Caves and Jungles of Hindustan was published. At the end of 1885, her magnum opus, The Secret Doctrine, was published, and The Key to Theosophy followed in 1889.

On May 8, 1891, in London, this magnificent woman died. Her eventful life, sketched here most briefly, continues to be a great inspiration to all students of the Ancient Wisdom the world over. Biographies of her life and reminiscences of her by friends and relatives continue to be published and are read everywhere with increasing interest. However, biographies just show her personality traits. Powerful as they were, they were overshadowed by her tremendously developed beingness. A highly developed being can tame the most flamboyant personality and use it to penetrate into and express the higher mind, the intuition, and still higher levels of beingness. Her true greatness, then, was the high level of her beingness, or Soul qualities, and the ability to express the great truths here on the physical plane perceived by that very beingness for the benefit of all mankind.

What, then, were these great truths which she sacrificed all to express? What philosophy did she give us that was so profound and useful for humanity that today thousands of students still eagerly study?

Out of many important contributions, the most important one was the revelation of the existence of the Masters of Wisdom. They are advanced Souls who, through self-sacrificing service, intense striving, and great thought, have conquered the physical plane. She revealed that these rare and glorious Beings, the Elder Brothers of humanity, really exist. Starting as ordinary human beings, they have raised themselves to such a height of achievement, of great beingness, that they have actually entered consciously the fifth, or divine, kingdom in nature. She further revealed that from this high point of achievement, these Elder Brothers of humanity are working ceaselessly for the benefit of mankind and helping all those who are struggling and sacrificing to raise themselves up also! In addition, she taught a small part of their great knowledge about the beginnings of our world and about the appearance of the various kingdoms on earth, including the human kingdom.

H.P.B. brought this teaching to us at precisely the right time. Nineteenth century science was developing its lower, strictly physical aspect so rapidly that the minds of men were in danger of swinging to the hopelessness of materialism. This "scientific" view was of a dead, mechanical universe running down without any more guidance than a kitchen clock. At the same time, institutionalized religions the world over had lost their tenuous spiritual ties, misplaced their Jacob's ladders, and were blindly following in the wake of this moribund "science" in the hope of still more temporal control and material riches than they had already collected.

At this critical juncture in human thought, H.P.B. appeared with her brightly lit lamp of Ancient Wisdom. The greatest scientific minds of her day; men like Crookes, Thomas Edison, and many others received the encouragement to explore the more unseen parts of nature and to begin to explore the world of energies. This became exemplified with Crookes' work with X-rays and Edison's invention of the electric light—visible light run by an invisible energy—ordinary electricity. Her work thus kept the door from closing on the spiritual world. It is definitely no exaggeration to state that the work of this extraordinary woman saved the world from hopeless materialism.

Chapter 2

The Masters of Wisdom

The Masters of Wisdom, the Spiritual Hierarchy, the Elder Brothers of humanity, as they are called, have always existed on our planet. There seems to have been no time during the existence of the fourth, or human, kingdom in nature that there were not teachers of humanity.

In the core of each human being there is a latent divinity, a Christ Consciousness, waiting to be unfolded to lead man on to his divine destiny. Because man was late in his development, as alluded to in The Secret Doctrine, he has always had teachers helping him. This help has always consisted, one way or another, in assisting him to find the keys to the unfoldment of his innate divinity and to see for himself that he is a part, an inseparable part, of the divine purpose. When he discovers this by raising his beingness to the divine realms and thus experiences that divinity directly, he will no longer need earthly teachers. Because his conscious penetration of divinity will allow him to experience every aspect of nature and her laws, he will know, by experience, where his rightful place is in the nature of things. Those Who already accomplished this banded together, forming the Spiritual Hierarchy to help the rest of the human race reach the same goal. They still teach, helping everyone who is ready to break the bonds of material limitation. It is the human being, each individual one, who has to do the work. There are no "free rides." However, no honest seeker is ever turned away, but is guided with advice, opportunity, and example. Having penetrated the veil of nature and seeing the purpose of divinity, or Will of God, as H.P.B. says, they formed a Plan based on this purpose, a Plan to help humanity reach the same goal as Themselves. The Plan of the Hierarchy has basically two objectives; to teach humanity to liberate itself from matter, superstition, glamor, and illusion, and to help humanity find its purpose as administrators of the will of God here on earth.

All world mythology points to the great teachers who came, taught, and left to come again. Some of these teachers are Hermes, Zoroaster, Hercules, Mithras, Vyasa, Krishna, Buddha, and above all, the Christ.[1] There are many others. However, the Christ was the only one the West accepted, and He with many misconceptions. Western thinkers rejected world mythology as fairy tales for simple people. The importance and the Hierarchical nature of the myths was completely lost until H. P. Blavatsky reintroduced these myths. They were based on real energies in nature, if not always real personages, and had the real effect of advancing the human race.

The Secret Doctrine, for example, is full of great, profound, and documented knowledge quoted from ancient sources. It proves that humanity, in its ever-upward struggle, passed through many stages of high civilizations and that there exists in the East knowledge and wisdom about philosophy, psychology, astronomy, astrology, alchemy, planetary, solar, and galactic cycles far more complete than we have in the West today. Furthermore, these and other teachings exist in their completeness only in the archives of the Spiritual Hierarchy. They are waiting for us to advance once more to our former greatness, learn what we have "lost," and pass on to even greater civilizations.

With all the official resistance that Western science and thought has to esoteric science today, we can well imagine how dreadful and hopeless the position of the human race would be today without H.P.B. and The Secret Doctrine. As the ideas presented in The Secret Doctrine took hold, she very cautiously began to reveal the existence of Those Who were the custodians of these ideas: the Masters of Wisdom.

Her first meeting with her Master, Master Morya, had taken place on her twentieth birthday in London. In her sketchbook, H.P.B. had written Ramsgate so that someone happening upon her papers would not connect the actual meeting with the Hindu princes who were in London that day.

---

[1] See Signs of Christ, by Harold Balyoz, chapters 1 and 4, Altai Publishers, 1979.

She wrote: "Memorable night! On a certain night by the light of the moon that was setting at Ramsgate on August 12, 1851 ... I met M.∴ the master of my dreams!!"

She had seen Master Morya in her dreams all her life, but this was her first physical plane meeting with Him. Master Morya was, and is, a tall, commanding presence, with dark hair and beard and flashing, piercing, dark eyes. He is the Master of Wisdom Who is the head of all esoteric schools in the world.

H.P.B. significantly continued in her sketchbook:

"...All the glories of Nature—the imposing silence of the night; the aroma of the flowers; the pale rays of the moon through the green tufts of the trees; the stars, flowers of fire strewn over the sky; the glow worms, flowers of fire strewn over the grass—all these have been created to render the Adept worthy of Nature, at the moment when for the first time she exclaims to Man, 'I am yours,'—words formed of a divine perfume of the soul, which, breathed forth, ascends to heaven together with the perfume of the flowers—the one moment of his life when he is king, when he is God; the moment which expiates and pays for with a whole life of bitter regrets.

"That moment—it is the price of all our miseries."

She concludes with: "Woman finds her happiness in the acquisition of supernatural powers—love is a vile dream, a nightmare."

In volume I of H.P.B.'s scrapbook she inserted a newspaper clipping:

"It is rumored that one or more Oriental Spiritualists of high rank have just arrived in this country. They are said to possess a profound knowledge of the mysteries of illumination ... If the report be true, their coming may be regarded as a great blessing, for after a quarter century of phenomena,[2] we are almost without a philosophy to account for them or control their occurrence. Welcome to the Wise Men of the East..."

---

[2]Note: spiritualistic phenomena. —H.B.

She wrote in the margin in red pencil: "At... and Ill... passed thro' New York and Boston; thence thro' California and Japan back. M.·. appearing in Kama-Rupa daily."[3]

In an article published in 1875, speaking of the Cabala, H.P.B. stated:

"As it is, the real, the complete Cabala of the first ages of humanity is in possession, as I said before, of but a few Oriental philosophers; where they are, who they are, is more than is given me to reveal ... The only thing I can say is that such a body exists, and that the location of their Brotherhood will never be revealed to other countries, until that day when Humanity shall awake in a mass from its spiritual lethargy, and open its blind eyes to the dazzling light of Truth..."

Another Master she identified was Koot Hoomi. He is an initiate of high degree and is a Kashmiri of noble presence. He is tall and fair with golden hair and has a golden beard. He has deep blue eyes which are full of love and wisdom. He has been in the West, having studied at Oxford, and speaks fluent English. In the future, he will assume the office of the Christ.

In a letter that Master Koot Hoomi wrote to A. P. Sinnett, a most improbable statement for the year 1882 was made. He wrote: "Science will <u>hear</u> sounds from certain planets before she <u>sees</u> them. This is a prophecy." Of course, his "prophecy" referred to our discovery of great non-luminous stars which emit enormous quantities of energy in the radio spectrum. Western science confirmed their existence to its satisfaction only after World War II and called them Quasars.

H. P. Blavatsky's most famous work, <u>The Secret Doctrine</u>, was written partly to destroy illusion and ignorance about the world and ourselves, and partly to reveal actual parts of the secret doctrine known to initiates of the sacred mysteries in all ages. She said that it was but the first turn of the key to unlock the sacred mysteries and that there were "seven turns of the key" to unlock them all.

---

[3]Note: At... and Ill... are Masters Atrya and Hilarion and M.·. is Master Morya Who was appearing to her daily on subjective levels. —H.B.

When these references are extracted from The Secret Doctrine, a fascinating and most remarkable teaching is revealed. These statements and fundamental ideas have travelled in handwritten and manuscript form all over the Western world for over one hundred years and have been taught to small circles of pupils by inspired teachers like Alice A. Bailey and T. Saraydarian. Those who have had the opportunity to study them have realized what a glorious teaching, what a great boon to humanity, what a great descending from divinity it is. They have realized also that their contact with this teaching has been due to the workings of their good karma. No other teaching has been so inspiring and liberating. The ones who studied it deeply, reflected on it profoundly, and really loved it soon learned that the radiance of the beauty of The Secret Doctrine's teaching was raising their own level of beingness.

Here, then, is part of the real secret doctrine taken from The Secret Doctrine and other writings of our most remarkable Helene Petrovna Blavatsky.

Chapter 3

The Secret Doctrine

Some Introductory Statements

Keynote:

The Secret Doctrine teaches that in order to become a divine, fully conscious God—aye, even the highest—the Spiritual, Primeval Intelligences must pass through the human stage.

When we say human, this does not apply merely to our terrestrial humanity but to the mortals that inhabit any world, i.e. to those intelligences that have reached the appropriate equilibrium between matter and spirit, as we have now ... Each entity must have won for himself the right of becoming divine, through self-experience.

Statement I

It is the *One Life*, eternal, invisible, yet omnipresent, without beginning or end, yet periodical in its regular manifestations—between which periods reigns the dark mystery of Non-Being; unconscious yet absolute Consciousness, unrealizable, yet the one self-existing Reality; truly "a Chaos to the sense, a Cosmos to the reason."

Statement II

The history of human evolution is traced in Heaven. Humanity and the Stars are bound together indissolubly because of the Intelligences which rule the Stars.

Statement III

Creation is but the result of will acting on phenomenal Matter, the calling forth out of it the Primordial Divine Light and Eternal Life.

Statement IV

"Let there be Sons of Light," or the Noumena of all phenomena ... these Beings are the Sons of Light because they emanate from, and are self-generated in, that infinite ocean of Light, whose one pole is pure Spirit lost in the absoluteness of Non-being, and the other pole, the Matter in which it condenses, "crystallizing" into a more gross type as it descends into manifestation. Matter is, in one sense, the illusive dregs of That Light whose Rays are the Creative Forces, yet has in it the full presence of the Soul thereof, of that Principle which none—not even the Sons of Light—will ever know.

Statement V

It is the Logos who is shown in the mystic symbolism of cosmogony ... playing two parts in the drama of Creation and Being—that of purely human Personality and the divine Impersonality of the so-called Avatars or Divine Incarnations and of the Universal Spirit, called Christos.

Statement VI

The Secret Doctrine established three fundamental propositions; the first is: an omnipresent, eternal, boundless and immutable *Principle* on which all speculation is impossible, since it transcends the power of human conception ... It is beyond the range and reach of thought.

Statement VII

The second fundamental proposition is: The eternity of the Universe as a boundless Plane; periodically "the playground of numberless Universes incessantly manifesting and disappearing" ... This is the absolute universality of the Law of Periodicity, of flux and reflux, of ebb and flow.

Statement VIII

The third fundamental proposition is: The fundamental identity of all souls with the Oversoul, the latter being itself an aspect of the Unknown Root; and the obligatory pilgrimage for every soul—a spark of the former—through the Cycle of Incarnation, or Necessity, in accordance with cyclic and karmic law, during the whole term.

Statement IX

The Wisdom-Religion is the inheritance of all the nations, the world over ... Its recognition parallels human evolution, Man can become a "Buddha of Wisdom unmoved."

Bodha......the innate possession of divine intellect or understanding.

Buddha....the acquirement of it by personal efforts and merit.

Buddhi.....the faculty of cognizing the channel through which divine knowledge reaches the Ego, the discernment of good and evil, also, divine conscience, and the spiritual soul which is the vehicle of Atman.

Statement X

Esoteric philosophy reconciles all religions, strips every one of its outward human garments, and shows the root of each to be identical with that of every other great world religion.

Statement XI

The goal and methods of attainment is summarized for us as follows: "The Maha Yogi, the great ascetic, in Whom is centered the highest perfection of austere penance and abstract meditation, by which the most unlimited powers are attained, marvels and miracles are worked, the highest spiritual knowledge is acquired and union with the great spirit of the universe is eventually gained."

Statement XII

Language is co-eval with reason and could never have been developed before men became one with the informing principles in them—those who fructified and awoke to life the manasic element, dormant in primitive man ... Thought and language are identical ... Logos is both reason and speech. But language, proceeding in cycles, is not always adequate to express spiritual thoughts.

18

H. P. Blavatsky gathered in <u>The</u> <u>Secret</u> <u>Doctrine</u> twelve main fundamentals of occultism that are universal in every presentation of the Ancient Wisdom. The Masters of Wisdom have taught these fundamentals to humanity along three lines of approach; religion, science, and philosophy. However, in whatever field one has encountered these truths, it must be remembered that all lead to the One Truth that stands behind these three fields as the cause does to its multiform effects.

<u>Fundamental I</u>

There is an omnipresent, eternal, immutable Principle, beyond the range and reach of thought.

a. The fundamental Law ... is the one homogeneous divine substance—Principle, the one radical Cause.

b. The Spirit and matter are the two poles of the same homogeneous substance, and the Root-Principle of the universe.

c. The first and fundamental dogma of occultism is universal Unity under three aspects.

d. Occultism sums up the one Existence thus: Deity is an arcane living Fire, and the eternal witnesses to this unseen Presence are Light, Heat and Moisture.

<u>Fundamental II</u>

The second assertion of the Secret Doctrine is the absolute universality of the Law of Periodicity ... in all departments of nature.

a. It is a fundamental law in occultism that there is no rest or cessation of motion in nature.

b. The universe is the periodical manifestation of the unknown Absolute Essence.

c. There is an eternal cyclic Law of Rebirth.

d. There is a cyclic, never-varying law of nature ... acting on a uniform plan that ... deals with the landworm as it deals with man.

Fundamental III

The fundamental identity of all souls with the Oversoul.

    a. Every atom in the universe has the potentiality of self-consciousness in it ... and is a universe in itself. It is an atom and an angel.

Fundamental IV

The Secret Doctrine teaches the progressive development of everything, worlds as well as atoms.

    a. The pivotal doctrine of the esoteric philosophy admits no privilege or special gifts in man, save those won by his own Ego through personal effort and merit through a long series of metempsychosis[1] and reincarnations.

    b. The whole of antiquity was imbued with that philosophy which teaches the involution of Spirit in matter, the progressive downward cyclic descent and active self-conscious evolutions.

    c. Occultism teaches an inherent law of progressive development.

    d. The upward progress of the Ego is a series of progressive awakenings.

Fundamental V

Analogy is the surest guide to the comprehension of the occult teachings.[2]

    a. Evolution proceeds on the laws of analogy in the kosmos as in the formation of the smallest globe.

    b. The evolution of man, the microcosm, is analogous to that of the universe, the macrocosm. His evolution stands between that of the latter and that of the animal, for which man is in his turn the macrocosm.

---

[1] The passing on of souls at death. —H.B.
[2] Or, as Hermes said, "as above, so below." —H.B.

c. The first law in nature is uniformity in diversity and the second is analogy.

Fundamental VI

Esoteric philosophy teaches that everything lives and is conscious, but not that all life and consciousness are similar to those of human or even animal being.

a. Everything in the universe throughout its kingdoms is conscious, i.e. endowed with a consciousness of its own kind and on its own plane of perception.

b. The capacity of perception exists in seven different aspects according to the seven conditions of matter.

c. Evolution proceeds along triple lines—spiritual, psychic, physical.

Fundamental VII

It is on the doctrine of the illusive nature of matter and of infinite divisibility of the atom that the whole science of occultism is built.

a. There is one universal element which is infinite, unborn and undying and all the rest—as in the world of phenomena—are so many various differentiated aspects and transformations of that One.

b. Spirit or cosmic Ideation and cosmic Substance ... are one and include the elements.

c. The occultist sees in the manifestation of every force in nature the action of the quality of the special characteristic of its Noumenon; which Noumenon is a distinct and intelligent individuality on the other side of the manifested mechanical universe.

d. Unconscious nature is in reality an aggregate of forces, manipulated by semi-intelligent beings (elementals) guided by high planetary Spirits, whose collective aggregate forms the manifested Verbum of the unmanifested Logos.

e. The whole universe is ruled by intelligent and semi-intelligent forces and powers.

f. Man himself is the separator of the One into various contrasted aspects.

<u>Fundamental VIII</u>

Matter is the vehicle for the manifestation of soul on this plane of existence, and soul is the vehicle on a higher plane for the manifestation of Spirit and those three are a trinity synthesized by Life which pervades them all.

a. Spirit is the matter of the seventh plane; matter is Spirit at the lowest point of its cyclic activity and both are Maya.

b. Ether, matter, energy—the sacred hypostatical trinity the three principles of the truly unknown God of science.

c. Matter after all is nothing more than the sequence of our own states of consciousness and Spirit an idea of psychic intuition.

d. Matter to the occultist is the totality of Existences in the cosmos which falls within any of the planes of possible perception.

e. Matter is regarded by the occultist as the eternal Root of all. The radiations from this are periodically aggregated into graduated forms from pure spirit to gross matter.

f. On the descending arc it is the Spirit which gradually transforms into the material. On the middle line of the base, spirit and matter are equilibrised in Man. On the ascending arc, Spirit is slowly asserting itself at the expense of the physical or matter.

<u>Fundamental IX</u>

The doctrine teaches that in order to become a divine fully conscious God, the Spiritual Primeval Intelligence must pass through the human state.

a. Man is identical in spiritual and physical essence with both the absolute Principle and with God in nature.

b. Man tends to become a god and then—God, like every other atom in the universe.

c. It is the spiritual evolution of the inner immortal man that forms the fundamental tenet of the occult sciences.

d. Nature (in man) must become a compound of Spirit and matter before he becomes what he is; and the Spirit latent in matter must be awakened to life and consciousness gradually.

e. Man is the macrocosm for the three lower kingdoms under him.

Fundamental X

Occultism teaches that no form can be given to anything either by nature or by man, whose ideal type does not exist in the subjective plane.

a. An idea is a being incorporeal; which has no subsistence by itself but gives figure and form unto shapeless matter and becomes the cause of manifestation.

b. According to the esoteric teaching there are seven primary and seven secondary creations; the former being the forces self-evolving from the one Causeless Force; the latter showing the manifested universe, emanating from the already differentiated divine elements.

c. Every power among the seven, once he is individualized has in charge one of the seven elements of creation and rules over it.

Fundamental XI

The Sun is the storehouse of vital force, which is the noumenon of electricity.

a. Eastern occultism insists that electricity is an entity.

b. The Sun is the Heart of the Solar World and its brain is hidden behind the visible Sun.

c. The solar system is as much the microcosm of the one Macrocosm as man is the former when compared with his own little solar cosmos.

Fundamental XII

The occultist accepts revelation as coming from divine, yet still finite beings, the manifested Lives, never from the Unmanifestable One Life.

The Secret Doctrine shows what were the ideas of antiquity with regard to *Primeval Instructors of Primitive Man* ... The genesis of the *Wisdom-Religion* ... dates from that period. So-called "Occultism", or rather Esoteric Science, has to be traced in its origin to those Beings who, led by Karma, have incarnated in our humanity and struck the keynote of that secret science which countless generations of subsequent adepts have expanded since then in every age, while they checked its doctrines by personal observation and experience. The bulk of this knowledge we now call "divine knowledge." Beings from other and higher worlds may have it entirely; we can have it only approximately.

It is from this *Wisdom-Religion* that all the various individual "Religions" (erroneously so called) have sprung, forming in their turn offshoots and branches, and also all the minor creeds, based upon and always originated through some personal experience in psychology. Every such religion, or religious offshoot, be it considered orthodox or heretical, wise or foolish, started originally as a clear and unadulterated stream from the Mother-Source. The fact that each became in time polluted with purely human speculations and even inventions, due to interested motives, does not prevent any from having been pure in its early beginnings. There are those creeds—we shall not call them religions—which have now been overlaid with the human element out of all recognition; others just showing signs of early decay; not one that escaped the hand of time. But each and all are of divine because natural and true origin, aye—Mazdeism, Brahmanism, Buddhism as much as Christianity. It is the dogmas and human element in the latter which led directly to modern Spiritualism.

24

The ancients considered religion, and the natural sciences along with philosophy, to be closely and inseparably linked together.

S.D. II, p. 106

There is not a religion worthy of the name which has been started otherwise than in consequence of *Visits* from beings on the higher planes.

Thus were born all prehistoric, as well as all the historic religions, Mazdeism, and Brahmanism, Buddhism and Christianity, Judaism, Gnosticism and Mahomedanism; in short, every more or less successful "ism."

Each of the Gnostic sects was founded by an Initiate, while their tenets were based on the correct knowledge of the symbolism of every nation.

S.D. II, p. 389

All are true at the bottom, and all are false on their surface. The *Revealer*, the artist who impressed a portion of the Truth on the brain of the Seer, was in every instance a true artist, who gave out genuine truths; but the instrument proved also, in every instance, to be *only a man*. Invite Rubinstein and ask him to play a sonata of Beethoven on a piano left to *Self-tuning*, one half of the keys of which are in chronic paralysis, while the wires hang loose; then see whether, the genius of the artist notwithstanding, you will be able to recognize the sonata. The moral of the fable is that a man—let him be the greatest of mediums or natural Seers—is but a man; and man left to his own devices and speculations *must* be out of tune with absolute truth, while even picking up some crumbs. For Man is but a *fallen* Angel, a god within, but having an animal brain in his head, more subject to cold and wine fumes while in company with other men on Earth, than to the faultless reception of divine revelations.

The "Serpent" and Dragon were the names given to the "Wise One," the initiated adepts of olden times ... When the Scandinavian Sigurd is fabled to have roasted the heart of Fafnir, the Dragon whom he had slain, becoming thereby the wisest of men, it meant the same thing. Sigurd had become learned in the runes and magical charms; he had received the "word" from an initiate of that name, or from a sorcerer after which the latter died, as many do after "passing the word."

S.D. I, p. 404

This word which is no word, has traveled once around the globe and still lingers as a far-off dying echo in the hearts of some privileged men ... but the "word" was known only to the ... chief lord of every college, and was passed to his successor only at the moment of death. There were many such colleges and the old classic authors speak of them.

S.D. II, p. 220

Enoch disappeared, "he walked with God, and he was not, for God took him," the allegory referring to the disappearance of the Sacred and Secret knowledge from among men; for "God" (the high hierophants, the heads of the colleges of initiated priests) took him, in other words the Enochs or the *Enoichions*, the Seers and their knowledge and wisdom, became strictly confined to the Secret Colleges of the Prophets, with the Jews, and to the temples with the Gentiles.

S.D. II, p. 532

An impenetrable veil of secrecy was thrown over the occult and religious mysteries taught, after the submersion of the last remnant of the Atlantean race some 12,000 years ago, lest they should be shared by the unworthy and so desecrated. Of these sciences several have now become exoteric—such as Astronomy, for instance, in its purely mathematical and physical aspect. Hence their dogmas and tenets, being all symbolized and left to the sole guardianship of parable and allegory, have been forgotten, and their meaning has become perverted... It is this secrecy which led the 5th Race to the establishment, or rather the re-establishment, of the religious mysteries, in which ancient truths might be taught to the coming generations under the veil of allegory and symbolism. Behold the imperishable witness to the evolution of the human race from the divine, and especially from the androgynous Race—the Egyptian Sphinx, that riddle of the Ages! Divine Wisdom incarnating on earth, and forced to taste of the bitter fruit of personal experience of pain and suffering generated under the shade of the tree of the knowledge of Good and Evil—a secret first known only to the Elohim, the *Self-Initiated "Higher Gods"*—on earth only.

S.D. II, p. 124

The "Kings Chamber" in *Cheops' Pyramid* is an Egyptian "Holy of Holies." On the days of the Mysteries of the Initiation, the candidate, representing the solar god, had to descend into the Sarcophagus, and represent the energizing ray, entering into the fecund womb of Nature. Emerging from it on the following morning, he typified the resurrection of life after the change called Death. In the great *mysteries* his figurative death lasted two days, when with the Sun he arose on the third morning, after a last night of the most cruel trials. While the postulant represented the Sun—the all-vivifying Orb that "resurrects" every morning but to impart life to all—the Sarcophagus was symbolic of the female principle. This, in Egypt; its form and shape changed with every country, provided it remained a vessel, a symbolic *navis* or boat-shaped vehicle, and a *container*, symbolically, of germs or the germ of life.

In India it is the "golden" Cow through which the candidate for Brahmanism has to pass if he desires to be a Brahman, and to become *Dvija* ("reborn a *second* time"). The crescent-form *Argha* of the Greeks was the type of the Queen of Heaven—Diana, or the Moon. She was the great Mother of all Existences, as the Sun was the Father.

S.D. II, p. 462

It was for divulging *The Secrets of the Gods* that Tantalos was plunged into the infernal regions; the keepers of the sacred Sibylline Books were threatened with the death penalty for revealing a word from them. Sigalions (images of Harpokrates) were in every temple—especially in those of Isis and Serapis—each pressing a finger to the lips, while the Hebrews taught that to divulge, after initiation into the Rabbinical mysteries, the secrets of Kabala, was like eating of the fruit of the Tree of Knowledge; it was punishable by death.

S.D. II, p. 396

It is from the 4th Race that the early Aryans got their knowledge of the "bundle of wonderful things," the *Sabha* and *Maysabha*, mentioned in the *Mahabarata*, the gift of Mayasura to the Pandavas. It is from them that they learned aeronautics, *Vimana Vidya* (the "knowledge of flying in air vehicles"), and, therefore, their great arts of meteorography and meteorology. It is from them, again, that the Aryans inherited their most valuable science of the hidden virtues of precious and other stones, of chemistry, or rather alchemy, of mineralogy, geology, physics and astronomy.

S.D. II, p. 426

The 4th Race had its periods of the highest civilization. Greek and Roman and even Egyptian civilizations are nothing compared to the civilizations that began with the 3rd Race "...after its separation."

S.D. II, p. 429

Do not the relics we treasure in our museums—lost mementos of the long "lost arts"—speak loudly in favor of ancient civilization? And do they not prove, over and over again, that nations and continents that have passed away have buried along with them arts and sciences, which neither the first crucible ever heated in a medieval cloister, nor the last cracked by a modern chemist, have revived, nor will—at least, in the present century.

S.D. II, p. 430

If modern masters are so much in advance of the old ones, why do they not restore to use the lost arts of our postdiluvian forefathers? Why do they not give us the unfading colors of Luxor—the Tyrian purple; the bright vermilion and dazzling blue which decorate the walls of this place, and are as bright as on the first day of their application? The indestructable cement of the pyramids and of ancient aqueducts; the Damascus blade, which can be turned like a corkscrew in its scabbard without breaking; the gorgeous, unparalleled tints of the stained glass that is found amid the dust of old ruins and beams in the windows of ancient cathedrals; and the secret of the true malleable glass? And if chemistry is so little able to rival even the early medieval ages in some arts, why boast of achievements which, according to strong probability, were perfectly known thousands of years ago? The more archaeology and philology advance, the more humiliating to our pride are the discoveries which are daily made, the more glorious testimony do they bear in behalf of those who, perhaps on account of the distance of their remote antiquity, have been until now, considered ignorant flounderers in the deepest mire of superstition.

S.D. II, p. 430

Had not Diocletian burned the esoteric works of the Egyptians in 296, together with their books on alchemy, Caesar 700,000 rolls at Alexandria, and Leo Isaurus 300,000 at Constantinople (VIII century) and the Mohammedans all they could lay their sacrilegious hands on—the world might know today more of Atlantis than it does. For Alchemy had its birthplace in Atlantis during the 4th Race, and had only its *Renaissance* in Egypt.

S.D. II, p. 763

Among other arts and sciences, the ancients—ay, as an heirloom from the Atlanteans—had those of astronomy and symbolism, which included the knowledge of the Zodiac.

S.D. II, p. 431

The Egyptian priests had the Zodiacs of the Atlantean Asura-Maya, as the modern Hindus still have.

S.D. II, p. 436

The forefathers of the Aryan Brahmans had their Zodiacal calculations and Zodiac from those born by Kriyasakti power, the "Sons of Yoga"; the Egyptians from the Atlanteans of Ruta.

The former, therefore, may have registered time for seven or eight millions of years, but the Egyptians *could not*.

S.D. II, p. 436

The builders of the Pyramid had the astronomical knowledge displayed in its perfect orientation and its other admitted astronomical features, and it is on this "knowledge" that the program of the *mysteries* and of the series of Initiations was based: thence, the construction of the Pyramids, the everlasting record and the indestructible symbol of these Mysteries and Initiations on Earth, as the courses of the stars are in Heaven. The cycle of Initiation was a reproduction in miniature of that great series of Cosmic changes to which astronomers have given the name of tropical or sidereal year. Just as, at the close of the cycle of the sidereal year (25,868 years), the heavenly bodies return to the same relative positions as they occupied at its outset, so at the close of the cycle of Initiation the inner man has regained the pristine state of divine purity and knowledge from which he set out on his cycle of terrestrial incarnation.

S.D. I, p. 314

Externally "The Pyramid of Gizeh" symbolized *The Creative Principle of Nature*, and illustrated also the *Principles of Geometry, Mathematics, Astrology, and Astronomy*. Internally, it was a majestic fane, in whose somber recesses were performed the mysteries, and whose walls had often witnessed the initiation-scenes of members of the royal family. The porphyry sarcophagus ... was the *Baptismal Font*, upon emerging from which the neophyte was "born again" and became an adept ... the narrow upward passage leading to the King's chamber had a "narrow gate," the same "strait gate" which "leadeth unto life," or the new spiritual rebirth alluded to by Jesus in Matthew VII. Verse 13 et seq:

S.D. I, p. 317

The ancient Hierophants have combined so cleverly the dogmas and symbols of their religious philosophies, that these symbols can be fully explained only by the combination and knowledge of *all* the keys. They can be only *approximately* interpreted, even if one finds out three out of these seven systems; the *Anthropological*, the *Psychic*, and the *Astronomical*.

S.D. I, p. 363

Without throwing any discredit upon time-honored beliefs, in whatever direction, we are forced to draw a marked line between blind faith, evolved by theologies, and knowledge due to the independent researches of long generations of adepts; between, in short, faith and philosophy ... From the very beginning of Aeons—in time and space in our Round and Globe—the Mysteries of Nature (at any rate, those which it is lawful for our races to know) were recorded by the pupils of those same now invisible "heavenly men," in geometrical figures and symbols. The keys thereto passed from one generation of "wise men" to the other. Some of the symbols, thus passed from the east to the west, were brought therefrom by Pythagoras, who was not the inventor of his famous "Triangle."

S.D. I, p. 612

Faith is a word not to be found in theosophical dictionaries; we say knowledge based on observation and experience. There is a difference, however, that while the observation and experience of physical science lead the scientists to about as many working hypotheses as there are minds to evolve them, our knowledge consents to add to its lore only those facts which have become undeniable, and which are fully and absolutely demonstrated. We have no two beliefs or hypotheses on the same subject... These theories may be slightly incorrect in their minor details, and even faulty in their exposition by lay students; they are facts in nature, nevertheless, and come nearer the truth than any scientific hypothesis.

What science in general will never accept as proof—the cumulative testimony of an endless series of seers who have testified to this fact. Their spiritual visions, real explorations by, and through, psychic and spiritual senses untrammelled by blind flesh, have been systematically checked and compared one with the other and their nature sifted. All that was not corroborated by unanimous and collective experience was rejected, while that only was recorded as established truth which, in various ages, under different climes, and throughout an untold series of incessant observations, was found to agree and receive constantly further corroboration. The methods used by our scholars and students of the psycho-spiritual sciences do not differ from those of students of the natural and physical sciences, as you may see. Only our fields of research are on two different planes and our instruments are made by no human hands; for which reason perchance they are but the more reliable. The retorts, accumulators, and microscopes of the chemist and naturalist may get out of order; the telescope and the astronomer's horological instruments may get spoiled; our recording instruments are beyond the influence of weather or the elements.

There is but one science that can henceforth direct modern research into the one path which will lead to the discovery of the whole, hitherto occult, truth, and it is the youngest of all—Chemistry, as it now stands reformed. There is no other, not excluding astronomy, that can so unerringly guide scientific intuition, as chemistry can...

It becomes evident that while pondering over the ultimate divisibility of matter, and in the hitherto fruitless chase after the element of negative atomic weight, the scientifically trained mind of the chemist must feel irresistibly drawn towards those ever-shrouded worlds, the mysterious beyond, whose measureless depths seem to close against the approach of the too materialistic hand that would fain draw aside its veil.

S.D. I, p. 581

The exact extent, depth, breadth, and length of the mysteries of Nature are to be found only in Eastern esoteric sciences. So vast and so profound are these that hardly a few, a very few of the highest Initiates—whose very existence is known but to a small number of adepts—are capable of assimilating the knowledge. Yet it is all there, and one by one facts and processes in Nature's workshops are permitted to find their way into the exact Sciences, while mysterious help is given to rare individuals in unraveling its arcana. It is at the close of the great Cycles, in connexion with racial development, that such events generally take place. We are at the very close of the cycle of 5000 years of the present Aryan Kaliyuga; and ... there will be a large rent made in the Veil of Nature.

S.D. I, p. 612

The ancient adepts have solved the great problems of science, however unwilling modern materialism may be to admit the fact. The mysteries of Life and Death were fathomed by the great masterminds of antiquity; and if they have preserved them in secrecy and silence, it is because these problems formed part of the sacred mysteries; and, secondly, because they must have remained incomprehensible to the vast majority of men then, as they do now.

S.D. II, p. 451

Every century an attempt is being made to show the world that Occultism is no vain superstition. Once the door is permitted to be kept a little ajar, it will be opened wider with every new century. The times are ripe for a more serious knowledge than hitherto permitted, though still very limited, so far.

There can be no possible conflict between the teachings of occult and so-called exact Science, where the conclusions of the latter are grounded on a substratum of unassailable fact. It is only when its more ardent exponents, over-stepping the limits of observed phenomena in order to penetrate into the arcana of Being, attempt to wrench the formation of Kosmos and its living Forces from Spirit, and attribute all to blind matter, that the Occultists claim the right to dispute and call in question their theories. Science cannot, owing to the very nature of things unveil the mystery of the universe around us. Science can, it is true, collect, classify, and generalize upon phenomena; but the occultist arguing from admitted metaphysical data, declares that the daring explorer, who would probe the innermost secrets of Nature, must transcend the narrow limitations of sense, and transfer his consciousness into the region of noumena and the sphere of primal causes. To effect this, he must develop faculties which are absolutely dormant—save in a few rare and exceptional cases—in the constitution of the offshoots of our present 5th Root-race in Europe and America. He can in no other conceivable manner collect the facts on which to base his speculations. Is not this apparent on the principles of Inductive Logic and Metaphysics alike?

S.D. I, p. 478

That which is true on the metaphysical plane must be also true on the physical.

Outside of metaphysics no occult philosophy, no esotericism is possible. It is like trying to explain the aspirations and affections, the love and hatred, the most private and sacred workings in the soul and mind of the living man, by an anatomical description of the chest and brain of his dead body.

S.D. I, p. 170

To make of Science an integral whole necessitates, indeed, the study of spiritual and psychic, as well as physical Nature. Otherwise it will be ever like the anatomy of man, discussed of old by the profane from the point of view of his shell-side and in ignorance of the interior work.

S.D. I, p. 588

The duty of the Occultist lies with the Soul and Spirit of Cosmic Space, not merely with its illusive appearance and behavior. That official physical science is to analyze and study its shell—the "ultima Thule" of the Universe and man, in the opinion of Materialism.

S.D. I, p. 589

Materialism and scepticism are evils that must remain in the world as long as man has not quitted his present gross form to don the one he had during the first and second races of this Round. Unless scepticism and our present natural ignorance are equilibrated by intuition and a natural spirituality, every being afflicted with such feelings will see in himself no better than a bundle of flesh, bones, and muscles, with an empty garret inside him which serves the purpose of storing his sensations and feelings.

S.D. I, p. 480

Let us pronounce the prayer to Shambhala:

> Thou Who called me to the path of labor, accept
> my ableness and my desire.
> Accept my labor, O Lord, because by day and by
> night Thou beholdest me.
> Manifest Thy hand, O Lord, because great is the
> darkness. I follow thee!

Chapter 4

Helena Roerich

There is a little known tradition in the spiritual affairs of the world that concerns the way some of the greatest teachings have been given to humanity. These are teachings that have been given by women, women who have carefully and deliberately kept their identities secret or at least their personalities hidden as much as possible as they presented their ideas. Mary, the mother of Jesus, is as highly revered as a teacher in India as is Jesus. Another "hidden" one, Mary Magdalene, is now known to have been a great teacher, maybe Christ's greatest disciple, although not a word of this is mentioned in conventional biblical writings. She is said to have always ended her talks with the phrase, "and thus He taught us," or words to that effect, always giving credit to her Teacher, and taking attention away from herself. We know, for example, of the deeds of Joan of Arc but nothing about her actual persuasive words. Her words must have been truly spectacular to arouse so many of her countrymen to united action.

Helena Roerich chose to remain in this tradition as much as possible while she presented her sublime philosophy to the world. She preferred, like many others before her, to let the teaching speak for itself while she kept her personality in the background. How many men are there who could, or would, do this? Yet, inspired by Master Morya, Who was also H.P.B.'s Master, Helena Roerich brought us the teachings of Agni Yoga, the highest known form of yoga. The Agni Yoga books, in thirteen slim volumes, carry no author's credit line in them, although they contain, without a doubt, the most advanced spiritual philosophy ever given to humanity.

Yoga means union with God and Agni Yoga, the yoga of fire, is the yoga that can link man with the highest divine principles.

In these relatively few pages, Helena Roerich has given us oceans of teaching. She tells us that by consciously developing our own innate virtues, virtues that have lain dormant in us through countless centuries of ignorance, suffering, wars, pain and exploitation, we can link up with the fiery virtues of divinity. These fiery virtues of divinity are nothing less than the higher laws of nature and they have their parallels deep within us in our own hidden nature. These virtues are there in us because we are the direct descendents of the highest divinity Who released a fiery spark of Himself into every single atom as He formed them. And our path back to our original home must be paved with our own virtues rediscovered and released into open expression through our own striving, sacrifices, and heavy labor.

What magnificent hope she brings us by showing us the way to release these virtues, develop and expand them, and enter into our ordained course toward the stars, so that we can again be a real working part of divinity! This is truly the future of the human race, the true future of man and woman advancing together into infinity.

Helena Roerich was born in Russia on February 13, 1879, the daughter of a prominent architect. She was very sensitive and frequently ailing. During illnesses, two very tall men would appear to her with help, but when the grownups objected to her accounts of them, she learned to keep her thoughts to herself. Her mother's sister, princess Putyatine, had an estate at Bologoye where little Helena spent her summers. All the domestic animals rushed to welcome her in the mornings when she would go out to feed them.

She learned to read at an early age and was seen carrying around heavy volumes of philosophy as well as Dore's illustrated bible. Her husband, Nicholas Roerich, commented that: "...Honesty, justice, a constant search for Truth and love for creative works—all this actually transformed the whole life around the strong, young spirit ... life became full of true labor." She also had a talent for music; she played the piano, and had a good eye for drawing and color.

When she met Nicholas Roerich, she found much in common with him and after accompanying him to many exhibitions and concerts, they fell in love and were married on October 28, 1901. Nicholas, one of the finest painters of his day, with an unparalleled command of color, was also very spiritually advanced. They had a happy family life together with their two sons, George and Svetoslav. The latter also became a fine painter. Svetoslav's portrait of his mother shows her to be a very beautiful woman.

In 1915, Nicholas became ill with pneumonia and they left their home in Petersburg for a better climate. In 1918 they went to England and in 1920 came to New York for Nicolas' first exhibition in the United States. By this time Helena was already in contact with Master Morya and the first Agni Yoga book: Leaves of Morya's Garden was written.

During their eventful life, they went to India where they organized their central asiatic expedition through India, China, Tibet, Mongolia and other countries. Both her husband Nicholas and son George wrote books about their adventures. Nicholas produced some of his most beautiful paintings then. Although Helena was an active participant, few personal details are known except that she never stopped writing, teaching, and helping others. Besides the thirteen published Agni Yoga books, she wrote numerous letters to disciples and aspirants all over the world. Some of these letters are published in her Letters of Helena Roerich, volumes I & II. She also wrote On Eastern Crossroads and Foundations of Buddhism, using different pseudonyms for each one. She died in 1949 and today far more people are gaining tremendous help and inspiration from her books, especially from the Agni Yoga series, than even in her lifetime. Her books are seriously studied in every country of the world.

Before we look at the real heart of her work, the Agni Yoga books, let us examine some of her ideas and advice from her letters collected in the Letters of Helena Roerich. In volume II, in the letter dated 12, July, 1938, she gives excellent advice to those who are approaching the Teaching and answers many questions of beginners. We also gain a sense of her personal approach in presenting her Teaching of Living Ethics to the world.

"Of course, now you will have to acknowledge that I was right in advising you not to discuss the Teaching amidst obviously hostile surroundings ... You write that someone asks by whom and in what way is the Teaching given. The answer to the first question is given in the Teaching, and its Author gives his name in several of the books. The answer to the second question is also given in the many pages of those same books. All such questions reveal how superficially the books are fathomed by their questioners.

"As to those who worry about whether any distortions have crept into the teaching, one may ask them, Did they not realize that it is just as easy for the Teacher to point out this or that mistake which slipped in as to give the next page? Yet, the rhythm of the Teaching is continuously increasing. But regrettably, mistakes by the printer and the copyist are unavoidable. However, they were corrected as far as possible. I do not know any book that does not have some misprints, and especially in our time of loss of quality in everything.

"I am also sufficiently acquainted with the gulf of human nature or consciousness, and I know that no assurances can ever convince anyone. Only our personal, inner conviction, which has its root in the accumulations of our past lives, can help in discerning the truth. Therefore my affirmations also will never be accepted by the doubting ones. I beg of you, be assured that we do not attempt either to persuade or dissuade anyone, and we rise up with all the power of our spirit against any forcing of the books of Living Ethics on anyone, and more so any kind of authorities. Each one must follow his path. Only he can deeply feel the truth of the Teaching and become aflame in his heart to the Call of the Teacher, who has in his former lives already approached the Teaching and the Great Teachers. Among those who approach for the first time there are always many waverings and doubts. But where doubt has made its nest, the fires of the heart cannot be kindled. Doubt is the most frightful poison. Nothing can be attained in any field of endeavor where there is evidence of doubt. No discovery could have been made if the searcher doubted the correctness of his theory; the proverb

'Faith moves mountains' has a profound meaning. Man does not realize that throughout his entire life he does things he believes. Precisely what to believe and how to believe comprises the solution of the problems of being. Man's free will or free choice molds his destiny.

"Those who wish to follow Christ exclusively should follow him. But let them clearly define which Christ they wish to serve, the evangelical Christ or the Christ of the latter-day churchmen. In this realization there will already be a shifting of the consciousness. None of the Great Teachers will ever demean any one of the Great Founders of ancient or later religions, because, verily, the very same Ego has many a time reincarnated in some of them.

"And to widely proclaim the hierarchical succession of Great Teachers was never permitted. A thinking disciple fully realizes the harm of such untimely announcements in doubting or hostile hands. Only novices, who do not understand that on each carelessly spoken word may hang the destiny and life of many people, ask questions the answers to which were given in remote antiquity during the highest initiations. Human consciousness has hardly changed since that time, and in many ways, alas, has become even coarser.

"You write that there are those who are indignant at the admonition encountered in the first book—'love Me'—and consider it a sort of importunity. To this I say, Apparently the hearts of these people have become petrified, and they do not know what is the fire of the heart, what is the flaming love of the disciple for the Teacher, and what joy these words of the Teacher awaken in the flaming heart of the disciple. For by this very declaration the Teacher not only accepts the love of the disciple but also brings him nearer and encourages him to follow this, the shortest and royal path. Subtle are the strings of the heart, and only when they are tempered by its fires, which are kindled by contact with the furnace of life, can they transmit to us the secretly resounding mysteries of man's being. Nothing coarse, nothing demanding, doubting, denying, deriding will find a key to any mystery of the higher Be-ness. Hence this hatred by the desiccated hearts of all Light, of all joy filled with the higher beauty of devotion and love for Hierarchy.

"I regret it if my opinion about certain books has deeply hurt a good man, but I cannot take it back. It would be dishonest for me to praise what I know to be a distortion of truth ... Truly, it is sad that there are people who speak negatively about the books of the Teaching and yet have not read any of them. And of those who regard themselves as respectable and educated men, who would renounce and speak disparagingly about that which he does not know at all or with which he has only a superficial acquaintance? Will such criticism be based on truth? Have not readers the right to demand at least a primitive honesty from the critics?

"But it is said that no Teaching was ever extolled by friends; always and in everything the fury of enemies helps. The Jinn build the temples. A sign from heaven was demanded even from Christ, and he was accused of ejecting the devils through the diabolical power of the prince of the devils. Read again the Gospel of St. Luke 11:15. Remarkable is the answer of Christ to these casuists, in the same chapter. Strange as it seems, those who attack the books of the Teaching and loudly denounce them are precisely those who do not know them, just as they do not know their own Scriptures.

"As to those who refuse to read the books of Living Ethics out of personal offense at my opinion about certain books, it remains but to pity them. We never refuse to read any book offered to us, in order not to somehow pass by a precious pearl. However, discrimination was placed in the foundation of discipleship, always and in all Teachings. H.P.B.[1] especially insisted on discrimination, which is contained in the fires of the heart, in straight-knowledge—this eye of the Dangma. And so, I will say once again that whatever is linked directly with H.P.B. is deeply revered by us...

"The Teaching speaks about the canon 'By thy God.' Therefore, tell those who, though accepting the Teaching, cannot accept its Source or those through whom it is transmitted, that they should not be disturbed by these questions. For them,

---

[1]H.P.B.: Helene Petrovna Blavatsky. —H.B.

let there be neither the Source nor the intermediaries. Let the Teaching speak for itself.

"Indeed, I agree with you that the refusal to accept the Source deprives the words of the Teaching of the highest magnet of the heart and of the higher beauty. But the refusal to accept the intermediaries *cannot* diminish the Teaching. Therefore, I beg you to assure everybody that I do not pretend to any authority and ask them to forget about my existence.

"Once again, I must say that to all questions and objections brought by you from the listeners and participants of the Agni Yoga group there are exact answers in the books of the Teaching. Having read the objections and questions, it becomes clear that no one troubled himself to get thoroughly acquainted with all ... books of the Teaching published to date.

"The Brotherhood of Light is based upon unity, and therefore all its participants are united in the one Stronghold. One could have answered these inquirers with the following words, 'And Jesus knew their thoughts, and said unto them, "Every kingdom divided against itself is brought to desolation; and every city or house divided against itself shall not stand."'

"Grievous is the atmosphere of disunity and blasphemy, I do not know any worse one; the greatest harm, including pernicious ailments, can be the result of it. Contemporary medical scientists assert that all moral principles have a purely biological foundation.

"If the Teaching is close to you, you will not carry it to the bazaar. From all my heart I wish that you may soon get out of the poisoned atmosphere.

All light to you.

"Have just looked through the copy of my letter to the person mentioned by you, and notice that I wrote about straight-knowledge, the accumulation of which gives us the possibility of penetrating into the very essence of things. Precisely, straight-knowledge is the sole criterion in all judgments. But nowhere did I liken straight-knowledge to inspiration or Hiero-inspiration. However, there is no doubt that only an accumulation of straight-knowledge gives the possibility of direct and constant communion with the Teachers, and thus being able to receive, not fragmentary information, but the entire Ocean of the Teaching. I am quoting here an excerpt from this letter: 'Indeed, the only true Teacher is the "Invisible" Teacher (the Teacher of the Great Brotherhood). But are there many who can have direct access to such a Teacher? This does not mean that the Teacher is inaccessible, no, verily, he is the closest. But this closeness cannot be endured by all. It is revealed without harm only to him who has carried the Image of the Teacher for many centuries in the innermost recesses of his heart. Without this age-old accumulation and the established magnetic link, it is difficult to absorb the rays that are sent by the "Invisible" Teacher, that may destroy the unprepared recipient. Even in the case of age-old tests and approaches, the new earthly envelope, or recipient, must become accustomed to this receptivity over many years. The invisible rays are very powerful and sometimes act more strongly than radium.'

"In view of having written previously to my correspondents about the acceptance of disciples and about the earthly teacher, to ease up my work I am enclosing here the existing copies of those pages. But now I will answer concerning your doubt regarding straight-knowledge. Indeed, it is difficult to develop or awaken straight-knowledge in oneself, yet there is no other criterion. Full discrimination comes only in this way. And the main difficulty is that straight-knowledge is not awakened in us while the feelings of selfhood, conceit, hypocrisy, or insincerity predominate in our heart. Only when these vipers are ejected does the voice of the heart take their place, and straight-knowledge becomes clear and infallible. Believe me, if someone is striving sincerely, he shall meet his earthly teacher and recognize him. But very, very rarely do these occurrences take place on our Earth. Let us recall the insignificant number of disciples that even the Great Teachers had during their earthly lives. Since those times humanity has not improved, and crucifixion and betrayal of the earthly Bearers of Light still continues. And the very same traitors, having only put on new masks, are contriving still more subtle methods of inquisition.

"Yes, it is most difficult for people to comprehend the law of Hierarchy. Yet, at the same time, precisely those who vociferate most of all against this cosmic law, are nevertheless blindly submissive to any hierarchy, beginning with standardized conditions, customs, and style, and ending with even accepting the hierarchy of evil and all its hidden multiformity. After all, the hierarchy of evil is much closer to the earthly spheres, and its numerous followers, the inhabitants of the lower spheres of the Subtle World, take delight in instilling in people the most abominable thoughts and in pushing them to the most fratricidal disunity and actions. During the days of Armageddon the forces of evil have become stronger, therefore it is so essential to cognize the Hierarchy of Light, and to strive upon this Path with one's whole heart. Of course, as it always was and will be, darkness itself will devour darkness. But how many of the 'lukewarm' ones will perish, who could have been saved if they had realized the danger in time and had taken strong hold of the Hand of Help stretched out to them."[2]

The following excerpts from her Letters of Helena Roerich show the remarkable depth of her philosophy and her great concern about people, especially women and children, and the possibilities for advancement along the spiritual path that are there for all of humanity.

"It is necessary to point out the harm of the widely growing craze for sports. Undoubtedly it is accompanied by a vulgarization of tastes. Sport of course has its place, but within limits and when co-measured with beauty. But all varieties of boxing can only evoke a profound disgust.

"It is most essential to develop from earliest childhood the ability to think. Precisely, as it is said, 'It is necessary to establish the science of thinking in schools, not as an abstract psychology but as the practical foundation of memory, attention, concentration and observation. True, apart from these four

---

[2]Letters of Helena Roerich vol. II, pp. 484-489

fundamental branches of the science of thinking, many other qualities require development; for instance, accuracy, resourcefulness, quickness, synthesis, originality and others. If even a part of the effort used in schools for sports were applied to the art of thinking, the results would be astounding.' But indeed, at the present time, this divine ability is a thing that frightens the mediocre. Most of all, people dread thinking. Small wonder that the leaders of the Mediaeval Church, in their cunning awareness, hastened to declare this awakening ability as a 'gift of the devil.' They knew their 'paradise' would become poor and empty as soon as intelligence manifested itself. And who would then lay at their feet the wealth of the earth won by the sweat of the people?

"Likewise, it is essential to point out one of the chief evils of modern religious instruction, i. e., the instilling into the human consciousness of a sense of irresponsibility. Precisely, a degenerating church, during the centuries, instilled into the consciousness of its flock an animal sense of irresponsibility. From childhood, people are allowed to believe that they may commit most terrible crimes because the priest, by the power given to him, can free the person of sin through confession and remission. Then, after this liberation, what is there to prevent the erring one from again committing the same sins and once more receiving remission, for perhaps a yet higher fee?

"Remember how it is said, 'Is not the forgiving of a repentant sinner for a fee the most heinous crime? Is not the bribery of Divinity with gold worse than the first forms of fetishism? This frightful question must be discussed from every angle.' Frightful indeed, as this ulcer is spread all over the world, in all religions. Recall the papal indulgences of the Middle Ages. But even now the old law is coming to life once more, and a Catholic does not have to bother to make a pilgrimage to Rome to do penance for his sins. All that is necessary is to send a certain sum for the indulgence, and the remission will permit entrance to Heaven.

"I have written all this to one of my correspondents, and therefore, in order to stress fully this evil, I shall quote from that letter of mine:

'...Indeed, by instilling into the minds of children the idea that the church, as a powerful intercessor, can for a tear of repentance and a fee give passage to the erring through the Gates of Paradise, the church commits the greatest sin. By removing from man the sense of responsibility, the church shuts him off from his Divine Origin. The church has discredited the great concept of Divine Justice. Losing the understanding of responsibility and justice, man will inevitably begin his involution, for those who fail to follow the cosmic laws are destined to deterioration.

'The whole Cosmos is built upon the law of responsibility, or, as it is more often called, the law of cause and effect, or the law of Karma. And it is quite impossible to ignore this law and to neglect it without bringing on, in the long run, self-destruction. All the ancient Teachings, without exception, taught this law of great responsibility, this pledge of the Divine in us ... Let us think ... of the words of Christ, "Ye have heard that it was said by them of old time, Thou shalt not kill; and whosoever shall kill shall be in danger of the judgment: But I say unto you, That whosoever is angry with his brother without a cause shall be in danger of the judgment: and whosoever shall say to his brother, Raca, shall be in danger of hellfire..."'[3]

"As to the question of the condition of our planet prior to the fall of Lucifer—according to Eastern writings and *The Secret Doctrine*, we know how advanced and beautiful was the civilization of the Third Race when it was guided and acclaimed by the Great Spirits from the higher worlds. The final fall of Lucifer took place in the Fourth Race, but his departure from the path of Light was already marked at an earlier time. When the human substance in him outweighed the divine, he became jealous and started the disastrous battle against the Great Brothers, which has now reached its limit. Remarkable is the fact that in order to achieve his goal of becoming the full and only ruler of Earth, his chief efforts were directed toward the humiliation of woman. He knew that with the demeaning of woman the coarsening and degeneration of humanity was unavoidable. There exists a most ancient saying, 'Where

---

[3]IBID vol. I, pp. 415-417

women are revered and safeguarded, prosperity reigns and the gods rejoice.' The New Epoch under the rays of Uranus will bring the renaissance of woman. The Epoch of Maitreya is the Epoch of the Mother of the World. It is remarkable to observe the rapid rise of the women of India. There one can see women occupying the posts of ministers and other responsible positions. Many women of India are excellent speakers. The Indians readily elect women, because they have faith in the common sense of their wives. But, of course, there are also opponents of the liberation of woman. In certain dominions in India where women are at the head of the government one sees many innovations, the temples are open for the lower castes, universities are founded, and also museums, laboratories, hospitals are patterned after European lines.[4]

"Of course, I fully trust your heart, and your aura is the guarantee of the best possibilities. You write that you are a novice in public life, but this is not to be feared, since experience comes with work; but the most important lies in the spiritual accumulation, in the quality of psychic energy, and no experience can replace the essence of this beautiful energy. Therefore in the basis of everything let us place precisely this gauge.

"I rejoice that you are paying attention to children. Indeed, the most urgent, and most essential task is the education of children and youth. In all countries very little and extremely poor attention at that is given to this question on which depends the entire welfare and strength of a people and a country. It is usually customary to confuse education with upbringing, but it is time to understand that school education, as it is established in most cases, not only does not contribute to the moral upbringing of youth, but acts inversely. In the Anglo-Saxon countries the schools are occupied mainly with the physical development of youth to the detriment of their mental development. But the excessive enthusiasm for sports leads to the coarsening of character, to mental degeneration, and to new diseases. True, not much better is the situation in home education under the conditions of the modern family. Therefore, it is time to pay

---

[4]IBID vol. II, p. 455

most serious attention to the grave and derelict situation of children and youth from the moral point of view. Many lofty concepts are completely out of habitual use, having been replaced by everyday formulas for the easy achievement of the most vulgar comforts and status...

"If one were to impart to children lessons of high morals from the lives of the heroes of all ages and all peoples, the sacred laws of existence could thus be imparted in the form of attractive narratives and examples from the life of all kingdoms of nature. The accumulated wisdom of the ages can be presented in the simplest forms, and thus many new vistas will be revealed. Actually, such lessons are remembered even better when they are presented to children, as you are doing, as short plays, with the children acting the parts of the heroes. Therefore I highly approve of your program. In their gatherings the children could use the name of their chosen hero.

"Also useful are studies of the arts and of the most prosaic handicrafts, as nothing awakens the latent abilities so well as the possibility of a direct personal accomplishment. Good are choral singing, folk dances, and all those studies which demand unified rhythm. And one should especially encourage children to express their opinions about all they have read, heard, and seen; such discussions will lay the foundation for thinking. It is equally important to conduct attractive studies and games that demand especial attentiveness. After all, memory is primarily attentiveness. In the senior groups, the keeping of diaries could be introduced, so that all the good that has been done during the day and all the acknowledged errors could be written down. And in beginning a new day, a resolution should be made not to allow certain conduct to take place during that day, such as irritation, rudeness, or lies, and, on the contrary, to stress special attentiveness, politeness, solicitude for those around, etc. Keeping such a diary, for the purpose of self-analysis, will help considerably in eradicating undesirable habits and affirming new and useful ones. Habits form qualities. Let us also not forget useful excursions for the children in order to become acquainted with various branches of labor, science, and art. It is absolutely essential to teach the children love for nature, in all its manifestations. In this respect, all kinds of picnics and walks are useful for assembling botanical, entomological, and mineralogical collections. All in all, assembling various kinds of collections greatly assists the acquirement of useful knowledge.

"In conclusion I shall quote for you one Discourse: 'You know to what an extent a word enters into a child's heart. Especially up to seven years of age one may recall memories of the Subtle World. Children feel how they sensed that special life. It is useful to ask children whether they remember some particular thing. Such touches are called the opening of memory. Even if with years the memory of the past again becomes dim, nevertheless there will remain a spark of beautiful existence. The Great Teacher[5] loved to uncover the memory. He brought the children close to Him and not only asked them questions but also touched them with His hand, thus increasing the vividness of recollection. He not only loved children but also saw in them the advance of humanity. He was right in treating them as grownups, for when the remote past or the Subtle World is recalled, the mind becomes that of a grownup. Children will never forget the one who approached them as an equal. They will retain this memory for their whole life. Maybe the children remembered the Teacher better than did those who were healed by him. Thus, one should remember that the minors will be the continuers of life, and everyone must impart to them his experience. But it will be wiser to awaken in them the memories of the Subtle World. The most profound spiritual life will be molded where the spark of the existence of the Subtle World began to glow, and where communion with the Invisible World was facilitated. The appearances of the Teacher in a subtle body strengthened the disciples in the reality of the Invisible World. Not all could be receptive to the substance of this World, but, nevertheless, the window was set ajar.'

"Thus, through cautious touches this knowledge will enter the consciousness of the growing generation. Truly, the work for the expansion of consciousness is without end. It is joyous to see how many hearts already respond to the forgotten truths.[6]

---

[5]The Christ. —H.B.
[6]Letters of Helena Roerich vol. II, pp. 456-459

"I am ... fond of the word 'warrior' and admire every heroic and courageous deed. By nature, I myself am quite courageous and militant. Nowhere is it said that we should practise non-resistance to evil. And did not Christ Himself drive away those who scoffed at and violated the sacredness of the Temple?

"Therefore, every mother must bring up her children in the spirit of great deeds, heroism and self-denial for the General Good. This is not approval of war in its usual sense; but we cannot deceive ourselves—we do live in the midst of the most dreadful and ruinous wars of all kinds. But the spiritual war is far more exacting than any other war. That is why it is so important to cultivate courage and fearlessness, the qualities which the disciple of the Masters of Light should first of all develop. However, if there is a strong bond with the Hierarchy, courage and fearlessness come absolutely naturally, as the Hand of the Hierarch will always hold back the final danger and will point out the way to victory. But I repeat, this is only so when the Image of the Master is constantly kept in mind. More than once have we had the opportunity of experiencing this wonderful influence. In a moment of danger we would become suddenly and amazingly serene and we knew that everything would be concluded perfectly.

"I, personally, prefer a courageous self-sacrifice in the performance of one's patriotic duty to such an attitude as that of the contemporary youth of a certain country which was expressed recently in a resolution not to fight for their country in time of war. You may ask, 'What about the Banner of Peace?' And you might even think that I am a secret supporter of war! No, for me war is unspeakably dreadful. I cannot imagine a manifestation of worse ignorance! But since we live in a world where physical power is still highly respected, we have to instill into the young generations the idea of the *illegality of killing and violence*. At the same time we must teach not to be afraid to perform one's duty for one's country, as this is beautiful and courageous. Who would wish to be a defenseless sheep in front of a wolf or a tiger? But tigers and wolves are lurking in every unprotected corner. Until there is a real cooperation among the peoples we shall be under the threat of constant wars and invasions.

"Let women remember about courage, so necessary for them in the fight for their lawful rights. But let them not understand courage as violence, as in the case of the suffragettes who used to break windows and burn mail boxes! Such measures are very ugly, but there are other ways of showing real courage. First of all, it will be in firm striving toward knowledge and beauty directed toward the General Good.[7]

"It is perfectly right that you pay so much attention to children's and youth's literature. This is a most essential problem, as not only in childhood but later on a person's mentality depends very much on the first, and therefore strongest, impressions. So often a good book could correct the results of imperfect surroundings of the family! Certainly there are many valuable books in the literature of the past. It is only necessary to choose correctly, and particularly to discard what is harmful.

"Almost everybody knows that the material and spiritual welfare of whole countries depend on foundations built into the consciousness of children. Nevertheless, almost nothing is done in this direction. I agree with you that books which deal with heroic deeds are most essential. Such books can influence a child's mentality and will guard against the terrible evil of today: the *superficial* attitude toward sacred concepts and the inferior quality of thought. Due to this, the whole structure of life is being built on sand, and it will crumble and disintegrate with the first shock.

"Teach children to understand the significance of each thought and each action, as well as of each manifestation of nature, which has its unfailing laws. Tell them that the violation of these laws is strictly punished. Point out that the vitality and creativeness of people, as well as of other creatures of the kingdom of nature, depend on the invisible world and the invisible vibrations of the great spiritual Sages of the past and present. Children are ready to accept the invisible as reality because their minds are not yet demoralized by destructive doubt. Moreover, today there are so many experiments with

---

[7]IBID vol. I, pp. 165-166

rays which prove the subtle influence of the invisible. Even such an example as photographic negatives will be most convincing to the child's mind. The most complicated scenes may be on a negative, but unless it is chemically developed, they will not be visible! Likewise, a sensitive film records the most distant stars which cannot be perceived through the strongest telescope. The same is true about scientific records of other manifestations invisible to the physical eye. It is necessary to impress upon the child's mind most emphatically the existence of the subtle spheres that surround us; and to eradicate the terror of death and of contact with the Subtle World. The Subtle World is as unavoidable as our earthly life, and when realized, being the sublimation of the earthly world, it will open to us unutterable beauty. Therefore, you must teach children not to be frightened of death, which is an illusion, and not to be afraid of so-called 'ghosts.' Usually, children who have an open psychic sight are not afraid of what they see until the grown-ups influence them either by their mocking attitude or by their stories about ghosts and 'that deadly cold of the grave.' This 'deadly cold' is nothing but a simple chemical reaction of the contact of the subtle with the gross.[8]

"I would suggest that from school age the importance of personal responsibility be advocated in simple and reasonable words. Children in school should be taught to be responsible for every motive, every thought, every deed. They should be given also a clear idea of the meaning and significance of their existence. From this will come the understanding of the necessity to fulfil the obligations of life. Such concepts should be laid into the foundation of the upbringing of the young generation.[9]

"The approaching great epoch is closely connected with the ascendancy of woman. As in the best days of humanity, the future epoch will again offer woman her rightful place alongside her eternal fellow traveler and co-worker, man. You must remember that the grandeur of the Cosmos is built by the dual Origin. Is it possible, therefore, to belittle one Element of It?

[8]IBID vol. I, pp. 150-151
[9]IBID vol. I, p. 505

"All the present and coming miseries and the cosmic cataclysms to a great degree result from the subjugation and abasement of woman. The dreadful decline of morality, the diseases and degeneration of some nations are also the results of the slavish dependence of woman. Woman is deprived of the greatest human privilege—complete participation in creative thought and constructive work. She is deprived not only of equal rights but, in many countries, of equal education with man. She is not allowed to express her abilities in the building of social and government life, of which, by Cosmic Law and Right, she is a full-fledged member. But a woman slave can give to the world slaves only. The proverb "great mother, great son" has a cosmic, scientific foundation. As sons mostly take after their mothers, and daughters after fathers, great is cosmic justice! By humiliating woman, man humiliates himself! This explains today the paucity of man's genius.

"Could the terrors and crimes of today be possible if both Origins had been balanced? In the hands of woman lies the salvation of humanity and of our planet. Woman must realize her significance, the great mission of the Mother of the World; she should be prepared to take responsibility for the destiny of humanity. Mother, the life-giver, has every right to direct the destiny of her children. The voice of woman, the mother, should be heard amongst the leaders of humanity. The mother suggests the first conscious thoughts to her child. She gives direction and quality to all his aspirations and abilities. But the mother who posesses no thought of culture can suggest only the lower expressions of human nature.

"The woman who strives to knowledge and beauty, who realizes her lofty responsibility, will greatly uplift the whole level of life. There will be no place for disgusting vices which lead to the degeneration and destruction of whole countries.

"But in her striving toward education, woman must remember that all educational systems are only the *means* for the development of a *higher* knowledge and culture. The true culture of thought is developed by the culture of *spirit* and *heart*. Only such a combination gives that great *synthesis* without which it is impossible to realize the real grandeur, diversity, and complexity of human life in its cosmic evolution. Therefore, while striving to knowledge, may woman remember the Source of Light and the Leaders of Spirit—those great Minds who, verily, created the consciousness of humanity. In approaching this Source, this leading Principle of Synthesis, humanity will find the way to real evolution.

"And woman is the one who should know and proclaim this leading Principle because from the very beginning she was chosen to link the two worlds, visible and invisible. Woman posesses the power of the sacred life energy. The coming epoch brings knowledge about this great omnipresent energy, which is manifested in all immortal creations of human genius.

"Western woman is awake and realizes her powers. Her cultural contributions are already evident. However, the majority of Western women—as with all beginners—start with imitation; whereas, it is in original self-expression that real beauty and harmony are found. Would we like to see man losing the beauty of manhood? The same is true about a man who has a sense of beauty. He certainly does not wish to see a woman imitating his habits and competing with his vices. Imitation always starts with the easiest. But we hope that this first step will soon be outlived and that woman will deepen her knowledge of Mother-Nature and will find true, original ways of self-expression.

"The Cosmos manifests unity of law, but there is no repetition in its variety. Why then does humanity alone strive toward uniformity in everything, while at the same time it violates the fundamental unity of law? Uniformity of perception, uniformity of life, and especially uniformity of thought is cherished by man. It is forgotten that uniformity of expression leads toward stagnation and death. Life and its power are in perpetual change of form. It is necessary to apply this life-giving principle in all the expressions of our life.

"Let us collect the most beautiful, heroic images of all times and countries, and with creative imagination let us apply their achievements in our life, taking into consideration the peculiarities of our epoch. Only such imitation will give the correct foundation for further progress.

"I shall finish my address to woman with a page from The Teaching of Life:

'When nations started disunity, the result was self-destruction. And only a return to balance can stop this self-destruction. Humanity does not apply the principles of creativeness in right proportion and thus violates the foundations of Being. When by the law of the Cosmic Magnet the lower forms are subordinated to the higher, this concerns only the energies which should be transmuted. But when the Origins are called to create and give life, it is impossible to remove one of the Origins without self-destruction. Therefore, humanity will start its real evolution only when both Origins are affirmed in life. All principles which do not include the understanding of the dual Origin can only increase the lack of balance. Humanity must understand the law of the Cosmic Magnet. Much can be done for evolution by the realization of the grandeur of the dual Origin which is the basis of Life.'

"Even this simple truth still does not find its place in the consciousness of man! Our scientists—biologists, chemists, physicists—should know the truth about the dual Element, or polarity, but they are silent. And such truth, in its most sacred and vital application, is scorned, and the rights of the strong selfishly dominate. The trouble is that the mind of man is disconnected from its source—the Cosmic Mind. Being part of the Cosmos, the human being yet does not see his solidarity, his unity with the Cosmos. And his observations of the manifestations of nature do not suggest to him any analogies. However, only in observations and comparisons with human nature is it possible to find the keys to all the mysteries of life, and therefore the solution to many problems of everyday life. People, like parrots, love to repeat the favorite ancient formula, 'Macrocosm is microcosm'! Much is said, much is repeated without the proper attention to its meaning! The enforced dogmas, human laws, and the standard of life have caused humanity to neglect the process of thinking; and the human mind, with rare exceptions, has become an automaton. Everybody is preaching various freedoms, but the most opposite schools of thought agree in one thing—they all are afraid of freedom of thought!

"Therefore, woman must defend not only her own rights but the right of free thought for the whole of humanity! Through the development of thinking, our abilities will expand. Let us think with the broadest, the purest thoughts. It is said:

'The kingdom is not made up of royalties or of subjects, but is created by cosmic ideas. Let us create our own cities, our countries, our planets! But let such thought be created by the heart, as only thought born of the heart is vital. The heart is the greatest Cosmic Magnet. All cosmic energies are attracted to the heart, and the heart assimilates them. The heart manifests in life all aspirations. The fire of space is attracted to the heart and the whole cosmic process lies in this principle. Therefore, the Cosmos exists in the attraction of the heart. Only the energies which are based on the attraction of the heart are vital. Thus, infinitely, the chain of life is forged by the heart.'

"Have you listened to your heart? Does it beat in rhythm with the Perfect Heart which embraces all of you?

"Thus, I shall finish with the words about the heart. Let woman affirm this great symbol, which can transfigure the whole of life. Let her strive to transmute the spiritual life of mankind.

"The mother, the life-giver, the life-protector—let her become also the Mother, the Leader ,the *All*-Giver, the *All*-Receiver.[10]

"And now let us turn to the subject of abortion. To deal with this problem now is quite timely. There appear currently the most disgusting articles about it and some of them are written with the approval of the clergy. On this subject I shall quote some paragraphs from the Teaching:

'The spirit is connected with the embryo at the moment of conception. It begins to enter in the beginning of the fourth month when the first nerve and brain channels are being formed. The formation of the vertebral column brings in the next degree of possession of the body. Wonderful is the moment of birth, when the consciousness of the spirit flashes up brightly and then

---

[10]IBID vol. I, pp. 6-9

blends with matter. There are even cases when words are pronounced at birth. The final possession of the body takes place at the seventh year of a child's life.' It is also said, 'Even as hunger directs toward food, so the spirit is directed toward incarnation, as only matter can give the new impulses.'

"Therefore, it is not hard to imagine how much suffering the spirit that is ready to incarnate endures from the forced interruption of life already begun, or from the averting of an incarnation even planned by karma. What a difficult karma the ignorant and criminal parents prepare for themselves![11]

"You mentioned a most painful problem of today's life—the question of the legality of abortion. Of course, there are no two opinions on this subject: abortion is most definitely murder. Therefore, only in cases where the mother's life is in danger should it take place. But it is wrong to think that a woman who is guilty of abortion always attracts low spirits. The karma of the whole family should be taken into consideration. Often we can notice that in a family where one of the children is worthless the other children are not bad. Karma ties groups of people for long, long thousands of years. And often, even a high spirit has not unimpeachable, irreproachable parents. And it is significant that the dark forces are especially against the reincarnation of highly developed spirits, and they try their best to prevent the reincarnations that are dangerous for them. And, once more, it is not the purgatory of the Subtle World that prevents spirits from reincarnating, but only the crime of the parents. There is not a more powerful purgatory than the earthly life, if all the potentialities of the individuality are intensified. It is said in the Teaching, 'As the one who hungers longs for food, even so, the spirit that is ready to incarnate longs for the new incarnation.'

"Of course, woman should not only be a giver of physical life; she has her other high duties. And for that purpose there is the most natural abstinance, which can easily be practised and the increase of the family thus regulated. This is quite possible when high interests occupy the head and the heart. Of course, I expect plenty of opposition; still, I insist on it. No doubt, in the

---

[11]IBID vol. I, p. 167

present state of the family it is quite difficult, but already there are such families and they will increase in the future. In remote antiquity, people knew how to regulate their families by the phases of the moon. Later on this was considered black magic, but nowadays even such measures would be better than the dreadful abortions that cripple women and therefore the coming generations.[12]

"Is it not mentioned in the Teaching about the high significance of woman in all the activities of life? Is it not indicated that the cause of so many miseries of our planet and of humanity is because of the loss of balance between the two sexes? Cosmos is based on these Origins, and on the Cosmic Scale both Origins are equally great and necessary, for one cannot exist without the other. But what do we see in life and in its customs made by people? Woman in some countries is degraded to the level of slavery, and even in more civilized countries all privileges belong to man.

"No doubt, in many respects, it is woman's own fault, especially now when she tries to imitate all the vices of man, instead of expressing her own character and originality. The result is an indecent caricature. Of course, there are no limitations in spiritual creativeness of either of the sexes. The creativeness of thought, art and construction of life are from the spirit and belong to both sexes. Both sexes have their characteristic features and this makes life more beautiful. And these features should be manifested most powerfully in order to revive the salutary beauty of romanticism and heroism. After the refinement of the consciousness and sentiments, the beautiful destiny of both sexes will be vividly expressed.

"In conclusion, I may tell you that many families have no right to such a term because they are united unlawfully. Verily, many unions which are legalized by all human laws should be considered illegal. True lawful union is a great science of the future. This science will be based on the immutable cosmic laws. Much was said and is said about the affinity of souls.

---

[12]IBID vol. I, pp. 179-180

But who knows and understands this truth in the grandeur of Cosmic Law?

"You remember that in the books of the Living Ethics it is said that people should be united according to the elements. Only parents who belong to the same element can give life to healthy and well-balanced children. 'And in life we often see that fire is united with water, and air with earth. The degeneration of entire nations is the outcome of such mixtures.' The time will come when this truth will be understood in all its glory and people will apply it in life as the most essential. The forms of life and all functions of humanity must be rebuilt according to the laws of Cosmos—that is, if humanity cares to continue its existence and evolution on this planet—otherwise, the destiny of Lemuria awaits us, i.e., destruction by fire.

"Certainly, I approve of the fight against abortion, but how will you fight this evil? There are no laws which can either preserve or forbid anything. That is why I, personally, think that first of all you must battle by uplifting the level of consciousness of the growing generations, directing it toward the right comprehension of the human cosmic mission in general and that of motherhood in particular. Thoughts should be directed toward creative work and broad problems of the General Good on a cosmic scale. It is important to establish *the world's scale*. Again, we return to the same fundamental question: *upbringing and education*. As the Great Mind expressed it, 'The source of all suffering is ignorance,' which is so true; and the history of humanity, with all its dark pages of persecution of the best representatives of knowledge, proves it.

"Without doubt, every mother and every child have the right to security, and here also there is no place for dividing into legitimate and illegitimate. But we may go further and say that every citizen has a right to security of work. So much has to be altered. And here the voice of the heart—woman—should help.[13]

"The process of outliving the accumulated karmic results is painful. But precisely this very process brings us quickest of all

---

[13]IBID vol. I, pp. 182-183

to the path of Service to humanity. Answer yourself honestly: was it not these blows of fate that made you seek the path of the true Light? Did not the contact with the horrible ulcers of reality broaden your consciousness and enable you to emerge from the conventional ways of thinking? I think you will bless this life of yours that opened to you the source of spiritual rebirth. Do you not experience joy when your consciousness ponders upon Being? Is this not the joy of a new comprehension of the purpose of existence, the joy of spiritual creativeness?

"Likewise, the attraction and love between the opposite Elements should be regarded as a manifestation of Cosmic Law. Verily, spiritually dead is the one who lacks this divine fire of inspiration and creativeness, given us by the Cosmic Law of existence. Unfortunately, even up to the present time there is no true understanding of this powerful foundation of cosmic structure. People have forgotten, or rather do not want to admit, the great cosmic significance of love. The materialism of our age puts love on the level of a purely physiological function. At best, love today is treated as a psychological process. But if the cosmic significance of love could be realized once more, people would see in love its highest function, i.e., the awakening of all the highest emotions and creative abilities. Precisely, this awakening is the chief purpose and the true keynote of love. Love is a unifying creative power. On the higher planes of Being everything is created by thought. But for the fulfilment of these thought forms, there must be the two Elements united by Cosmic Love. There is a great deal of misunderstanding surrounding the fundamental concept of the dual Element. Religions are to blame for this, and especially Christianity. The church profaned the greatest Cosmic Mystery by demeaning marriage and degrading the woman, by its contempt of love and its vows of celibacy and monasticism, and by declaring this spiritual impoverishment to be the highest achievement of the human spirit. This frightful fanaticism brought about terrible consequences, among which the mortification of the flesh was and is not the worst. Let us recall the criminal hypocrisy, the dreadful sexual perversions and crimes that resulted from these prohibitions and condemnations, which are completely against Cosmic Law. Likewise, the words of Christ, 'But I say unto you, That whosoever looketh on a woman to lust after her hath committed adultery with her already in his heart' are entirely misinterpreted. These words should be understood in the light of the Cosmic Law, which has in view the affinity of souls and the true lawfulness of marriage. (I have written about this before.) The science of correct marriage will give to humanity the necessary equilibrium. Precisely, most unions which constitute marriage today are, from a cosmic point of view, adulterous, and they threaten to ruin the whole planet. The right comprehension of this great mystery, and the giving of due respect to woman can regenerate the world. People should understand love in its highest manifestation, and should look for its reflection here on Earth. And, indeed, the posterity that would result from this love would be much higher than that which issues from chance unions. Marriage entered into just for the sake of progeny is an ugly and sacrilegious manifestation. We should always remember that man is a destined creator of the world. Therefore, all types of creativeness should be manifested by his spiritual substance, which is possible only if he becomes kindled by the highest love. Love alone reveals all concealed fires. Thus, in the foundation of each creation is laid the great Attraction, the great Love. All that is in the world depends on love and is sustained by love. Love must lead to the higher comprehension.

"How beautiful is the Image of the Mother of the World! So much beauty, self-renunciation and tragedy is in this majestic Image! Aspire in your heart to the Highest, and joy and exultation will enter your soul. The whole creativeness of man, all mystic exaltation, is the result of that same Love, be it expressed or concealed. And we should remember that for the pure, all is pure.[14]

"Who can tell where woman's rights—rights given to her by Nature—begin and where they end? The same question could be asked about man's rights. Only evolution gives the answer and points out the direction. There is no indication in Nature that woman should be restricted to her hearth! Verily, she is the Mother and the Custodian of the World. Hence, there is not a single domain of life where man could rule alone. *It is precisely*

---

[14]IBID vol. I, pp. 372-373

this domination of the one Element that has created the dark epoch. Creativeness is given equally to both Elements. In man it is more pronounced at the moment only because woman has been deprived of equal education and has not had the same possibilities for exercising her creative forces on a broad scale. Even today an ignorant belief prevails that the brain of the woman is lighter and smaller than that of the man, and that therefore woman is more stupid, etc. I remember how amazed were the scientists when, after the death of a brilliant writer, Anatole France, his brain was weighed and was found to be amazingly light—almost like a child's brain! Likewise, when someone once said that the more developed is the animal the bigger is its brain, I remember that the Teacher pointed out that some insects are cleverer than animals. Take as an example the ants or the bees. A heavy weight of brain signifies great physical endurance, but not refinement. Entirely different are the signs of great intelligence. The convolutions of the brain have great significance. However, here also, only a partial conclusion may be reached, as very little is known about the mysteries of the inner man. There was another, still more ridiculous, theory of the anthropologists that the bigger the skull is, the more intelligent is the man. Here again, Nature proved the contrary, as it was found that the size of the skull of the island savage is larger than that of the average witty Frenchman. Today, many have come to the conclusion that there are no grounds for considering the mental abilities of woman below those of man.

"The dark epoch tried to make out of woman a concubine and a nurse. But if woman stands high as a mother, it is not only as mother of the family, but as Mother and Great Teacher of the consciousness of nations! Thus, as it is said in the Teaching, 'Woman, who gives life to people, has the right to govern their destiny. We want to see woman taking part in government, in the councils of ministers, in all constructive activity.' But it is said at the same time that '...the struggle between the two Elements will be hard, and woman herself will have to recapture her rights which she voluntarily relinquished.'

"But the violated equilibrium has had such a terrible effect on the life of the whole planet that it is now in danger of destruction! And cosmic justice and goal-fitness once more come to the rescue by bringing forward more and more talented women. In the younger countries destined for evolution, one may observe the way in which woman expresses herself. Thus, in America, there are already women ministers, women diplomats, ambassadors, state governors, directors of the largest firms, aviators, lawyers who win the most complicated cases. Also, a trusted personal secretary of the President is a woman. Indeed, in America women are the main promoters of education and culture. Even most of the 'wunderkinds' are to be found among little girls. All these are good omens of the coming epoch.

"And now ponder deeply on the following: In the process of evolution Nature will remove the imperfections of physical conception, birth and helpless babyhood (this eventually will depart into the realm of the legendary); for the formation of the body of the incarnating spirit the forces of both mother and father will be necessary and will participate in this process of densification, and nourishment in general will not require a smoky hearth. Could it then be possible that the sphere accessible to woman may become still narrower until she is limited to the role of 'amuser' of man? No, it is time for the best people to think about this and to be ashamed at the poverty of imagination that has been revealed thus far.[15]

"...let us remember that only an enlightened heart or a mind illumined by the light of the heart can become a reliable guide in reading all the Sacred Scriptures. Religions which allowed, or rather affirmed the humiliation and subordination of woman are destined to extinction. By humiliating woman, the later religions were indeed serving Satan; knowing the power of woman, the Prince of this World, for the fulfillment of his plan, first of all schemed to demean her—the bearer of the higher energy.

"But when woman (who, by a strange paradox, is the main supporter of the church) awoke and understood where her age-long oppressors were hiding, the downfall of the church took place. Religion, or rather quests of the spirit will never leave the

---

[15]IBID vol. I, pp. 460-462

people, but the awakened consciousnesses will demand new forms and new ways from spiritual teachers and leaders.

"The most ancient Teachings always highly regarded the Feminine Principle, and even female divinities were considered by them to be the most sacred. We can now find traces of these most ancient cults among the American Indians, whose priesthood is headed by women; women also head the clan, and the whole line of inheritance is considered as coming from the woman's side. Likewise, there is no distinction between the two Origins in the Teaching of Buddha, and woman, as well as man, can reach the state of Arhatship. And even now in India, in spite of the fact that the later Brahmins humiliated woman because of greed and self-interest, the cult of the Goddess Kâlî is nevertheless spread most widely. The last of the known sages of India, Râmakrishna and Vivekananda, were worshippers of the Divine Origin in its aspect of the Mother of the World. Indeed, it is the ignorant and avaricious distortion of the cosmic law that has placed woman in a subjugated position.

"Certainly it would be wrong to blame the Masculine Principle alone for the situation created; woman, too, is at fault. Many women welcomed being constantly in custody as wards, and precisely this weakened their strength and dulled their abilities. Therefore, nowadays a reverse order is necessary. Woman must accept the struggle against life's obstacles in order to temper her strength and manifest her true nature. True, the struggle for her lost rights will be a hard one, but with the refinement of thought and acceptance of the higher, psychic energy much will be eased. Indeed, not a single high experiment with the subtlest energies can be performed without the presence of the Feminine Element. The famous philosophers' stone cannot be discovered or created without the participation of woman. Thus, Cosmos itself, Nature herself, affirms the equilibrium of the Origins in their higher functions. And one may say, 'To confirm rights does not mean to possess them.'

"The first task which faces women is to insist in all countries upon full rights and equal education with men; to try with all their might to develop their thinking faculties, and, above all, to learn to stand on their own feet without leaning altogether upon men. In the West there are many fields which are now available to women, and one must admit that they are quite successful in all of them.

"It is necessary to awaken in woman herself a great respect for her own Origin; she should realize her great destiny as a bearer of the higher energy. Indeed, it is woman's intuition which should again, as in the better periods of history, lead humanity on the path of progress. And meanwhile, one can only profoundly grieve and, at times, watch with inexpressible shame how woman humiliates herself in her desire to win the admiration of the stronger sex. The combinations of the luminaries are favorable for the awakening of women, and I believe that the new influx of psychic energy will be utilized by women for lofty tasks and in search of new achievements for the good of humanity. Let the fire of achievement in the name of great service be truly kindled in woman. The quality of self-sacrifice is fundamental in woman, but she should learn not to limit her self-sacrifice to the narrow concept of home life, which is often nothing more than encouragement of the family's egoism—she should apply it on a world scale. I believe that woman should be even more educated and cultured than man, for indeed it is she who instills in her family the first concepts of knowledge, culture, and understanding of statesmanship.[16]

"According to the Sacred Teaching, the fall of humanity began from the time of the abasement of the Feminine Principle. Therefore, with the beginning of the Epoch of the Mother of the World woman should realize that she herself contains all forces, and the moment she shakes off the age-old hypnosis of her seemingly lawful subjugation and mental inferiority and occupies herself with a manifold education, she will create in collaboration with man a new and better world. Indeed, it is essential that woman herself refute the unworthy and profoundly ignorant assertion about her passive receptivity and therefore her inability to create independently. But in the entire Cosmos there is *no* passive element. In the chain of creation each manifestation in its turn becomes relatively passive or active, giving or receiving. Cosmos affirms the greatness of woman's

---

[16]IBID vol. II, pp. 304-305

creative principle. Woman is a personification of nature, and it is nature that teaches man, not man nature. Therefore, may all women realize the grandeur of their origin, and may they strive for knowledge. Where there is knowledge, there is power. Ancient legends actually attribute to woman the role of the guardian of sacred knowledge. Therefore, may she now also remember her defamed ancestress, Eve, and again harken to the voice of her intuition in not only eating of but also planting as many trees bearing the fruits of the knowledge of good and evil as possible. And as before, when she deprived Adam of his dull, senseless bliss, so let her now lead him on to a still broader vista and into the majestic battle with the chaos of ignorance for her divine rights.

"In conclusion I want to add that women must without delay begin to perfect themselves in all fields, and this is not done at a moment's notice. First of all, we women have so much to outlive. Let us develop primarily a sense of our own dignity and learn to lean courageously on our own strength and knowledge, in order to join in, as well as accept, responsibility for the great structure of General Good.[17]

"In one of my letters I already wrote that I consider marriage a sacred concept, and also that I will never cast a stone at a woman who, because of self-sacrificing love, ignored the established conventions, providing, however, that she does not build her happiness on the misfortune of others. It seems to me that this is spoken broadly enough, and I would not want to enter into further explanations regarding all cases when it is permissible to break the conventions. After all, every sensible human being well understands the significance of the inviolability of marriage and of the harmony of the family for the growing generation and in the structure of the state. It is said in the Teaching that the family is the prototype of the state. The welfare and the well-being of the state rest upon the firm foundations of the family.

"If, however, one were to cite the most immutable cosmic truths that establish the inviolability of marriage, the majority

---

[17]IBID vol. II, pp. 359-360

would undoubtedly use these proclaimed truths to vindicate the violation of it. Thus, if one were to affirm to them that the sacredness and inviolability of marriage has as its basis the great truth about twin-souls, with an eased conscience they will at once start to look for the half which belongs to them, and without fail will find it at someone else's fireside. There are not a few who explain all their infatuations as cosmic attractions. Is it possible to explain to these people that precisely the purity of their married life will bring them faster and closer to finding the kindred soul? If one were to tell them that during moral licentiousness twin-souls feel an especially sharp antagonism toward each other, they would not believe it and would become indignant. Whereas, only where there is purity of feeling are the most beautiful unions and best possibilities attainable. Owing to the moral degradation of contemporary humanity, a harmonious union is rarest of all, yet only then are the greatest achievements possible in all worlds.

"It is shocking to observe how light-mindedly people approach the Teaching, which demands from them the most serious, the most penetrating attitude toward all vital questions together with a realization of one's full responsibility not only for each action but also for each thought. The Living Ethics, though primarily setting forth the moral foundations, also demands a full realization of responsibility, fulfillment of one's duty and all accepted obligations, and honesty in everything and toward all. Each lie, each deceit, each hypocrisy is severely condemned. A man who has entered the path of the Teaching of Living Ethics must account for all his deeds and should know that his violation of the moral foundations will entail redoubled consequences for him, for he cannot say that he acted because of ignorance.

"Thus, purity in married life is an absolute condition for all true disciples. How can one approach the Covenants of Light if the soul is full of unbridled feelings? One of the Teachers says that 'In ancient times the master who purified silver had to sit before the crucible in which was melted the mass of metal until he could see his face reflected in the purified metal. The improvement of the human essence—the law of evolution—refines crude forms of life in accordance with a perfect pattern and must bring these forms to that point of development where this pattern shall be reflected in each organic cell of these forms, in all conditions and states—physical, mental, and spiritual; and fire, i.e., pressure, tension, and sufferings are the only levers by which the mass—the human race—can be raised from the crucible. The physical substance must be raised into the light of the substance of higher mentality, where the renunciation of any attachment to the lower conditions of the substance—*the passions*—will make possible the manifestation of more refined and perfected spiritual forms...

'Any sensible man cannot fail to see the great necessity of changing the methods of instituting marriages and of certain stipulations in existing marriage laws if we wish to see a better race of human beings, which is on the way to replace ours. But the rejection of the present marriage laws, a conscious lowering of ideals, and the acceptance of a lawlessness that was dominant in antediluvian times, can only have one result—*degeneration.* Humanity will not acquire strength and knowledge through regression deep into past centuries; only a purifying, progressive motion creates evolution. Therefore, education and upbringing should be directed toward finding a true union of both sides in marriage, and monogamy must be established instead of the existing disorderly mixing of sexes...

'A good gardener, desiring to cultivate a beautiful flower of a certain family, collects seeds or takes a graft from the best sample of the chosen species and combines it with another sample of the same family; and when he receives in this manner a pefected variety he will try not to mix its seeds with the lower specimens of the same family. The same laws are also applicable to the human race. Therefore, no refutation can make out of that which is usually called 'sexual freedom' anything but freedom for the satisfaction of lower desires...

'In the future more perfected race true marriages will be just as common as they are rare at present...

'Of course, it is unthinkable to insist on the continuity of marriage bonds between people who are antagonistic, faithless, and cruel to each other, for this would be the worst kind of tyranny, but it is essential to institute a careful choice, and to use natural means for establishing a wise combination. A wrong or unfavorable aspect of the planets, covetous considerations, or an abnormal sexual attraction approaching an unhealthy state are responsible for the majority of unhappy and unnatural marriages at present.

'Humanity is now developing under a different aspect of the universal law from the one that ruled the birth and evolution of man during the early centuries of this Cycle. The law of differentiation—disunity—ruled in the far-off past, whereas now, primarily, the law of unity acts, and those who, because of egoistical desires, attempt to oppose the preordained Divine Plan exclude themselves from the evolutionary current...'

"In conclusion, I will give one more quotation: 'Woman of the present race approaches the highest point in the coming Cycle, and every woman who can save man from his lower "ego"—in that she herself does not succumb to the temptations that her lower nature places also on her path, thus affirming the existence of a higher phase of life—this woman, in the coming Cycle, will do more for the salvation of the race to which they both belong than any man, no matter how great he may be. The coming epoch is the epoch of woman, and therefore, in the end precisely woman, far more than man, will be summoned to the austere responsibility for the immorality of our age. The coming time affords a great possibility for woman, therefore I again appeal to you, daughters of Light, pray that God who is within you may help you to preserve purity...'[18]

"What really is terrible is the intolerance of some churches. Verily, '...most difficult of all is to reveal the true Image of Christ,' as one of the Great Teachers expressed it. The main cause of intolerance is ignorance. But things cannot continue this way, and the new generation already demands a new explanation of the problems of Being. If the spiritual authorities do not want to be entirely ignored, they should consider this demand and should be able to satisfy it. The consciousness of the masses grows and expands, and it is impossible to keep it locked within mediaeval torture chambers! The Western Church

[18]IBID vol. II, pp. 519-521

is also alarmed, but in order not to lose entirely its authority, it begins to watch the movement of science and even some of the Eastern Teachings. Some of the clergy even admit the existence of the Great Brotherhood. And truly speaking, what is the Hierarchy of Light if not 'Jacob's Ladder'? Others pay attention to the law of Reincarnation. The New Testament, the words of Christ Himself, confirm this law, which was a cornerstone of all the most ancient religions. From these sources Christianity later borrowed all its symbols and ceremonies. A recent Conference of Bishops in the United States proposed to study the works of the great Origen. This is a great step forward, as the studying of the Origen may broaden the ecclesiastical framework and its dogmas. We should not forget that the law of Reincarnation was rejected only in the sixth century by the Council of Constantinople. And we are supposed to accept as revelation and dogma the authority of the Fathers of the Church who, with great seriousness, discussed such problems as 'How many spirits may be placed on the end of a needle?' or such similar pearls as 'Has woman a soul?' And these reverend Fathers, the educators of our consciousness, did not hesitate to slap each other and tear each other's hair and beards! Even now, there are some people, quite educated in some respects, who sincerely believe that they will be raised from the dead in the last day of judgment—in their physical bodies! That is the main reason why they are so against cremation. How to understand this self-delusion, by hypnotism or by atavism?

"It is time to understand that the world needs vivid souls, able to perceive quickly, intensely and profoundly that the essence of the events of today is evident proof of the uselessness of outlived ideas and structures, and that amid unprecedented destruction the new ideas of great tolerance and cultural leadership are engendered, like heat lightning against a black sky.[19]

"If the great example and sacrifice of Christ kindles the fire within our hearts, and if we apply his Covenant, it can be said that he did not suffer in vain, and that precisely the Cup that he accepted, sealed his Covenant. But if we imagine that,

---

[19]IBID vol. I, pp. 175-176

regardless of what we do and what crimes we commit, the blood that was shed by Christ will save us forever from the power of the devil, then we ourselves become these very devils! No one can save another. Only by personal efforts can the spirit ascend into the preordained beautiful worlds. 'Faith without works is dead.'

"All the Great Teachers are called Saviours of the World, because again and again they point out to us the Path of Light. However, They are able to help and safeguard us only so far as we ourselves accept Their protection. The whole of Cosmos is based on the law of reciprocity or mutuality, and where there is no response, there is no result. This explains why Christ could not perform miracles where there was no faith in him, and where there was no striving of the spirit toward his healing ray.

"The Sacrament of the Great Sacrifice has its origin in the most ancient Mysteries. At the last initiation, the neophyte was offered a cup filled with the juice of pomegranates (symbolizing blood); accepting it, he had to spill the contents in four directions as a sign of his readiness to give his soul and body for the service of the world, that is, to suffer for Truth. Thus, Christ also wished to affirm this symbol among his disciples, in order to infix the memory of his sacrifice and Covenant for future generations. But no mechanical communion is able to save our souls, for 'faith without works is dead.'

"I remember my conversation with a woman missionary about Christ's sacrifice. She was beating her breast and shouting hysterically that she knew that Christ had suffered for her, and so had saved her from eternal damnation. To which I answered, 'You are mistaken. Christ suffered not for you, but *because of you*.' Of course, we never met her again, were proclaimed pagans and spies, and were rewarded by other corresponding titles.

"Nothing seems more sacrilegious to me than the concept of an All-Merciful Father-God, who sacrificed his only begotten and consubstantial Son for the sins of the people, the people whom, according to the Scriptures, he himself created! It reminds one of a certain Akkadian ruler who sacrificed his son in an attempt to avoid the consequences of his own sins.

Ancient history recorded and condemned such a barbarous concept of fatherhood. Is it possible for later generations to accept such an example of parental love and to elevate it to the stature of Divinity? Every truly loving earthly father or mother would gladly sacrifice their lives for the salvation of their son. Can a Divine Father be morally inferior to the people whom he himself created!

"It is by voluntary sacrifice or self-renunciation that the world is held together. In the higher worlds the chalice of self-sacrifice is radiant with all the fires of unutterable joy, and only on our plane, the plane of tests and sorrow, is this chalice full of bitterness and poison. The Spirit that has realized the joy of self-sacrifice is in itself the highest Beauty. Beauty and self-sacrifice lie in the foundation of Being.

"You ask how to understand the appalling example of betrayal by Judas. We know the occult law that Light attracts darkness; therefore, the stronger the light, the denser the darkness. Thus, on all great paths, the encounter with the servants of darkness and with betrayers of varying degrees is inevitable. They follow the Source of Light like shadows. Indeed, the very hatred of the dark ones binds them to the object of their hatred. The potentialities of such betrayal definitely were hidden in Judas himself. That is why the dark forces used him, as well as the priests' and Pharisees' hatred, as a tool for accomplishing their criminal purpose. Therefore, Judas can be regarded as the representative of a collective betrayal.

"People are not fully cognizant of the extent to which the visible and invisible worlds participate in their deeds and in events, and of how often they become the semiconscious and subconscious instruments of the servants of darkness. Indeed, one can assert that two-thirds of all the actions of people are performed under the influence of visible and invisible counselors. And, alas, because of the mental state of mankind those counselors are for the most part denizens of the lower spheres adjacent to Earth. The influence of the lower spheres is more easily assimilated by the denizens of the earthly plane, whereas the pure, higher influences can be received only by a pure vessel.[20]

"You assume that 'the dark doers of harm are confident that it is they who do good.' But I do not agree with this assumption. All conscious doers of harm, in the depths of their consciousness know full well the covetous cause of their actions. Even the so-called unconscious ill-doers, for some reason, are always trying not to suffer personal harm, and chiefly, not to their pockets. The degrees of consciousnesses are without end, and we can still see not a few animal-like consciousnesses. Verily, there is no greater misfortune than ignorance.

"However, the cannon 'By thy God' must be applied in life, practically on every step. During each conversation, when there is no unity of consciousnesses, our first duty is not to infuriate our companion by contradiction and censure of his convictions, but, starting with his best possibilities and considering the level of his consciousness, we should gradually and patiently broaden his horizon. Thus, speaking with a Moslem, you will not begin by praising Lord Buddha or demeaning Mohammed, but you will interchange with him all that is beautiful in his religion, and when opportunity arises, you will explain more deeply and broadly the meaning of some sayings of Mohammed that have entered the treasury of world wisdom. Thus you will also do in any other situations in life. You will not speak with an avid chauvinist against his country, but you will discover the best expressions and qualities of his nation, and you will point out to him new ways for developing its particular qualifications. Your breadth of understanding of national beliefs will smooth over the factor of chauvinism and, unexpectedly for him, his limited consciousness will begin to respond to the note of containment. And so, one should learn to carry on timely conversations without animosity but evaluating your companion with friendliness. Precisely, carry them on with PATIENCE and respect for your adversary, not permitting irritation, derision, and other unworthy means. And in each conversation one should know how to sacrifice one's self, one's knowledge, and

---

[20]IBID vol. II, pp. 211-212

not to boast of one's enlightenment. Remember that it is said in the Teaching that only a pompous ignorance loves to spread on window sills the dry, small twigs of its knowledge, but he who truly knows does not fear to snip off a piece of his knowledge when it can oppress and humiliate his companion. In this manner, the cannon 'By thy God' is merely a manifestation of selflessness, without which nothing can be achieved. It is a great error to liken it to non-resistance to evil. If you wish, accept this canon as a manifestation of mercy. And so, the cannon 'By thy God' is fully compatible precisely with resistance to evil. One can put a stop to evil by various means, and straight-knowledge should prompt the *limits* of possibilities when applying the given cannon.[21]

"One should not overestimate the achievements of Hatha Yoga and think that 'the adepts of Hatha Yoga are equal to those of Raja Yoga in ability to awaken the kundalini and to acquire various siddhis,' and that 'they reach bliss and liberation from matter.' It is not so! The degree of bliss reached by such adepts is very relative, and they *never* reach liberation from matter (in the sense which is meant by the Great Teachers) by means of Hatha Yoga. As it is said in the Teaching, 'We know of no one who reached the goal by way of Hatha Yoga.'

"Even the development of the lower siddhis, to which the Hatha Yogis come by stubborn and terribly difficult mechanical exercises (Western literature has no idea about even half of these horrors), is not lasting, and in their next incarnations they may lose all these siddhis. Only those achievements are valuable and permanent that come naturally, for then they are the result of inner spiritual development and can never be lost. Only in such a way can the all-powerful manifestations be reached. Exercises in Hatha Yoga should not go beyond a slight and very careful pranayama, which strengthens health, as otherwise they might be dangerous and could lead to mediumism, obsession and insanity.

"Quite correctly, the Hindu people of high spiritual development consider Hatha Yoga most undesirable, and they

[21]IBID vol. II, pp. 525-526

say that at best it is useful 'for fat and ill people.' Even Vivekananda, who is so often mentioned now, though he cited examples of fearful demoniac persons whom he knew who were able to peform the most amazing miracles and cure the hopelessly sick by a glance, was very much against the so-called siddhis and these miracles.

"Therefore, the main test for all spiritual Teachers is the magnet of their own hearts, their occult ability to change spiritually the surroundings and to transform the consciousness and the very nature of their disciples. It is by no means their ability in so-called miracles. This requires the fiery ray of synthesis, which is inherent in the opened centers but not in the lower siddhis. No pranayama can give the necessary purification and high results if the consciousness does not correlate with the High Ideal. The higher forms of Yoga do not need pranayama. Every coolie in India knows about pranayama; the average Hindu performs it every day, but nevertheless they are far from spiritual achievement. Therefore, do not rely just upon pranayama![22]

"One should also take into consideration that Hatha Yoga is dangerous because, in a peculiar way, it strengthens the astral body and holds it for a very long time in the lower astral spheres, which prevents the evolution of spirit. In the temples of India there was, and still is, a custom of keeping Hatha Yogis for certain lower phenomena of the astral type. They are supposed to lead a very pure life, but even then are never initiated into the higher spiritual powers. And if such a Hatha Yogi leaves the temple, he is not accepted back again, for, by becoming free from the higher control while having an easy access to the lower strata of the Subtle World, such a yogi becomes a victim and sometimes even an instrument of the darkest forces. Here is also the reason why the Hierophants of Egypt never accepted mediumistically inclined disciples, and even avoided lymphatic servants. Not a single medium, not one lymphatic, can become a true Agni Yogi.

---

[22]IBID vol. I, pp. 203-204

"The Great Teachers are grieved because of the predomination of lower psychism at the expense of true spirituality. Without the understanding and application of the Living Ethics, without spirituality, the lower psychism can lead to the most grievous results. Therefore, in order to be accepted as disciples it is necessary, first of all, to practise self-perfection, to improve morally and spiritually, and to apply the Teaching in life. This will broaden the consciousness and bring the necessary balance. The Teaching is beautiful and true when it is realized, but no tricks of pseudo-occultism and magic will lead to true discipleship. In order to fill one's vessel from the High Source, one has to establish the corresponding high vibrations. The application in life of the Living Ethics is the quickest way to reach the goal.[23]

"It is most essential to point out the difference between mediumship, psychism, and true spiritual development. Much harm has been done by books about all kinds of Hatha Yoga exercises. What ignorance is displayed in thinking that the highest and subtlest can be achieved by purely mechanical methods! You are quite right when you say that people, in striving for spiritual development (which to them so often means the achievement of psychic powers), forget that without active service to the General Good this development will be one-sided and unstable. Our inner fires are kindled only through contact with people. Only thus can we test ourselves; only thus shall we be able to sharpen and temper the blade of our spirit. Undoubtedly, certain isolation and *periodic* retreat is essential for the restoration of our forces. However, constant seclusion will never provide that tension of our forces which alone can bring their refinement. Many statements in the Teaching confirm this. For example, in the second book of *Leaves of Morya's Garden*, on page 47, it is said: 'Christ, Buddha, and their closest co-workers did not use magic formulae but acted and created in full blending with the spirit. Therefore, in the new evolution the former artificial methods must be abandoned ... The mechanics of yogism are no longer suitable for the regeneration of the world.' And further on, 'Many times have saints returned to

---

[23]IBID vol. I, p. 206

Earth because they had conveyed to the crowd too much of their exaltation instead of the structure of life. We are absolutely averse to monasteries, for they are the antithesis of life ... *Indeed, through life one must attain.*' Likewise, in the book *Agni Yoga* it is said, in the middle of paragraph 161, 'Raja Yoga, Jnana Yoga, Bhakti Yoga are all isolated from their surrounding reality [from active participation in life]; and because of this they cannot enter into the evolution of the future.' And in paragraph 163, 'This most unifying [Agni] Yoga exacts an obligation *to construct* the entire life in conformity with a discipline externally imperceptible.' This means that while constructing and working, one should take certain precautions and should follow the indicated regimen for maintaining health. Thus, if we study the lives of the Great Teachers of humanity, we shall discover that none of them *shut themselves off* from life, but poured all their forces, spiritual and physical, into the service for the General Good. Thus, in everything let us follow these great examples in a lofty attainment of self-renunciation. The crown of self-renunciation is glorious![24]

"And now as to your question about karma. In each life a person can neutralize a certain part of his old karma, which reaches him in this incarnation, and certainly he then starts new karma. But if his consciousness is broadened he can outlive more quickly the accumulated karma, and the new karma he then creates will be already of higher quality. Moreover, the old karma will not be as fearful because of the purified thinking; therefore the purified aura will react entirely differently on the return blows. And in this way man can emerge from the spellbound circle of karma. But this concerns only the earthly karma, which attracts him to Earth, for karma cannot be entirely eliminated so long as there is consciousness and thought. Karma which corresponds with the cosmic laws will infinitely improve its quality, entering new cycles and coming out of them, and so unto Infinity.

"Individual karma is always the basic one. And firstly, it is formed by the inclinations, thoughts and motives of

---

[24]IBID vol. II, pp. 27-28

man—actions are secondary factors. The Buddhists say, 'Karma is thought.' If it were otherwise, man could not rid himself of his karma. Verily, the individual karma, being fundamental and determinative, can influence the creation as well as the liquidation of all other types of karma. By injuring himself a person injures others. Everything is linked in the Cosmos; everything is intertwined, and nothing can be dismembered from all the rest of karma. Therefore, individual karma also cannot be dismembered from other types of karma, such as group karma, race karma, etc. It is said in the Teaching, 'With difficulty do the sparks of creativeness seep through on the path of karma; and even less understood is the truth of karmic action. Not from without comes the proper estimation of karma. Every cell contains within itself its karma. The spirit carried its achievement and weapon within.'[25]

"Your question regarding animals is rather complicated. Certainly, the killing of harmless animals for the sake of food, when the whole of nature provides us with plenty of other sustenance which is bloodless, cannot be excused in principle. But then, life is so complex! It is impossible to bring to Earth immediately all the conditions of the higher worlds. Our Earth and its population are not yet ready to accept higher laws and higher conditions. Therefore, one is obliged to tolerate the present customs and circumstances, striving at the same time to improve and ennoble them as much as possible. But in order not to be entirely lost in this labyrinth of most complicated and at times almost insoluble problems, we have to bear in mind the following rule, which should become our guiding principle: 'From two kinds of evil, select the lesser; from two kinds of good, the greater.'

"Thus, our first concern should be for people, with the concern for animals secondary. I quite understand your feelings, but remember that only gradually, with the broadening of the consciousness and with the refinement of the human organism, will many concepts find their true application. Also, I remember that when I once remarked that plants do not react to pain as much as fishes I was told, 'Not necessarily so, as the

---

[25]IBID vol. II, pp. 196-197

consciousness of some flowers is not below that of many fishes and insects.' After this statement, we can hardly insist that a plant or vegetable does not feel any pain when cut or plucked. This is proved on the basis of the modern scientific experiments with plants, conducted in the Calcutta Institute of the Hindu scientist, Jagadis Bose. These experiments have shown that the sensitiveness of the nervous system of plants is amazing.

"We can do nothing but accept the great law which is laid in the foundation of the life of the entire Cosmos, the law of the Great Sacrifice. Indeed, everything in Nature lives at the expense of something else. But with the growth of the consciousness, this sacrifice becomes subtler and loftier, at the same time remaining a sacrifice. And only in the highest worlds is this giving and renouncing transformed into a source of highest joy. Do not the Greatest Spirits sacrifice their forces in sending forth their spiritual emanations, which sustain us in the truest sense of the word? Do They not sacrifice their well-deserved joy of permanent, immutable creation in the spheres that are rightfully theirs, and remain instead in the earthly spheres for the sake of directing the evolution of humanity? At its present stage, humanity is a dreadful vampire, draining and robbing the forces of the Great Spirits who are on eternal watch, as well as the energies of everyone who is a trifle higher in spiritual development than the majority. Often this causes complete exhaustion, and sometimes even premature death. But without the flow of the spiritual power, which is sent by the Highest Spirits, humanity would have been lost long ago. Therefore, first of all one must think about human beings and help them *not to exhaust and not to kill each other*. By *improving* people, we shall improve the destiny of animals.

"Hence let us love and be compassionate to animals, but let us not make idols of them, and let us not place them above man. Let us accept the law of the Eternal Sacrifice, this eternal churning and whirling of exchanging energies which, in the Furnace of Cosmos, transmutes everything in its eternal striving toward perfection.[26]

---

[26]IBID vol. I, pp. 420-421

"Indeed, God is love, and the whole existence of the Universe is based on love and nothing else! But how ugly and sacrilegious is the understanding of this love! Truly the concept of love is very far from the understanding of our present humanity. Into this highest cosmic concept people inject their cannibalistic, or devouring ideas. And that is why it is so hard, and at times even shameful, to utter the word love. This word, on the lips of many bipeds, has become the greatest profanation.

"I cannot agree with you that no one can be blamed for anything. Indeed no, all are to blame, and for everything. Since the whole Universe is an endless chain of causes and effects, how can we, particles of this Universe, be excluded from this cosmic law? The predestination that you mention exists and materializes only because it is the result of causes. Therefore I cannot agree with the statement that after death and passing into the Subtle World people will immediately find there satisfaction, happiness, and the whole meaning of all they sought on Earth. This would be contradictory to the basic cosmic law just mentioned. Undoubtedly, those who sincerely seek for the meaning of earthly existence and who strive after the highest ideals will find them there, in full accordance with their striving and thoughts. There is no scale of justice more precise than that which man carries within himself; for his own aura, which is woven out of energies, motives, and thoughts, is that true scale. Precisely these energies carry his spirit to the level which he himself has built.

"The Subtle, or astral, world is the world of effects, therefore those thoughts and strivings that did not find application on Earth will do so there, because there the inner man lives and acts with all his feelings and strivings. But can one expect that a man sunk in crime and possessed of an animal mentality could find happiness and satisfaction there? Inasmuch as an effect is the exact development of a cause, how can an evil-minded murderer, a seducer, or an idiot experience a condition of well-being in the higher spheres, which would be unbearable for him owing to their subtle vibrations! And more than unbearable, for the very approach of a being from the higher spheres causes incredible pains to such as he; furthermore, from contact with the higher energies, he decomposes. Great GOAL-

82

FITNESS and precise affinity of virbrations reign in the whole Universe. Indeed, we live in a Gigantic Laboratory, and we ourselves are kilns, as it were; therefore, it is easy to imagine how the energies or chemical ingredients that enter our aura act upon our environment and, in turn, absorb or repel the energies around is. Reciprocity is everywhere and in everything. The world is based on the principle of equilibrium, and this law runs like a thread through all the Teachings of antiquity. In achieving equilibrium man becomes free of the attraction of Earth, and is able to act consciously and simultaneously on three planes—earthly, subtle, and spiritual or mental. With such an expanded existence, with such an illumined consciousness, life becomes full of meaning, beauty, and a special joyous wisdom. A broadened consciousness points out to us the paths of evolution, the paths of the future, and our mind gives humble gratitude to the grandeur and wisdom of the One Law of Love, which is expressed on Earth as the law of karma. (I foresee the protest of many people regarding such a definition of karma.) Therefore, I may say, any and all violence is certainly against the laws of the Universe and inevitably must cause explosions and destructions.[27]

"People think that they have advanced in many ways, and they proudly point to their mechanical achievements. But they are very little advanced in the knowledge of spiritual and ethical foundations. Man has perfected himself in ways and means of fratricide, but he has lost the ability to think about the foundations of existence. Indeed, those problems which could improve life remain neglected. Try to question the world at large and you will behold a shameful spectacle. Only a minority will manifest some striving toward the foundations mentioned above, and even this minority will *timidly* whisper about the Subtle World, about the continuity of life, about the significance of thought and the need for ethical concepts. Acceleration of mechanical discoveries does not lead to concentration of thought. If we were to write the history of knowledge concerning these foundations, it would speak clearly about the

[27]IBID vol. II, pp. 53-54

immobility of consciousness. Therefore, if humanity wishes to flourish, it should think of the foundations.[28]

"I often receive information about the reincarnation of H. P. Blavatsky. Several English Theosophists have identified her in a little English girl born in India. Besides this, I myself often receive letters in which people address me as H. P. Blavatsky, and ask permission to come and see me! But I assure you that I *am not* the incarnation of H. P. Blavatsky. H. P. Blavatsky reincarnated about forty years ago, and in 1924 she safely arrived at the main Stronghold in her physical body.

"I am very much touched by your reverence toward H. P. Blavatsky. It would be wonderful if you could write an article about this lion-hearted woman. It would be good if someone would lay a first foundation stone in reverence to her memory.[29]

"It is said by the Great Teacher, 'Only Blavatsky knew,' and it is our duty to rehabilitate the memory of this great woman martyr. If you only knew all the slanderous literature about Mme. Blavatsky, all the betrayals and the perfidy around her, you would be horrified. So much ingratitude, viciousness and ignorance. Of course, all hideousness results from the latter.[30]

"I must tell you that, definitely, H. P. Blavatsky was a fiery messenger of the White Brotherhood. Most certainly she was the bearer of the entrusted knowledge. Definitely, of all the Theosophists, only H. P. Blavatsky had the privilege of receiving the Teaching directly from the Great Teachers in one of their Ashrams in Tibet. She was the great spirit who accepted the bitter task of giving to humanity, lost in dead dogma and on its way to atheism, the impulse to study the great sacred Doctrines of the East. Precisely, only through H. P. Blavatsky was it possible to approach the White Brotherhood, as she was the link in the Hierarchic Chain. But some of those who surrounded her were very much beneath her fiery spirit and heart; yet in their self-conceit they thought of reaching alone the Heights, ignoring the Hierarchical link as well as her merit. In

---

[28]IBID vol. II, p. 393

[29]IBID vol. I, p. 255

[30]IBID vol. I, p. 207

their jealousy, they slandered, criticized and inveighed against her, the one who had given them everything, who trusted them. But all those self-deluded, arrogant people achieved nothing, for the law of Hierarchy is immutable. For the benefit of the general work, the Mahatmas corresponded with some of her co-workers; however, not one of those people was admitted into discipleship. In the writings of H. P. Blavatsky, and in *The Mahatma Letters*, you will find the statement that H. P. Blavatsky was the Hierarchical link which, if neglected, would cause complete failure. And now the self-deluded ones who have passed into the Subtle World and are surrounded by their followers are probably even further away from the Stronghold of the White Brotherhood than ever. Whereas, our great compatriot, because of her fiery striving, was incarnated (in Hungary) almost immediately after her death, and now it has been ten years since she arrived in her physical body at the main Stronghold and under the name of Brother X is working for the salvation of humanity. *Thus acts Cosmic Justice.* H. P. Blavatsky was a great martyr in the real sense of the word. The envy, slander and persecution of the ignorant killed her, and her work remained unfinished. The concluding volume of *The Secret Doctrine* could not be given. Thus people deprive themselves of the highest.

"I must revere the great spirit and fiery heart of our countrywoman, and I know that in the Russia of the future her name will be fittingly honored. H. P. Blavatsky should truly evoke our national pride. Great martyr for Light and Truth! May Glory always be with her![31]

"We must emphasize the significance of action or labor for awakening and developing psychic energy, since psychic energy, first of all, needs to be exercised. It must not be limited by accidental impulses; only constant, systematic, and rhythmic labor can attune its current. The correct exchange of psychic energy is based on rhythm. Do emphasize the harmful effect of laziness, which stops the action of psychic energy in us and thus ruins our entire evolution, finally leading to complete destruction. Indeed, it now becomes obvious that the busiest

---

[31]IBID vol. I, pp. 299-300

people live the longest, provided there is rhythm in their work and no excessive poisoning of their organisms. It must also be pointed out that each labor should be performed with complete consciousness. Also, striving toward the betterment of the quality of each labor and each action is the best method for growth and for intensification of the psychic energy.

"But it is also necessary to state that an excessive outflow of psychic energy is dangerous. Co-measurement should be applied in everything. A person who immeasurably expends his psychic energy disturbs the balance of his organism, thus opening himself to the possibility of infection and also to the attacks of evil forces, consequently damaging his health and energy. When it is said that the more the spirit gives, the more it receives, this does not mean giving it out excessively at one time, but constant rhythmical use of it. Certainly the mastery of divisibility of spirit can be achieved only when psychic energy is considerably developed.[32]

"Do not be unhappy because of the necessity for spending so much time earning your living. We must all earn our bread. Indeed, all should be accomplished without retiring from life and by earthly hands and feet. Therein lies great beauty. Is labor performed in comfort and prosperity of great value? And do we ever hear much about such labor? No, all the giants of thought created amidst most trying circumstances. The work performed in ease and affluence cannot bring about the necessary tension of all the centers.

"Verily, material prosperity and ease are our most dangerous enemies. Nothing extinguishes the inner fire so quickly as security for the morrow. We do not know such security, and we work on the border of exigency and possibilities. However, at a difficult moment, when all are forces are tensed, when we have applied all our resourcefulness, help comes, but at the last moment—such is the law. All earthly burdens are necessary for the growth of the spirit. Thus, the best flowers of joy grow beside thorny roads. In time, new conditions will come into existence and the tasks will become broader. Possibly there will

---

[32]IBID vol. II, pp. 299-300

86

no longer be worries about earning a living, but there will be
new problems, far more complicated and difficult. But if the
Image of the Teacher lives in our hearts, can we worry about
tomorrow! That which is considered the worst, from a human
point of view, sometimes becomes our salvation and a step
toward new possibilities. Verily, if our service is unselfish, not
one hair will fall from our heads without the knowledge of the
Great Teacher.   Unselfish service, sincere devotion, and
gratitude weave a strong thread by which all that is needful
comes to us.

"Thus, let us courageously meet the inevitable trials, and let
us nurture the spirit through communion with seekers of Light.
Events are ripening, one may expect many changes. But if we
serve the great Light, the most destructive wave can only bear us
upwards. Let us, therefore, in complete confidence in the
Leading Hand create the light-bearing work."[33]

[33]IBID vol. II, p. 30

Chapter 5

Quotations from Helena Roerich

The following quotations are from the thirteen published Agni Yoga books that Helena Roerich brought to the world. They and the two volume Letters of Helena Roerich are available from the Agni Yoga Society, Inc., 319 West 107th Street, New York, New York 10025.

Leaves of Morya's Garden vol. I

13. The daughter of the world may vanquish destiny. The New World approaches—sacrifices are the steps of ascent. The growth is quickened by faith if the spirit is ready to receive. My friends! Hasten past the first steps, that, purified, you may ascend to the glory of your motherland. And if I offer thee the allurements of gold, or flowers, or jewels—refuse.

45. The miracle of Beauty in the adornment of our daily lives will exalt mankind. Uphold thy light. Illumine the beauties of My Temple. Teach the Joy of Beauty. Teach the Happiness of Wisdom. Teach the Bliss of Love. Teach the Glory of Unity with God. I will grant thee the power and fleetness of Mercury.

72. The Spirit of Christ breathes across the desert of life. Like a spring It wears Its way through the solid rocks. In the milky firmament It radiates in myriads of lights, and rises upward in the stems of flowers.

73. We lay stones for the steps to the resplendent Temple. In the name of Christ we carry the rocks. Erect Thy Altar, O Lord, in our garden. The rocks are too large for the garden. Too steep the steps for the flowers. On a cloud He approaches. On the grass shall He sit beside us. I rejoice, O Lord, to give to Thee my garden. Depart not, O Manifested Lord. Desert not

our garden. With stars is Thy Path adorned. Among them shall I find Thy Way.

I shall follow Thee—My Lord. Should the worldly sun disperse Thy starry signs, Then shall I invoke the aid of storm and wave to veil its rays. Wherein its use if it obscure Thy starry tokens?

77. There is no love greater than love.

78. Naught occurs by accident. My Power is with thee.

83. Know to spread happiness—condemn not.

88. Unpreparedness is not transgression. Love the unhappy, have compassion upon the humble.

94. Prayers to the Creator are offered not only in temples—the wax of the candle is consumed in the labor of life.

147. Half of human life passes on the astral plane, but men do not remember. Men search for knowledge but peceive it not. Blessed are you who comprehend the knowledge of the future and its ever-changing outlines.

By love will you learn the boundaries of the new order of life. The miracle of perception into the future will come without the sound of cannons. But the bell will summon each wayfarer lost within the forest.

149. We shall assert Our Existence. We shall unfold the pure teachings of the happy journey of life. Harass not thyself—after thou understandeth the different aspects of Our Teaching, thou wilt walk the broad highway. Be benevolent not by impulse but by constant striving. With pure spirit must thou work, and all will follow without effort.

180. In the schools of the future the ways of spiritual growth will be taught by those who have gained full ascent. My chosen ones will bring My simple Word of what must be rendered to the great nation. And personal love, national love, and universal love will render praise and sacrifice to the Creator of Love. We send to thee Our Help and Blessing.

183. Thou must aspire. For the way of aspiration provides a new window, and the window leads to the open. Who desires—receives. All things have their significance.

232. The path of virtue is not a singing of psalms but labor and service. If Karma be diverted, it will react against thee. The travail of the spirit is the one ladder of the shortest way. The suffering of a decade is crowded into a day in the lives of the chosen ones. Better a full cup of misery than a life of mild sadness. Pay thy accounts in the hostelries on the way, and with obeisance they will carry thy trunks onto the ships. O Lord, give strength to my heart and power to my arm. Because I am Thy servant. In Thy Rays I shall learn the eternal Truth of Being. In Thy Voice I shall listen to the harmony of the World. My heart I give to Thee, O Lord. Sacrifice it for the sake of the World. They will ask thee how to traverse life. Answer: Like crossing an abyss upon a taut string—Beautifully, carefully, and fleetly.

Leaves of Morya's Garden vol. II

3. Christ said: "Not in a temple, but in spirit shalt thou pray." Verily, religious prejudice is the worst vulgarity. Often even religious ecstacies result in more harm than good. Out of them the crowd has made a vulgar spectacle. Therefore, it is important to show the vitality of Those Who stand upon all rungs of the Ladder.

It is time to cast off the diamonds which desecrate the holy Images. It is time to burn the relics, following the covenant of Christ. It is time to enter into the Temple of Spirit-understanding, consecrating one's forces which perfect the knowledge of the true power of spirit.

Not in remote laboratories, not in monastic cells, but in life shall you gather the truthful records. Where Christ, not in the folds of a chiton but in the beauty of toil, gathers the seekers of the freedom of the spirit...

Only the seminars of life, communities of the best manifestation of labor, shall find Our assistance. Indeed, through life one must attain. It is precisely the generally-accepted religiousness that is unnecessary. The facts of conscious Communion with the Abode of Light are needed. Let us say we wish to bring help, so we proceed consciously without magic to the practical Source. In this simplicity is contained the entire current secret, as yet so inaccessible to men who walk up to their waists in prejudice. It is difficult for them to understand simplicity, beauty and fearlessness.

4. Fearlessness is Our leader. Beauty is Our ray of understanding. Simplicity is Our key to the secret doors of happiness.

Simplicity, beauty, and fearlessness—Christ and Buddha spoke of nothing more. And it is a blessing if the spirit vibrates to these covenants.

15. The Teaching about sacrifice was already given to you. Sacrifice is power. Power is possibility. Consequently every sacrifice is first of all a possibility.

It is time to cast aside the hypocrisy that sacrifice is deprivation. We do not accept deprivations, but We give possibilities.

Let us see what possibilities are born from the so-called sacrifice. Where is a true sacrifice which can demean? In Our Treasury there is a large collection of sacrifices, and each one was useful to the one who made it. We dislike to speak about sacrifices, because a sacrifice is the most profitable undertaking.

Small tradesmen love to cry about the expenditures and to feign a loss. But a real provider in life considers each expenditure as only a business guarantee. You have lost not through sacrifice but pillage.

Christ advised to distribute spiritual wealth. But, as the keys to it are far away, people have applied this advice toward the distribution of pillaged money. First to steal and then to give away with a tear and become enraptured by one's own goodness. As if in speaking of distribution the Teacher could have had in mind chairs and old coats! The Teacher meant imponderable wealth. Only the spiritual gift can move the cup of the scales.

Let us examine the row of coworkers. Was anyone deprived of anything? No, all have been enriched. Is it not enrichment to become a ruler of a new kingdom? So rich is that kingdom that without too much harm we can break a few dishes. Positively the hands are growing, and the book of gratitude can be examined.

I advise the providers in life to have substitutes for all positions.

In large enterprises the business stands upon the business, and not upon personality.

Who can justly assert that he has been the giving one? We will open Our account books and show how much every one received. For it is not at all easy to sacrifice when a sacrifice is a possibility, and the possibility is a benefit, and the benefit is a sound cooperation, and the cooperation is the Alatir-Stone, which either resurrects or consumes.

But self-abnegation can open the Gates of Understanding, and the decrepit sacrifice of unneeded things will swing upon one branch with self-love.

2. What I will say now is very important. The canon, "By thy God," is the higher, and this canon is the basis of the New World. Formerly one said: "And my spirit rejoiceth in God, my Savior." Now you will say: "And my spirit rejoiceth in God, thy Savior."

Solemnly do I say that therein is salvation. "Long live thy God!" So you will say to everyone; and, exchanging Gods, you will walk to the One.

There where one might otherwise sink one can tread softly, if without negation. There where one could suffocate one can pass, by pronouncing "Thy God." There where matter is revered one can pass only by elevating the earthly matter into the Cosmos. Essentially, one should not have any attachment to Earth.

Why is there a legend about the descent of Christ into hell? The Teacher addressed the lower strata of the astral world, saying: "Why, by cherishing earthly thoughts, bind oneself eternally to Earth?" And many revolted in spirit and rose higher.

Thus, find the God of each one and exalt Him. One can understand it in mind, but it is more important that it be accepted in the smile of the spirit. When the most difficult becomes easy, like the flight of birds, then the stones themselves unite into a Dome, and Christ the Mason will appear to each one.

11. I have already told you that the Mother of the World conceals Her Name. I have already shown you how the Mother of the World veils Her Face. I have already made mention about the Mother of Buddha and Christ.

Indeed it is time to point out that the one Mother of both Lords is not a symbol but a Great Manifestation of the Feminine Origin, in which is revealed the spiritual Mother of Christ and Buddha.

She it was Who taught and ordained Them for achievement.

From times immemorial the Mother of the World has sent forth to achievement. In the history of humanity, Her Hand traces an unbreakable thread.

On Sinai Her Voice rang out. She assumed the image of Kali. She was at the basis of the cult of Isis and Ishtar. After Atlantis, when a blow was inflicted upon the cult of the spirit, the Mother of the World began to weave a new thread, which will now begin to radiate. After Atlantis the Mother of the World veiled Her Face and forbade the pronouncement of Her Name until the hour of the constellations should strike. She has manifested Herself only partly; never has She manifested Herself on a planetary scale.

14. Healer, tell the ailing ones that the use of wine diminishes by half their chances, that the use of narcotics takes away three quarters of their vitality. Certainly in My pharmacy there is no place for narcotics. Before using My medicines one must spend three years amidst prana.

5. Do not live on income from money. This profit is stained. The best interchange of goods is by direct exchange of objects; or if necessary they can be allowed to be exchanged into money to be reconverted immediately.

Do not be displeased except with yourself. Do not let others do what you can do for yourself, and in this way you will abolish the thralldom of servants. Do not say twice what needs to be said once. Do not re-tread the same path, for even a stone threshold will wear away. Do not swim where one has to fly. Do not turn back where one should make haste. Do not distort your mouth in ill-speech where you should pass in silence. When the steel of achievement is needed, do not cover yourself with rays. No need for a saddle where wings are growing. Not the fist but the hammer drives in the nail. Not the bow but the arrow reaches the mark. Not by my God, but by thine. Do not be bounded by a fence but by the fire of thought.

6. Regard nothing as belonging to you; the easier for you not to damage things. Think how best to adorn each place; the surer will you protect yourself from rubbish. Consider how much better than the old must each new thing be; by this will you affirm the ladder of ascent. Think how beautiful is the morrow; thus will you learn to look forward. Think how cruel is the condition of animals; thus will you start to pity the lower. Reflect how small is the Earth; thus will you improve your understanding of relationships. Think how beautiful is the sun hiding behind the Earth's sphere; thus will you restrain yourself from irritation. Think how white are the doves in the sun's ray; thus will you strengthen your hope. Think how blue is the sky; thus will you approach eternity. Think how black is darkness; thus will you guard yourself against the cold of retreat. Think courageously about the Images of the Great Ones; thus will you follow the line of unity. Think what happiness it is to walk upon the crust of the planet, imbuing it with the consciousness of the spirit. Think what happiness it is to walk under the rays of constellations, being a focal point of rays millenniums of years old. Think about Our Hand, which guides vigilantly; thus will you prolong the thread of life.

7. When someone bars your way, step aside in silence if you know your path. When you have to find shelter, find good words for the host. If your path is broad, when the hour of departure strikes, find good words for those remaining. When a tree blossoms by the roadside, do not break it; maybe it will give joy to those coming after you. When you hear a call of greeting,

do not spoil it. When you hear a singing bird, do not shake the tree. When you see children approaching, say, "We have been expecting you." When you are hurrying for supper, step on dry stones. When you go to rest, set your thoughts in order. When you hear something pleasant about yourself, do not write it down in a note book. When you think about an offense, look back for the dust on the floor.

8. "It is better to accept an urgent message than to hide from the messenger. It is better not to paint brightly the gates on a dusty road. It is better to let one's horse into a vegetable garden than to make it step on stones. It is better to forgive a village policeman than to have a lawsuit with the magistrate. It is better to give up carrots than to be deprived of peas. It is better to fall asleep on a wooden plank than on an ant hill. It is better to receive sound reprimands than to smirk at syrupy speech. It is better to be friends with a donkey than to listen to a fox. It is better to call a physician than to bleed a demon. It is better to shudder at the torments of the past than to be in doubt about the future. It is better to judge in the morning and forgive in the evening. It is better to think by day and fly by night." Thus is it said in the book "The Pearl of Dreams," written in China.

13. Two signs of the authenticity of the Teaching are: first, striving for the Common Weal; second, acceptance of all previous Teachings which are congruous with the first sign. It must be noted that the primary form of a Teaching does not contain negative postulates. But superstitious followers begin to fence in the Covenants with negations, obstructing the good. There results the ruinous formula: "Our creed is the best," or, "We are the true believers; all others are infidels." From this point it is a single step to the Crusades, to the Inquisition, and to seas of blood in the name of Those Who condemned killing. There is no worse occupation than forcible imposition of one's creed.

Whoever wishes to follow Us must first of all forget negation and freely bear the renewed life without constraint of others. People are attracted by beauty and by luminous knowledge. Only that Teaching which contains all hope, which makes life beautiful, which manifests action, can promote true evolution. Certainly life is not a market, where one can make a fine bargain for entrance into the Heavenly Kingdom. Certainly life is not a grave, where one trembles before the justice of an Unknown Judge!

In keeping with their opinion, scholars have proposed the ingenious consolation: "Man begins to die from the moment of his birth"—a scanty and funereal comfort. But We say that man is eternally being born, and particularly at the moment of so-called death.

The servitors of distorted religions encourage their wards in the purchase of places in the cemetery, where through their advance arrangements they will lie more advantageously and honorably than others more indigent and hence undeserving of lengthy prayers. The incense for these poor ones will be adulterated and the prayers abominably sung.

Ask people, finally, what authentic Teaching has enjoined this monstrous practice? Verily, we have had enough of graves, cemeteries, and intimidations!

One may know how loftily the Teachers have regarded the transition to future manifestations, and least of all have They been concerned about a cemetery site.

The attitude toward death is a very important indicator of the character of the Teaching, for in it is contained the understanding of reincarnation.

I urge you to consider reincarnation strictly scientifically.

If you can propound any other structure of the universe, We shall reserve for you a chair as professor of theology and promise you a first-class funeral; for indeed in the eyes of the enlightened you will have already decided to die.

Read attentively the writings of the Teachers published by you, and you will be amazed at how unanimously in all ages They speak about the change of life.

The Path of Light will appear when you venture to look scientifically and without prejudices.

The daring ones are with Us—joy to the daring ones!

Community

5. The path of life is one of mutual help. Participants in the great task cannot be humanity-haters. This term denoting a shameful hatred is a long one. But perhaps people will the better remember it and be ashamed.

8. Cooperation must be based upon sound rules. This teaches orderliness; that is, it helps the acquirement of a rhythm. Thus even in daily work are expressed the great laws of the Universe. It is especially needed to become accustomed from childhood to continuous labor. Let the better evolution be built upon labor as the measure of value.

9. And another absolute condition must be fulfilled. Labor must be voluntary. Cooperation must be voluntary. Community must be voluntary. Labor must not be enslaved by force. The condition of voluntary agreement must be laid into the foundation of advancement. No one may bring dissolution into the new house. Workers, builders, creators, can be likened to high-soaring eagles. Only in a broad flight does the dust and rubbish of decay fall away.

12. There should be instilled respect for craftsmanship, in order that it be understood as a higher distinction. Ancient working community-guilds left testimony of their vitality. One can see how people cultivated their skills toward perfection. They knew how to shield each other and how to guard the dignity of their community. So long as people do not learn to defend the merit of their fellow-workers they will not achieve the happiness of Common Good.

71. First of all forget all nationalities, and apprehend the fact that the consciousness is developed by pefecting the invisible centers. Some await a Messiah for a single nation, but this is ignorant; for evolution of the planet can be only on a planetary scale. Precisely, the manifestation of universality must be assimilated. Only one blood flows, and the external world will no more be divided into races of primitive formation.

102. It is necessary to guide the education of a people from the initial instruction of children, from as early an age as

possible. The earlier, the better. You may be sure that overfatigue of the brain occurs only from awkwardness. The mother approaching the cradle of her child utters the first formula of instruction: "You can do everything." Prohibitions are not needed; even the harmful should not be prohibited. It is better instead to turn the attention simply to the more useful and the more attractive. That tutorage will be best which can enhance the attractiveness of the good. Besides, it is not necessary to mutilate beautiful Images for the sake of an imagined childish non-understanding; do not humiliate the children. Firmly remember that true science is always appealing, brief, precise and beautiful. It is necessary that families possess at least an embryo of understanding of education. After the age of seven years much has been already lost. Usually after the age of three years the organism is full of receptivity. During the first step the hand of the guide must already turn the attention to, and indicate, the far-off worlds. Infinity must be sensed by the young eye. Precisely, the eye must become accustomed to admitting Infinity.

It is also necessary that the word express the precise thought. One must expel falsehood, coarseness and mockery. Treason, even in embryo, is inadmissible. Work "as grown-ups" is to be encouraged. After its third year the consciousness easily grasps the idea of the community. What a mistake to think that one must give a child its own things! A child can easily understand that things may be held in common.

The assertion "I can do anything" is not idle boasting but only the realization of an apparatus. The most wretched being can find the current to Infinity; for each labor, of quality, opens the locks.

116. Shield children from everything false; guard them against worthless music; protect them from obscenity; protect them from false competitions; protect them from affirmation of selfhood. The more so, since it is necessary to inculcate a love for incessant learning. The muscles must not gain the upper hand over mind and heart. What sort of heart takes a liking to blows of the fist?

Once, according to an old legend, there came a messenger from a distant world to give people equality, brotherhood and joy. Long since had people forgotten their songs. They remained in a stupor of hate. The messenger banished darkness and crowdedness, smote infection, and instituted joyful labor. Hatred was stilled, and the sword of the messenger remained on the wall. But all were silent and knew not how to begin singing. Then the messenger assembled the little children, led them into the woods, and said to them: "These are your flowers, your brooks, your trees. No one has followed us. I shall rest—and you fill yourselves with joy." Thereupon, timidly they ventured into the forest. At last the littlest one came to a meadow and sighted a ray of the sun. Then a yellow oriole sounded its call. The little one followed it, whispering. And soon joyously he sang out, "The sun is ours!" One by one the children gathered upon the meadow, and a new hymn to Light rang out. The messenger said: "Man has again begun to sing. Come is the date!"

195. Write down about psychic infection. It is an old theme, yet up to now unapplied in life. As before, people fear physical infection even to excess, forgetting the main channel of all infections. Is it possible to keep on killing, cursing and raging without spatial stratifications resulting? All is precipitated solidly and heavily, creating above the site of an event a shroud similar to harmful gases. Can it be expected that the poisonous radiations of malignant energy will be dispersed? On the contrary, they will become condensed and will affect the prana. Never settle on bloody places.

New works must be on a new place.

251. Contemporary industry and the entire production of objects has become so unbalanced, in quantity and quality, that for the time being they preclude the possibility of a proper distribution of things. Forcible and indiscriminate distribution engenders craftiness and lies. Can one expect new possibilities in inaction, or should one deepen the consciousness in its essence? You remember the words of Buddha about the disciple surrounded with things yet consciously renouncing personal ownership. It is useless to try to take away objects forcibly and thus create a passion for trash. The most important thing is to

carry out rationally an educational program on the debasing significance of possession. It is not important that someone remain in his own armchair, but it is important that youth realize the absurdity of having its own chair. It is necessary that this consciousness be manifested not as a denial but as a free conquest. When, liberated from craftiness, people will learn of the impracticality of personal ownership, then a collective of coworkers will grow up.

252. The poisonous breath of possession can be destroyed only by a clearly conceived school program. Literature against possession does not exist. Only a few have conquered the dragon of trash. But many dream about personal acquisitions. How veracious must historical comparisons be! How strictly must be collected biological details, in order to demonstrate the illegality and the futility of possession. The laws of the properties of matter testify that possession does not conform to the nature of man.

Understand, it is necessary to put oneself wholly into the conquest of the fundamentals of liberation. Be able to look courageously into a shallow well—how quickly the surface grows scummy, and there is a thorny growth above the stagnant water. Let us deepen what has been started.

Agni Yoga

14. The world has lost its happiness, because happiness is in the spirit. Those who have turned away from the spirit must endure unhappiness, because how else can they return? Therein lies the meaning of great events.

To seek happiness through lies and through murder! One may rejoice that degeneracy is hastening evolution. Crimes are fanning the fire of the defunct world.

15. The poison resulting from irritability is called "imperil"—a commanding danger. This poison, a quite substantial one, is precipitated against the walls of the nerve channels and thus spread through the entire organism.

If modern science would try impartially to examine the nerve channels, giving heed to the astral currents, it would encounter a strange decomposition of the astral substance during its passage through the nerve channels—this is the reaction to imperil. Only rest can help the nervous system to overcome the dangerous enemy which can call forth the most diverse irritations and painful contractions of the organism.

He who is afflicted with imperil must repeat: "How beautiful is everything!" And he will be right; because the flow of evolution is rational, in other words, beautiful. The more subtle is the nervous system, the more painful is the precipitation of imperil. This same poison, by the addition of one ingredient, may contribute to the dissolution of matter.

27. Homelessness is a necessary attribute of the Teacher. The Teacher has a dwelling place, but not a home. The Teacher enters life, but does not display conventionality. The Teacher beautifies a discussion, but does not prolong it. He pities, but does not bewail. The Teacher defends, but does not gesture. The Teacher affirms, but is not confused. He forewarns, but delays not. If necessary He smites, but never wounds. He is grateful, but does not forget. He evaluates the motives, but does not show weakness. Cautiously He guards, but does not oppress. He fears not, yet is not reckless. And so, cherish the Teacher, Who is revealed for the growth of the spirit. Consciously must the spirit be nurtured.

28. Hatha Yoga cannot be regarded as an independent form. The growth of the spirit changes it into Raja Yoga. It is impossible to name anybody who attained through Hatha Yoga. Besides, in the astral world the accomplishments through Hatha Yoga may even bring harm, by stressing especially the astral body. The fakirs may adapt themselves to the astral plane and unwittingly weaken the ascent of thought. Even an immobile person, meditating, can attain further; because thought is the Raja of all that exists. Beauty is born through the lightning of thought. Truly, a flaming Bhakti can kindle new worlds with a thought. And the step of a Jnana will be but the smile of a Raja-Bhakti. Therefore Hatha and Jnana are not self-sufficient. What sage of wisdom would not be the lord of love?

42. One should distinguish three groups of medicines—life-givers, preservers and restorers. Let us leave for our enemies the fourth group—the destroyers. Let us first turn to the life-givers, because they act first of all upon the nervous system. The nerve centers and secretions of the glands indicate the future trend of medicine. Through these domains humanity will discover the finest energy, which for simplification we call spirit. The discovery of the emanations of this energy will be the next step in the development of culture.

Metalization in the cultivation of plants will yield useful secretions of the roots. Therefore it is necessary once again to direct attention to the vegetable kingdom. Besides, observe the nourishing properties of vegetables and grains and you will have many surprises. The lack of discrimination in the choice of man's nourishment is astonishing. I speak of the quality.

44. Do not say, "I do not remember." Say, "I failed to observe." Do not condemn the memory but glance back at an impotent observation. People would sooner fall downstairs than watch the steps.

Do not say, "I do not know." Say, "As yet I have failed to learn." Nor age, nor health, nor conditions of life, vindicate the funereal "I do not know." Audacity in life teems with eagerness to learn.

Do not say, "I have decided." Say, "This seems fit for the goal." It is easy to increase the goal-fitness, but to change one's decision is unworthy.

Chiefly, do not invoke unhappiness persistently, as is usually done.

72. Have you finally learned to rejoice at obstacles? Can We be assured that the seeming obstacle will tenfold multiply your resourcefulness? Can We term you conquering warriors? Can We send you the arrow of help, assured that you will catch it in flight? Can We pronounce the word of the New World in unison with you? Can we believe that for the sake of the beauty of creation you have burned your outworn garments? Can the Mother of the World entrust to your vigilance the texture of Light? Can the "Lion" hasten to your aid? Can the Light

illumine your way? Victory knocks. And finally, do you understand how to apply to yourself the given Teaching? Can We trust you with the wearing of the given signs? Can We despatch the ray of perfectionment? Can We vouch for your vigilance? Can We construct a rampart from your understanding of self? Can We rejoice at the steadfastness of your path? Can the Mother of the World name you the just? Could the "Lion" become the guard at your dwelling? Can the Light bathe the new steps? Unbolt your portals!

Let us pronounce the prayer to Shambhala:

> Thou Who called me to the path of labor, accept
>   my ableness and my desire.
> Accept my labor, O Lord, because by day and by
>   night Thou beholdest me.
> Manifest Thy hand, O Lord, because great is the
>   darkness. I follow thee!

161. Let us see wherein lie the similarities and differences between Agni Yoga and the preceding Yogas. Karma Yoga has many similarities with it, when it acts with the elements of earth. But when Agni Yoga masters the ways to the realization of the far-off worlds, then the distinction becomes apparent. Raja Yoga, Jnana Yoga, Bhakti Yoga are all isolated from their surrounding reality; and because of this they cannot enter into the evolution of the future. Of course, an Agni Yogi should also be a Jnana and a Bhakti, and the development of the forces of his spirit makes him a Raja Yogi. How beautiful is the possibility of responding to the tasks of the future evolution without rejecting the past conquests of spirit! One should not boast of innovation, because only the combination of elements renews the possibilities.

166. Every one has aligned himself with some type of Yoga, even if only in an elementary stage or in a distorted form. People may be classified according to the elements, and one may also divide them according to Yogas. Often in a bigot you find the perversion of Bhakti Yoga; in an unbearable athlete, Hatha Yoga; in a zealot, Raja Yoga; and in a hypocrite, Jnana Yoga. But what surpasses the contribution of the true Yoga, which links the earthly consciousness with the cosmic pulse? Can one

imagine anything that could replace the fundamental striving of the incarnate spirit; something that could imbue the astral understanding; something that would justify the existence of mankind? But the study of Agni Yoga brings man closer to the far-off worlds.

You may ask Me what physical exercises are useful in Agni Yoga. I advise short pranayama in the morning, no longer than five minutes. One should abstain from meat, except smoked meats. Vegetables, fruit, milk and cereals are always acceptable. All wines are also barred, except for curative purposes. Opium is the enemy of Agni Yoga. The clouds in the sky weigh upon an Agni Yogi. I advise to insulate the footwear with rubber and to walk in the morning, avoiding smoke. With valor must the various communications of life be received, as it is impossible otherwise to decide where is the good and where the bad. He who transmits into life the true Yoga fulfils his great mission. Thus before us is the foundation of Agni Yoga.

185. Some of the young may ask, "How should one understand Agni Yoga?"

Say, "As the perception and application in life of the all-embracing element of fire, which nourishes the seed of the spirit."

He will ask, "How may I approach that knowledge?"

"Purify your thoughts, and after determining your three worst defects sacrifice them to be burned in a fiery striving. Then choose a Teacher on earth and, comprehending the Teaching, strengthen your body with the prescribed medicines and pranayama. You will behold the stars of the spirit; you will see the flames of purification of your centers; you will hear the voice of the Invisible Teacher and you will acquire those subtlest perceptions which transform life.

"Help is ready for you who have entered, and the mission is given. You have realized that joy is a special wisdom. You will not return to the old shore of the stream. You have realized the battles of space. Blind evidence no longer exists for you. You are an attaining coworker and brother!"

186. For an Agni Yogi, carpentry, blacksmithery, and laundry are harmful. One must be prepared to withstand the battles of space. One must also understand to what an extent the fire, called to life, refines the organism. I, the Hierarch, have justly decreed that the achievement of transmitting the new Yoga is superior to all other missions.

256. The Keeper of the Seven Gates grieved. "I have visited people with an endless stream of miracles, but they do not perceive them. I provide new stars, but their light does not alter human thought. I plunge whole countries into the depths of the seas, but human consciousness remains stilled. I erect mountains and the Teachings of Truth, but the people do not even turn their heads to the call. I send wars and pestilence, but even terror does not impel people to think. I offer the joy of knowledge, but people make a gruel out of the sacred feast. I have no further signs to hold humanity from destruction."

To the Keeper spake the Most Exalted: "When the builder lays the foundations of the building, does he proclaim it to all who labor on the structure? The least of these knows the given dimensions, but only to few is disclosed the purpose of the building. Those who dig the stones of past foundations will not comprehend a single new foundation. But a builder should not be grieved if there be no realization among his workers of the real import of his plan. He can only distribute the work proportionately."

Thus, as to the consciousness of people, we shall know that those who cannot contain nor hearken will fulfill only the lowest work. Let him who has understood be firm as a hundred thousand sages. And the signs, as inscriptions, will unfold before him.

451. Once a French nobleman said to St. Germain, "I cannot grasp the nonsense going around you."

St. Germain answered, "It is not difficult to understand my nonsense if you will give it the same attention you give your own, if you will read my reports with the same attention as the list of dancers at the court. But the trouble is that the order of a minuet is of more importance to you than the safety of the Earth."

Just in these words is contained also the calamity of our times. We have an unlimited time for all kinds of degrading occupations, but we do not find an hour for the most vital.

610. Many think about the peace of the whole world. But if you venture to pronounce these words you will be exposed to the most insolent and hypocritical attacks. People are afraid of peace, for their consciousness cannot contain this bliss. But those who have accumulated consciousness must reiterate about the opening of the gates of peace.

Infinity vol. I

20. It is customary to consider the karma as the will and recompense determining the course of one's life. It is also customary to consider karma as a retribution. But in its true significance, karma means labor. Do not limit the work of the laboratory of the spirit and you will see the results.

When the spirit is seduced by Maya and by the manifestations of self-satisfaction, then a hammer and the development of straight-knowledge are required. When the spirit is dazzled by the glamor of wealth, without realizing its impermanence and considering that a bar of gold leads to happiness, then let us recall all the menaces of sickness and disaster.

But the warrior of spirit glows as a manifestation of light; he is illumined by the rays of the fires of Infinity. The response must be understood, and one must strive to the Cosmos with all fires and all flowers.

Upon the summit of consciousness is affirmed the path of the Lord. On the summit of consciousness achievement and evolution resound in unison. Eternal, indefatigable is the labor of ascent! This eternal motion is your karma!

You are right—only currents of will direct the karma. But to stop the course of karma is as perilous as to invoke eternal night. With what will you fill the Chalice of Amrita if you sink into the pool of darkness? We shall answer that the ocean of actions is verily more beautiful!

44. When We summon to the far-off worlds, it is not for a detachment from life but for a discovery of new ways. Only in realizing participation in Infinity may one reach the upper spheres. If we trace the development of the human spirit from the very primitive forms, we will perceive that the variety of forms of the primary spirits branch out into corresponding manifestations. One may call the forms of the present day forms aspiring toward perfection. The forms of the future correspond to the far-off worlds. Having deprived itself of the knowledge of cosmic vistas, humanity has dissociated itself from the manifestations of Infinity and has lost the thread of unity with the beauty of life and with cosmic energy. This cleavage is cruel, and the lost thread turns into a thin cobweb of reality.

We, the Brothers of Humanity, know that there exists a great unembellished and indestructible Reality. Affirm yourselves in the acceptance of the great beauty of Infinity!

Let the far-off worlds live in the consciousness of men as a wondrous kingdom. This is just as indisputable and just as real as the fact that a growing seed gives birth to a flower. The far-off worlds are interpreted only as something illustrative of the concept of distance. But let us regard the far-off worlds—the life there is affirmed in beauty and in striving for achievement; there are the fires of spirit; there is the fire of love; there the seeming excrescences of Earth are transformed into creations of Fire. The fires of the spirit carry knowledge that the passing of the present and the striving into the better future will be the ladder upon which we shall ascend.

We, the Brothers of Humanity, sound the summons to the far-off worlds!

72. We bring to humanity the most creative possibilities. We lead humanity toward realization of Truth. We proclaim the cosmic life as embodiment of the principle of perpetuity. One should accept the manifestation of cosmic energy as a fact of daily life, as the herald of new lives.

We manifest the Brotherhood as the affirmation of cosmic power, and Our symbol is the material result.

The books of Agni Yoga are a gift to humanity. I affirm the gift of the spirit; the approach of Fire will give to mankind a newly inscribed line, leading to the highest manifestations. We consider as most important and valuable the high manifestation of spirit which is linked with the appearance of the fires. We respect a high straight-knowledge and can impart Our treasures to the spirits closest to Us.

If people could but understand the call of Space and the true Image of an Arhat! Even the best people do not recognize the fire of the spirit; dimly glows their understanding of an Arhat.

73. In rejecting responsibility, man deprives himself of a most wonderful feeling and of a personal, affirmed, creative force. Man, transmuting the fires of Space into forms, cannot cast aside his responsibility. Each form created in Cosmos will correspond to the form of the spirit. All generated forms will correspond to the forms created by the spirit in its ceaseless striving toward perfection. The feeling of responsibility must raise the cosmic creativeness.

When the spirit develops in the direction of Infinity, then the feeling of responsibility acquires the power manifested by the Creators of Cosmos. Begin to realize personal responsibility and strive toward cosmic responsibility. There is the step of personal responsibility, the step of responsibility for human thought, the step of responsibility for human evolution, the step of responsibility for a better future. When thinking will be perfected, it will be possible to say that the time of construction of a better future is near.

In Cosmos lives that power of reason which is called the cosmic rhythm, and the whole of human life depends on the cycle of this rhythm. But let us assume that the cycle, which generates reciprocally with the Cosmos, has been affirmed, and that the psychic energy is defining the current of evolution.

The mutual interrelation of responsibility is limitless.

156. It is truly told about the power of love for humanity. Can one love a garden and despise its flowers? Can one

worship the power of beauty and not show respect for love? I attest that the Power adorning Our Universe is confirmed as Our Mother of the World—the Feminine Origin! Indeed, one may cite many scientific examples indicative of the creative destiny of woman. Those who deny the evidence of woman's creativeness should reflect that woman gives voluntarily. It does not mean that those who possess the rights are the ones who affirm them. Hence is the woman's path termed one of voluntary giving. Certainly in Cosmos everything is interwoven, but humanity transgresses the laws of the Higher Reason. Truly, the Feminine Origin is most beautiful! Verily, the pinnacle of Be-ness cannot exist without the Feminine Origin. How badly people have mutilated the great cosmic laws! How far people have departed from Truth!

The one who possesses the full Chalice We call a voluntary giver.

176. For the instruction of humanity, a complete parallel comparison can be made between the activity of a medium and the activity of an Agni Yogi. Humanity will soon learn how greatly it errs in regarding the medium as an exponent of the highest cosmic forces, and how greatly its existence is enriched by the Agni Yogis. Verily, the Fire of the higher spheres is trying to break through! We confirm the achievement of the Mother of Agni Yoga as a guiding radiant symbol!

The emanations of the luminous images give joy and sustenance to the spirit. We, Brothers of Humanity, call these emanations the vital fiery streams. These streams are most powerful creations of the spirit, and the activity of the Agni Yogi is most fiery. The fiery spirit of the Agni Yogi can austerely melt down the encumbrances which accumulate upon the path. The fiery spirit of the Agni Yogi creates through his own light. Each act asserts the self-sacrifice of spirit-creativeness.

203. The pearl of the heart is the most subtle tension. Only with that tension do We create worlds. The world of striving builds a future. The source of love unites all that exists!

295. Humanity's understanding of cosmic reality, as well as its concept of void, is incommensurate. How can reality be assigned only to the surface? When the presence of pain

provokes convulsions, how can one deny the cause which gave rise to the pain? How is it possible not to perceive reality in the confirmation of all manifestations? The spheres of reality should be understood as the very substance of Cosmos. The laws cannot be based on the nonexistent! In Infinity we should realize the relativity which governs our concepts. Thus let us close the circle of life, beyond the concept of void. Thus does reality make tense every moment of our existence!

316. The destiny of man on this planet is but little understood. The existence of a cosmic being certainly should have its predestination, but humanity is striving so blindly to its own narrow horizon that it cannot discern its cosmic destination. The creativeness of Cosmos grants a purpose for being to even the smallest worm. Everything in Cosmos creates with a purpose, and, as the relative connection between man and the lower beings is evident, so does there exist the relative connections of the higher spheres. The creativeness of the Cosmic Magnet predetermines each action, as well as the role which the beings are predestined to enact. Thus, the human spheres are designated for cooperation. The Great Reason strains all cosmic spheres; hence, the destiny of man has as its basis the cooperation and beauty of Infinity.

360. When humanity will come to understand the Cosmic Oneness, the cosmic construction will be affirmed. The chief task of humanity is to unite the world of matter with the world of spirit. The demarcation line between the spheres is very sharply drawn; hence, the correlation of the predestined with the mechanical world in which men are submerged is rare. When the planetary consciousness is directed toward unification of all factors, the manifestation of cosmic shiftings overtakes all spheres. Hence, the planetary consciousness establishes the cosmic energy. The striving of an Agni Yogi and the work of the centers help to determine the cosmic consciousness. Therefore, the most important affirmation of the energy is the broadening of consciousness. The creativenss of Our Brothers is directed toward the development of cosmic consciousness in humanity. Therefore is the cooperation of the centers so affirmed by Us.

Verily, We value the transmuting power of the fires!

<u>Infinity</u> vol. II

51. The spirit shudders at the thought of death. But when consciousness penetrates the essence of Be-ness, the conception of Oneness is confirmed. When the spirit understands how ceaselessly the manifestations of life flow, the continuity of all chains may be indicated. The chain of thought, the chain of action, the chain of effects, the chain of strivings, the chain of lives—each chain predetermines the succeeding one. The creativeness of the magnet of life lies in these chains. The spirit must shudder not at the thought of death and change but at the thought of sundering the chain. If one could observe the records of disrupted chains borne in space, the spirit verily would shudder. When the great shifting is brought about, only he will succeed who has adhered to the oneness of evolution.

52. How much striving is dissipated by humanity in the search for phenomena, without heed to the voice which directs it toward the power of spirit-understanding. Does the materialization of objects have such powerful attraction that the understanding of the transmissions of spirit and energy can be erased? How can materialization, which suffocates the consciousness and which leads only to visible manifestations, direct the spirit to the far-off worlds? Each manifested form is of itself a cosmic phenomenon. Humanity has arrested itself upon the step of search for visible manifestations. In speaking of the far-off worlds, one should accept the entire broad understanding of infinite growth. Let us confirm our consciousness upon the thought of the far-off worlds. The stimulus of spirit creativeness comprises the entire boundlessness of striving. In it is preserved the great cosmic striving. Only with the understanding of invisible materialization can there be true striving, because in that great impulse of the Universe is comprised the entire cosmic creativeness.

56. Humanity regards all uninvestigated energies as nonexistent. It is not striving but denial that impels humanity to reject the subtlest energies. When the cosmic creativeness

strains its levers, the preordained forms are generated. But humanity, in not aspiring to accept the new forms, certainly rejects further progress. Everything soars around humanity, but the energies only then take form when they come in contact with the human consciousness. Hence, the surging tide toward deaf receivers is bringing but isolation from the cosmic treasury. Thus humanity deprives itself of the most precious.

60. One should seek Truth beyond the boundaries of human understanding. The destruction of the broad fields of vision, the cosmic, has not led to progress. When thought dwelt in the lower sphere, the striving manifested was in conformity with the scope of this sphere. When instead of a striving for expansion there was substituted the striving toward a limited sphere, that of the visible, the horizon indeed was narrowed. Cosmic creativeness aggregates its manifested forms according to expressed affinity. The attraction of correlated particles by the Magnet corresponds to the sphere of the spirit. You spoke correctly about the spheres saturated by the spirit. Only when spiritual striving leads to the realization of the nature of the dimensions of various spheres is the realization of the higher worlds affirmed. One may join in evolution limitlessly.

113. Wherein, really, lies the wealth of humanity? In the construction of new steps. Spatial thought holds the tension for the creation of new worlds. Each spatial thought is man's possession. Hence, the stratifying of the space should be the paramount care of humanity. How then is it possible not to give importance to this factor? Even a simple daily formula says that the construction of a step depends upon the degree of striving. Hence, each step reflects a creative direction. Thought is dependent on the direction imparted by the spirit. Hence, the spatial thought reflects the collective thinking. Let us accept this law about spatial thought for the sake of clarification of cosmic vistas. The crumbs of thought also have their consequences. Thus, humanity must choose between pure striving and spatial contagion.

The path to the Infinite lies through a perfect consciousness.

118. The great purpose in Our actions is to aid humanity in the shiftings of consciousness. Our disciples are appointed as

such helpers. Each shifting of thought produces its effect. Therefore, Our mission is to lead human consciousness into a shifting, and the mission of Our disciples is to set the pace with the Cosmic Magnet. Our Stronghold contains the essence of the shifting of the consciousness and the directing of it toward the center of evolution. Hence, the shifting of thought is the paramount healer of mankind.

140. Humanity is saturated with cravings. When the spirit yields to the asserted cravings, the step into evolution is limited by the visible. The opposite striving of the spirit establishes the step of affirmed evolution. The two opposites are always mutually confirmed. While one part strives to possess the visible, the other part strives toward the invisible. Thus, in an epoch of cosmic reaction, humanity may be divided into slaves and those who strive for cosmic cooperation. The planet is populated by slaves to possession and by those who carry the cosmic fires. Thus, Our Carriers of Fire do battle, and the clutching hands are of the slaves bereft of spirit. Only those striving to Infinity can understand the beauty of Be-ness.

168. With what does humanity enshroud the Earth? The most opaque sphere is that of egotism. The most worthless sphere is that manifested by the worm of jealousy. The most destructive sphere is that manifested by conceit. These spheres destroy families, empires, churches and all kinds of organizations. Whereas, Cosmos summons to cooperation. The approaching change can sweep away the human accumulations, but each participant in these accumulations carries the karma of the planet. The human creativeness is reduced to destruction. The spirit striving to Infinity participates in cosmic cooperation.

178. Nations fashion their destinies upon the principle of independent action. Each country builds its principles around its seed. Thus each country acts, straining different energies. Creativeness which lacks the higher principles produces a karma of destruction. Parasites which suck all the sap from the trees bring the karma of extermination upon themselves. Hence, when Our law proclaims cooperation, it must be realized that without this principle the better step cannot be created.

179. When the nations create a new future, the energies are assembled by the power of the spirit. When the power strives to establish the Cosmic Right, the departing power tightens its snares. A difficult time manifests always new possibilities. Hence, the Cosmic Right is creating its channels.

295. People are afraid most of all of expansion of consciousness. Everything within the boundaries of the customary is very close to man, and each new thought arouses opposition. Therefore, when We send someone for an achievement, We first impart the urge toward a new consciousness. Only limitless striving toward expansion of consciousness and reaching for the unusual can advance the consciousness toward evolution.

296. The expansion of consciousness is the goal of Our striving, and when Our co-workers carry this vessel a full cooperation is affirmed. Thus Our Brothers create, expanding the consciousnesses. The great experiment of Agni Yoga will bestow upon humanity the expansion of consciousness and the greater understanding of the two worlds.

298. Every thought of an Agni Yogi is like a pearl for the regeneration of consciousness. Thus is the space imbued by Our Brothers. Certainly, a country propelled by a mechanical system cannot achieve much without the destruction of the old. Therefore, We value each creative thought, and the gold of the entire world will not buy the growth of thought.

377. Beautiful is the thought about Brotherhood upon Earth. Each disciplining of spirit produces striving. Only the will can give discipline to the spirit. But when the thought rambles, asserting selfhood, then verily there is no channel for true vital action. Every applied thought will bring growth to the spirit. Thus, each applied thought furthers the expansion of consciousness.

428. Knowledge, knowledge, knowledge! If people would ponder upon the fact that knowledge is the only salvation, there would not be a particle of the present suffering. All human sorrow is the result of ignorance. Therefore, every expansion of consciousness is cooperation with evolution. Every manifestation that obstructs the expansion of consciousness is

antagonistic to evolution. Hence, the actions of the enemies are criminal and their karma is dreadful. Knowledge, let us reiterate, will put an end to the suffering of mankind.

429. Again one has to remind the scientists that the theories of Einstein do not upset the laws of Euclid but encompass them. Just as the third dimension does not nullify the laws of the plane, but is infinitely larger than the latter, so also the laws of spiritual knowledge encompass all your laws, being infinitely broader. Therefore, lay antagonism aside as an impediment to evolution.

Hierarchy

38. Each growth of spirit requires burdening through circumstances. There exists an ancient legend that out of human sufferings are created precious stones. Thus it is, and when I say, "Burden Me," it does not mean that I bring a sacrifice, I am only multiplying the power of the spirit. Likewise, people must realize how much closer the latest discoveries bring them to the solution of cosmic problems. For every call flashes throughout the worlds; and as the ordinary photographic apparatus can make a print of the astral world, so every wave of any current can unite the threads of the far-off worlds.

It is time to understand the responsibility and the privilege afforded by earthly incarnations. Yet people often avoid listening to the waves of space and catching the echoes and answers which come from various strata of the Universe. We are repeating about the privileges of spiritual development, but the matter is so distorted that a well-meaning denizen even fears to mention anything that is linked with the radiant region of spirit. Try to speak of the light of realization and the bliss of spirit and you will be feared like robbers and murderers. But even robbers were disciples of Christ and Buddha; hence do not fear human epithets, but harken to the Voice of Eternity, which leads to Bliss and Light.

Fear not, fear not, fear not!

47. One yogi won the reputation of being a practical joker, because he would unnoticeably rearrange various objects in homes, and when asked why, he answered, "I am observing whether you have become blind." Verily there are few who notice changes in their surroundings. But the first sign of an "eagle-eye" is to notice the minutest changes, since on them depends the vibration of the whole.

49. Attentiveness can be tested by a very simple method. Place an object in a new place; if it remains unnoticed, enlarge the size of the object and observe what elephant finally attracts the "sharp" eye. In general, test yourself and others. Apply tests for fear, for irritation, and for negligence, and in all cases where the litmus paper may blush from shame. There is no need of complicated invocations, simple attentiveness will permit one to advance many steps. Thus one should begin to develop the "eagle-eye."

62. In all religions the one departing from Earth has been accorded an accompanying Intercessor in the aspect of a saint, angel, or departed relative. Thus was affirmed the existence of a world beyond the grave and the need of a Guide. One should become accustomed to this thought of the need of a Guide. Thus in all religions the Guide and the Teacher were affirmed. Hence when We speak of the Teacher, We remind of that which is inevitable. The Teaching can live, or turn into the embrace of death. But it is easy to enhance life by turning to Light.

71. One may prosecute ignorance, but one should especially chastise superstition and hypocrisy. Like a leprous film, superstition covers weak brains. We are not against laboratories and Western methods, but We ask that honesty, efficiency, and the courage of impartiality be added to them. How can one think of cooperation when birdlike brains impede each experiment? One can produce the most stupendous manifestation if the horns of the devil do not impede in the test tube. People believe more in devils than in saints!

79. Already you know how tense is the time; and to those who are seized with fear, say that when the Lord lives within the heart, no hair will fall from one's head, and to each one a palace for body and spirit is allotted. But preserve your heart in purity,

in order that I may enter there and surround you with armor. Remember that if you give in spirit to the Lord what has been taken from you, He will reward you a hundredfold. Thus, direct your thought to the Lord and let the Lord enter your heart. Without the Lord it will be narrow in the empty heart, and, like peas in a dried sheepskin, wrath will jar within the empty heart. Fill your heart with the Lord so fully that no enemy can force his way through. Peace unto you.

99. The chief error of men is that they consider themselves to be outside of all that exists. From this issues a lack of cooperation. It is impossible to explain to the one who stands outside that he is responsible for what happens inside without him. The father of egoism has sown doubt and self-deception in order to sever the current with the treasury of Light. Nobody wants to consider that Light is the effect of thought, but the multitudes that inhabit the interplanetary spaces will willingly acknowledge the power of mental cooperation. They realize cooperation and understand responsibility. One can enroot oneself in a universal thought and thus acquire wings in heaven and on Earth—the foundation. Many valuable reminders about the link with far-off worlds are spread everywhere.

103. Controversies are the carpet of the father of lies. The one who treads on it cannot see a man without maligning. The controversies in science usually stand upon the same carpet. It is amazing to what extent people fill themselves with interpretations in which they do not believe. The contemporary churches are the best example of why the highest manifestation does not alter life. Therefore, let us protect the all-embracing heart.

117. Earthquakes, volcanic eruptions, storms, fogs, shoaling, changes of climate, sicknesses, poverty, wars, revolts, heresy, treason—what other signs does humanity expect of the threatening time? Prophets are not needed, the most insignificant scribe may testify that never as yet have so many dreadful forerunners of Earth's disintegration been gathered. But deaf is the ear and obscured is the vision. There has never been such an hour of disintegration as this planetary year! It is as if a path were being laid for the waves of fire, and the obsolete monsters of other days creep away unwilling to realize

the price of that which takes place. Verily, the world is sustained by Magnets as imperceptible as the air and the flame of space, and just as indispensable as light. The Magnets sent by Us for Our manifestation are like the anchors of a ship tossed in the storm.

145. Unfortunately, the present time fully corresponds to the last period of Atlantis. The very same pseudoprophets and a pseudosavior; the same wars, the same treasons and spiritual barbarism. We take pride in the crumbs of civilization; the Atlanteans likewise knew how to fly across the planet in order to speedily cheat each other. The temples likewise became defiled, and science became a subject of speculation and dissension. The same occurred in construction, as if they did not dare to build solidly! Likewise, they rebelled against Hierarchy and were stifled with their own egoism. Likewise, they disturbed the equilibrium of the subterranean forces, and by mutual efforts a cataclysm was created.

162. The science closest to spirit is higher mathematics, if correctly understood. Thus abstraction becomes reality. The mist of knowledge can be illumined through Infinity. Certainly we must strive to all that can lead our consciousness beyond the boundaries of our planet. Only thus can the true values be understood. He who can understand synthesis will understand Hierarchy. One may reiterate much about Hierarchy, and We shall emulate the woodpecker until the knots of the bark are broken through. I repeat, if you do not understand Hierarchy in spirit, understand it at least for the benefit of your health. Manifest reverence.

174. Certainly the path of Service can bring one to higher knowledge. Only ignorance could bring the planet to its present condition. Humanity has lost the understanding of the beauty of aspiration, and construction has been established upon the stupidity of isolationism. For this reason, unity of Service has been revealed as salvation for humanity. The entire power of constructiveness is based on Hierarchy. Thus the mighty thread unites the entire Cosmos. Verily, only in full realization of Great Service can the beauty of Spirit and the Might of Hierarchy be understood. Space summons to the fulfillment of

the great Law. Yes, yes, yes! Thus the steps of true evolution are built.

176. Verily, if you realize yourself as being constantly in the solemn presence of the Lord, you are already on the shortest path to Us. People loathe especially the routine of daily life; for them it is the symbol of weariness and descent, whereas for us the daily routine is perfectment and ascent; it opens the gates to Infinity. One can learn to love this daily routine, because it tempers the spirit and gives one courage to contemplate the endless chain of the ages of labor. For some, these ages are a menace, but a refined consciousness will accept them as the source of endless creativeness. Beautiful cults became dulled on account of daily routine, but how wondrous is the realization that daily devotion and a flaming love are offered to Hierarchy. If I shall say, "I love Thee, O Lord, and I am devoted to Thee, O Lord, and I reverence Thee, Teacher," by what a mighty choir will this song of praise be transformed on the far-off worlds! Thus, in each act of devotion one can open new locks; and how wondrous it is to feel the inexhaustibility of great concepts. The Ordainment can be concise: "Be aflame in heart and create in love!"

280. Let us turn back to the concept of love. In each book a considerable place must be allotted to that fundamental concept, especially because under the concept of love much of the opposite is understood. It is correctly pointed out that love is a guiding and creative principle. This means that love must be conscious, striving, and self-denying. Creativeness requires these conditions. And if love is marked by self-enfeeblement, disintegration, and service to self, it will not be the highest concept of humanity, which extols the concept of achievement. The heart filled to the brim with love will be active, valiant, and will expand to its capacity. Such a heart can pray without words and can bathe in bliss. How greatly in need is humanity of the realization of the fire of love! A purple star of the highest tension will correspond to this fire.

316. Healing through the fragrance of flowers, resins, and seeds goes back to hoary antiquity. Thus, a rose not only possesses a similarity to musk but also prevents imperil. A garden of roses was considered by the ancients as a place of

inspiration. Freesias are beneficial for the sympathetic nervous system, which vibrates so much in a Yogi. The seeds of barley are unsurpassed for the lungs. You know already about mint, about the resin of cedar and other resins. Perfumes are now bereft of meaning like all other desecrated values, yet the origin of fragrance underlies a useful but forgotten knowledge. Certainly the poisons of antiquity were very subtle. The newly invented narcotics are comparitively crude; chiefly, they destroy the intellect—in other words, precisely that which sustains the balance in all psychic experiments. A flaming heart without spiritual balance is an impossibility. Thus one must remember all details that bring one close to Hierarchy.

367. Who is the giver? The one who possesses. But lest one become exhausted one should receive from the inexhaustible Source. Let us turn toward Hierarchy.

380. Are there not enough earthquakes? Are there not enough wrecks, storms, excessess of cold and heat? Has not the fiery cross risen? Has not a star shone by day? Has not a fiery rainbow flared? Have not the signs sufficiently multiplied? But humanity amidst chaos does not wish to be aware of the apparent signs! And so We shall not insist upon a visible sign when doubt has blinded the people. But amidst these blind and deaf the children of fire are found. To them We send signs, that they shall know of the approach of Light.

395. Humanity has sunk in the mire of outworn survivals, in old thoughts, beyond the realization of affirmed Existence. Thus the spirit of the shifted nations smolders under the departing energies of bigotry and superstition. The basis of this smoldering—the church that sows terror—is intolerable. A state that acts by means of treason cannot live. Thus, the regeneration of the spirit must eliminate these horrors which engulf the planet. Hence, only the Chain of Hierarchy can restore the human image. Thus, a new affirmation is being built by means of eternal Hierarchy.

396. When the world is convulsed and humanity heaves in turmoil, there remains only one path to salvation. How is it possible not to realize the highest, and the creative, path of the ascent of the spirit! Just now when all the old ways are

destroyed, when all the old energies are out-lived, when the planet itself shifts its crust, how is it possible not to adopt with one's entire spirit the new affirmations and the regenerating energies emanating from the might of the Chain of Hierarchy! Only thus can humanity be attracted to the higher energies. Following the foundations of the Cosmic Magnet, the highest manifestation will attract the spirit to the Highest. Thus, the highest law of Hierarchy creates through beneficence, affirming a better future.

418. Diseases are divided as sacred, karmic, and those that are admitted. The first two concepts are easily understood, but precisely in the book *Hierarchy* one should mention the admitted ones. How or what permits these diseases? Certainly ignorance and the horror of non-realization. It is not enough not to think about them. Children likewise do not think of them, yet become infected. One should protect oneself in consciousness and create an invulnerable armor of nerve emanations. Even severe epidemics cannot develop if people master their consciousnesses. An experiment with the substance of psychic energy would indicate what powerful antiseptics people carry within themselves. For this, two conditions are necessary: the first—realization of psychic energy; the second—realization of Hierarchy as the sold path for the increase of psychic energy. One should not look upon Hierarchy as something abstract. One should realize firmly that it is the most powerful life-giver. We call it the primary remedy. But even a pill must be swallowed and an ointment applied. There is no effect from a remedy that is in a trunk. Likewise, the Benefaction of Hierarchy must be taken by striving. Thus, an irrevocable striving will afford a healing result.

427. Despair is the death of faith. But faith is knowledge. Therefore despair is the death of knowledge, the death of all accumulations. Despair is always connected with a feeling of issuelessness. The usual method of the dark ones is to confine their victim in a circle without issue and then urge him to crime. Indeed, where can the victim turn if he is not aware of the path upward? For those who know the Bliss of Hierarchy there can be no such thing as issuelessness and despair. Thus, one can trace to what an extent the Teaching has in mind an essential,

direct benefit, which can be given to everyone who knows how to look upward.

432. How, then, does humanity hope to save its Karma and advance its evolution? Certainly not by denial of the great foundations, not through disparaging the highest principles, not by destruction of the affirmed and manifested Origins! Still, humanity continues to base its principles upon destruction, not realizing that breaking away from the great Hierarchy carries it to the abyss. Thus, self-destruction is the fate of all servitors of darkness. Thus, as long as humanity directs itself to the limitations established by darkness it will not find the path to the Highest Light and salvation.

437. Truly, in the days of perturbations there exists only one salvation for humanity. Thought that leads to the understanding of Hierarchy is the only way by which humanity can be brought to the goal of realization of the highest affirmed Hierarchy. Thus, in the days of chaos one can say that only by following the Hierarchy can one reach the best step, for the leadership of the spirit is the all-comprising and all-encòmpassing might. Thus it can be asserted when the Cosmic Magnet transmits its might to humanity through the leadership of the spirit. Therefore, one should adopt progress through Hierarchy as the salvation of the planet.

456. Everyone whose consciousness can already contain the significance of Hierarchy must first of all renounce blasphemy of the spirit. Much unworthy blasphemy is uttered and thought amidst the usual work of day and night. The most dangerous poison is produced by these imperceptible treasons. Often their consequences are more dreadful than one misdeed through crass ignorance. It is not easy to break the habit of the abomination of blasphemy, for the boundary between the white and the black is complicated. We call this contamination a black ulcer similar to cancer. Besides, the meaning of cancer in general is not far distant from the consequences of a spiritual abomination. Like striving to the Guide, one should develop in oneself comprehension of the Highest Hierarchy. Ponder that in concluding our notes about Hierarchy We do not conclude anything, but only open the next Gates.

458. Fear generates ugliness. Nothing that proceeds from fear can have a worthy importance. It is impossible to approach Hierarchy through fear. It is not possible to understand the application of the Highest Chain before realizing the harm of fear. There are many ways to Hierarchy. But the slippery unsteadiness of fear will not endure the ascent upon the rocks, and a trembling hand will not feel the handrails which have been carefully prepared. The condition of fearlessness must be understood equally with devotion. Broad is devotion, but you remember how multicolored is fear. A man who is not even bad may be frightened, and this infection can forever deprive him of ascent. Hence, one should cure oneself of fear.

Besides psychic energy, musk is useful, because it strengthens the nervous system and kindles the protective net. Thus the strengthening of the centers of the heart and Chalice gives a necessary strength to the protective net. Heart, fiery Chalice, illumine ye the path of the ascending ones!

Heart

1. To behold with the eyes of the heart; to listen with the ears of the heart to the roar of the world; to peer into the future with the comprehension of the heart; to remember the cumulations of the past through the heart; thus must one impetuously advance upon the path of ascent. Creativeness encompasses the fiery potentiality, and is impregnated with the sacred fire of the heart. Therefore, upon the path to the Hierarchy, upon the path of Great Service, upon the path of Communion, synthesis is the one luminous path of the heart. How can the manifested rays be radiated if the flame is not affirmed in the heart? It is precisely the quality of the magnet that is inherent in the heart. The highest creativeness is imbued with this great law. Hence, each consummation, each union, each great cosmic unification is achieved through the flame of the heart. By what means can the foundation of the great steps be laid? Verily, only through the heart. Thus the arcs of consciousness are fused by the flame of the heart.

Thus, we shall keep in memory the beauteous attraction of the magnet of the heart, which links all manifestations. Verily, the silver thread that links the Teacher with the disciple is the great magnet of the heart. The union between Teacher and disciple affirms the essence of all evolutions.

6. Doubt is the destruction of quality. Doubt is the tomb of the heart. Doubt is the source of ugliness. Doubt must be mentioned in each talk, because where can we go without quality? What shall we understand without the heart? What shall we attain without beauty?

They will ask, Why first *Infinity*, then *Hierarchy*, and only then *Heart?* Why not the reverse? But first comes the direction, then the connection, and then the means. One must not spoil this sacred recourse by doubt. Let us regard the quality of the pulse of a man in doubt and also at the hour of devoted striving. If doubt can alter the pulse and the emanations, how physically deteriorating will be its action upon the nervous system! Psychic energy is simply devoured by doubt.

After doubt, let us recall treason itself, for who is closer to doubt than the traitor? But one can overcome that darkness only by adherence to Hierarchy, to the most inevitable, like the radiance of the sun. Truly, it burns, but lacking it there is darkness!

7. The heart is the focal point, but of all it is least egocentric. Not egoism dwells in the heart, but pan-humanity. Only reason enshrouds the heart with a cobweb of egocentricity. Mercy is measured not so much by so-called good actions, the cause of which can be too varied, but by the inmost kindliness; it kindles the light which shines in the darkness. Thus, the heart is verily an international organ. If we accept light as the symbol of the aura, then its parent will be the heart. How necessary it is to learn to feel one's heart not as one's own, but as the universal one. Only through this sensation can one liberate oneself from egoism, safeguarding the individuality of accumulations. It is difficult to contain individuality with universal containment, but not vainly is the magnet of the heart connected with the Chalice. One can understand how the heart radiates a special light, which

is refracted in every way by the nerve substance. For the crystal of psychic energy can be variedly tinted.

22. Advise to develop thinking and observation. The heart cannot fulfill its destination if instead of a thought there are fleas and instead of observation, a mole. With such fellow travellers one will not go far! Now is the very time to deepen the trend of thought, else the masses will not find an application for the treasures received. Overproduction is the sign of a trivial trend of thought and a lack of observation. It is said that schools should introduce hours for training in observation and thinking. The heart cannot be nurtured externally only, it must be supported also by earthly strivings. Firmness of striving will be attained also by sharpness of cognizance.

25. Without exaggeration it can be said that the majority of heart diseases originate because of wealth. Therefore, people who have embraced the Teaching depart from wealth to remain only its guardians.

43. Magic is like a massage. A massage artificially limits and restores the forms of the body and circulation of the blood. Magic also artificially connects and restores the communion with the Invisible World. Massage is not necessary for a normal organism. Magic is not necessary for a developed spirit. Massage is concerned with unhealthy organs. Magic propounds the teaching of conditions, of palliatives, without opening the simplest approach to the Higher World. When beginning massage, it is necessary to increase it, otherwise the tissue will be threatened with abnormal growth and destruction. Turning to magic, it is necessary to increase its conquest, otherwise the elements will begin to press the retreating one. Thus, comparing the bodily and spiritual worlds, we see the same vital laws. The same laws indicate how much closer to a developed consciousness are the simplest paths. During moderation the stomach will not grow. The heart will not become silent during the refinement of the spirit.

44. It is necessary to establish forever that Yoga is not magic. First of all, there is nothing artificial in Yoga. The relationship and harmony of the laws of Be-ness are opposed to everything coercive. A Yogi may not disturb the Primary

Energy without extreme necessity. With a Yogi, complete cooperation is created with nature. Thus, a Yogi's knowledge is based primarily upon straight-knowledge; upon this pure surface are inscribed the signs of experience.

87. Vengeance is justly condemned by all Teachings. The original wrong itself may be but little realized and even unintentional, yet vengeance is always thought out and consciously intensified in the heart. Vengeance is like a megaphone for the wrong; therefore its harm, in the spatial sense, is very great. Vengeance only slightly resembles indignation. Indignation, like an impulse to threaten may pass quickly, but premeditated acts of vengeance widely poison the atmosphere. It is said that intention is equal to action, but one must have in mind the action of thought. It is most difficult for humanity to get accustomed to these considerations. To contemporary humanity thought has been transformed into an inconsequential cerebral contraction. Since the eye does not peceive the consequence of the thought, this means that it does not exist; but then we will arrive at denying the process of thought completely! The heart is in a better position; it makes motion and noise—thus, the heart can knock.

100. Healers are divided into two groups; one heals through the laying on of hands or through the direct glance; the other sends a heart current from a distance. Of course, for future construction the second means is preferable. With the heart's radiation, one does not need to strike many centers of the patient, but without burdening his attention, the sick part alone can be reacted upon, thus sustaining the organism in the battle for balance. You know how imperceptible are Our touches, in order not to infringe upon independent activity. You also remember how We avoided physical manifestations, permitting them to the extent that was necessary for the evidence of a certain step. We strive further as soon as We see understanding. We call a lazy person the violator of the law of life. Healers through the heart current act in the physical as well as in the subtle body. Attention should be paid to the phenomenal side of life, it is far more substantial than it seems.

113. Mankind is terrified by every so-called supernatural thing, forgetting that nothing can be supernatural—above that

which exists. Therefore, insist strongly that Agni Yoga and the Teaching of the Heart cannot contain anything supernatural. Be especially cautious with the young people up to thirty years, when not all the centers can function without harm to the heart. It is necessary to point out that Our Yoga contains no enforced sorcery and never will be a producer of chaos. It is necessary to kindle the young ones to heroic action which will transform their natures and, imperceptibly to them, prepare the heart for future perfection. Thus, it is necessary with the utmost simplicity and joy to sail to the White Island, as We sometimes call Our Site.

155. There are many occult books, but the majority of them cannot be utilized now. The chief reason is that everywhere they take into account only some specially chosen people. But Our Teaching has in mind all, all, all! Only through these calls to all can abstract ethics be replaced by the Teaching of Life.

158. One must wisely understand the final clash of the two worlds—the one that departs and the one that is born. Signs of madness can be seen in the first and of daring in the second. How long it is since I pointed out the division of the world! Thus one can see to what an extent the cleavage has already begun. It must be understood how near the decisive time has come and how unitedly it should be met.

302. It is instructive to compile a book about the harm resulting from bad thoughts; for oneself, as well as others. These thoughts are the source of many sicknesses. Formerly, only psychic illnesses were connected with evil thoughts, but it is time to discern the multitude of the most varied physical illnesses that are born of thought. Not only diseases of the heart, but most of the stomach and skin diseases are the consequences of destructive thoughts. Likewise, infectious diseases can be transmitted, not only by predisposition but through thinking as well.

This is not only autosuggestion but one may see cases when infection was spread by one person among many. One can see how physical effects proceed entirely parallel with spiritual manifestations. In this regard, it is noticed how certain organisms unconsciously spread a definite infection without being themselves subject to it. Already in ancient times such carriers of infection were known, but afterward the scientific knowledge was forgotten, and everything was attributed to the so-called evil eye.

303. It means that even in purely physical illnesses it is necessary to seek the cause in the quality of thought. Therefore, direct the thoughts of those who surround you gradually toward good. You already have an example of how much pain is caused by cursing and profanity, even at far distances. It is necessary attentively to direct the heart upon existing reality. Especially can those obsessed ones act who contact the aura, even slightly. Thus, it is very necessary to pay attention to the very first impression of people when the heart is able to give its sign. One can easily imagine what type of infection-carriers obsessed people may be, therefore it is necessary to avoid them.

331. Refinement of the heart predicates the eschewal of a meat diet; furthermore an understanding of the Subtle World not only indicates the harm of assimilating decaying products but also reveals what neighbors decomposition attracts. Truly, it is difficult to decide where lies the greatest harm—from the assimilation of meat or from attraction by meat of undesirable guests. Even the dried and smoked meats, which are relatively less harmful, nevertheless, by their odor, attract hungry ones from the Subtle World, and if they are welcomed by abominable speech, the most harmful associations result. As you have heard, many partake of food in silence, or accompany it by worthy conversation. Of course, no decay is permissible, even vegetables must not be permitted to decompose. People need little—two fruits, some cereal, and milk. Thus one not only may be purified internally but also rid oneself of many neighbors. Is it not necessary for the physicians who study the means of fighting cancer and gallstones to pay attention to this elementary prophylaxis? People speak of burning incense and of the use of perfumes. But certain poisons are aromatic and kill the consciousness! This study also should not be forgotten.

390. Whoever loves flowers is on the heart's path. Whoever knows the striving to the summits is on the heart's path. Whoever thinks purely is on the heart's path. Whoever knows of the highest worlds is on the heart's path. Whoever is ready for Infinity is on the heart's path. Thus shall we summon

all hearts to the realization of the Source. It is correct to understand that the substance of the heart belongs to the Subtle and also the Fiery World. One can perceive worlds within the heart, but not within the mind. Thus, wisdom is contrary to intellect, yet it is not forbidden to adorn the mind with wisdom.

405. Events are bearing away the corrupted world. This period was indicated in all scriptures. Nevertheless, people do not think of what is taking place. They cannot even begin to think of the future. Thus, one should not produce a book without indicating the Teaching of the time which has come. One cannot assume that something will still alter the direction of the current created by people. On the far-off worlds there is already a horror of the fiery inevitability, yet Earth continues to shroud itself in a dark cover. That which necessitated a century now occurs in five years—the progression of accelleration acts according to law. Therefore, when I speak of the heart it means that salvation can be found along this channel. Do you hear? I repeat about salvation! Not arguments, not doubt, not uncertainty, but salvation will be the sign of that hour. One must understand still more firmly how unfit by now are the old measures. Only one bridge remains from the highest worlds—the heart. Let us approach the source of the sensing of Light. Let us understand that even in the fiery furnaces the youths were not consumed when they ascended by way of the heart. The time is a difficult one! Thus we shall repeat, fearless of the derision of the ignorant. They do not have even an idea of the significance of the heart.

406. When you are asked how to pass an hour of difficulty, say, "Only in expectation; only in striving to the Teacher, or in labor." Say, "Verily, in all three measures." Thus, labor must be like the gathering of all values for the distant voyage. The quality of labor opens the gates of the heart.

408. The education of the heart must begin at the age of two. First of all, one may advise mother's milk or goat's milk—but using a wet nurse is a hideous practice. Besides, the mother's milk is often more digestible and already contains particles of the heart energy. But until now this was not taken into consideration; even the simplest people feel the truth more than the cold dogmatists.

426. The development of observation will lead to fearlessness. We should not fear that which surrounds us. And thus we shall disclose new structures which only yesterday were imperceptible or invisible. Thus, one should become accustomed to the apparently most unusual. That which was forbidden yesterday through ignorance will tomorrow become the participant and inspiration of life.

450. A Rishi sent small pieces of linen or palm leaf or birch bark to the needy and sick. Those who received these ridiculed them and said, "Is it not ridiculous to waste one's forces in sending blank fragments?" They paid regard only to words. But those who were wise applied what had been sent to the affected part or the heart, receiving relief. They understood that the Rishi had placed his hand upon it and suffused what had been sent with his psychic energy. There are also known miraculously transmitted images or imprints of hands which become apparent under heat or light. Naturally, any physician will have faith in the crudest plaster or salve, but he will admit to no belief in the significance of the magnetism of objects. Perhaps one may even pacify the physician by pointing out to him the fatty precipitations, but in all higher matters a dog shows himself to be more understanding. Thus, it is unprecedentedly difficult to instill into the human brain all that uplifts man's dignity.

458. Indeed, not long ago the potato was regarded as the devil's apple. Let us not become proud, for these examples of ignorance are innumerable. One may even prefer the ignorance of savages, because they can be enlightened more easily on the possibilities of the distant worlds. Reincarnation itself remains a curiosity or superstition. All the indications regarding nature's laws do not yet lead to significant conclusions. I do not repeat this for you but for the cowardly ignoramuses who seek to cloak crime with irresponsibility. How afraid they are of death! But at the same time, they fear also to cross to the other shore of the river. Sometimes it is necessary to disturb their ignorance. Those who slumber are often in need of a blow.

472. Prejudice—whether negative or positive—is wrong. It is opposed to every Yoga; it cuts off the phenomenal aspect of ascent. One often confuses prejudice with straight-knowledge,

yet these qualities are directly opposed to each other. Prejudice is an offspring of the mind, whereas the abode of straight-knowledge is in the heart. Thus, one cannot compare the offspring of the mind with those of the heart. The acceptance of such a thing is not only erroneous but also harmful, disparaging the activity of the heart. It can be observed how strata of prejudice are accumulated until the entire life is turned into a self-erected prison. But straight-knowledge concerns cosmic truth, hence, in itself it does not contain anything disparaging. The self-development of straight-knowledge induces solemnity of feeling. Thus, through different gates we approach the Abode of Solemnity.

473. He who has not experienced the sacred quiver of solemnity cannot understand the harm of prejudice. It is developed not in great deeds, but in each minute action. Thus, the slave of prejudice awakens cursing a dream that did not fit into the limitations of his being. The entire day he will condemn and curse, because he does not possess measures of the heart. And he will fall asleep in condemnation and will visit the sphere befitting condemnation.

474. The dying out of generations of human and animal life as well as the exhaustion of nature's generative forces indicates the end of Kali Yuga. This process evolves before your eyes, but only few take the trouble to notice this cosmic manifestation. Even you at times are prone to ascribe to chance the evidences of the austere law called into action by humanity. It would seem impossible not to perceive the occurrences of recent years! Yet people nevertheless lull themselves with the consolations of yesterday, but should they perceive menacing signs anywhere, they fall under the spell of animal fear. Still no one harkens to the word about the heart. The great salutary substance remains unapplied.

You desire to gather Our talks for the General Good; let it be so, but the readers may be counted on your fingers. Many will turn over the leaves of this book and smile at the childish reasoning about the heart, about Armageddon, about the depletion of generative forces. It has already happened thus more than once. The very same must be repeated, and one can only wish that the end of Kali Yuga may not become The End!

475. However, not many firm spirits are required to change the perilous situation. A few flaming hearts can rise in self-sacrificing vigil and weave the firm net of defense. Not the supernatural, or magic, simply a flaming aspiration of the heart will unite the worlds. I have already spoken of the end of Kali Yuga, but some think of hundreds of years that seemingly remain. No allowance is made for the possibility of accelleration, although simple chemical experiments prove that reagents quicken manifestations.

554. The savage in his prayers pleads primarily for mercy for himself, whereas the wise anchorites pray for beneficence for the world—therein lies the difference between a savage and the wise ones. This should be set into the foundation of all thoughts. It is neither fitting nor useful to plead for oneself. Only the crude heart presumes itself to be the most important. But it is much wiser to pray for the world, in which you yourself will also find a drop of Bliss. Especially now it is necessary to proceed along the great path, only thus can the heart be reached.

591. Each despair signifies limitation. The heart signifies Infinity.

592. Suicide is a profanation against the heart, and the extreme limit of ignorance. A premeditated murder is likewise against the heart.

599. A legend of the Uighurs speaks of the giant who captured the Black Dragon and chained him with many fetters. The giant left his sister to guard the dragon and himself hastened to the end of the Earth to announce his victory. But when the giant reached the distant lands he heart his sister's call, and understood that the dragon was rending the chains. The giant hastened back, but when he saw the seas, he realized that he would be late if he continued by this way. Hence the giant determined to go from one mountain to the other, avoiding the seas, the forests, and the marshes; only thus did the giant arrive in time. And as the dragon was cleaving through his last chain the giant again chained the Black Dragon.

Let us remember this parable and hasten along the summits. Thus, proceeding from summit to summit we shall more easily

132

meet those who are in various lands, various garbs, but who live by one heart. Thus let us approach the Fiery Gates.

Fiery World vol. I

69. The quality of observation is one of the principal fiery qualities, but it is not attained easily. It is acquired as slowly as is consciousness. You noted correctly that consciousness is strengthened by life itself; observation is strengthened likewise. There can be no abstract consciousness, nor can there be theoretical observation. But human absent-mindedness is monstrous, it creates a seemingly unreal world. In their egoism people see only their own delusions. In such wanderings there can be no discourse about the New World. Hence, by all means, training in observation should be introduced in schools, even for small children. An hour devoted to observation is a true lesson in life, and for the teacher this hour will be a lesson in resourcefulness. Begin the refinement of observation upon everyday objects. It would be a mistake to direct the pupils too rapidly to higher concepts. If, for a beginning, the pupil is capable of observing the habitual contents of a room, this will already be an achievement. This is not so easy as it seems to an unobservant eye. Later, by a series of experiments we can accelerate the ability to form impressions. We can propose that the pupil pass through an unfamiliar room at a run and yet with concentrated observation. Thus, it is possible to reveal blindness and assert true keenness of vision. It is necessary to outline a program of tests for all the senses. Thus is fiery action expressed in a simple exercise. Children are very fond of such tasks. Such exercises of consciousness carry one into the higher spheres. The most ordinary routines can become the gateway to the most complex. Imagine the exultation of the child when he exclaims, "I've seen more!" In this "more" can be comprised an entire step. The same joyous exclamation will greet the first fiery starlet that is observed. Thus, true observation begins.

75. The associates of the black lodges themselves distinctly recognize each other. There actually exist obvious signs. Thus, if you notice an inhuman cruelty, be assured that this is a sign of

the dark ones. Each Teaching of Light is primarily a development of humaneness. Remember this definitely, for the world has never before been in such need of this quality. Humaneness is the gateway to all other worlds. Humaneness is the basis of straight-knowledge. Humaneness is the wings of beauty. The essence of humaneness is the substance of the Chalice. Therefore, above all, on Earth let us be clothed in humaneness and recognize it as an armor against the dark forces. A fiery manifestation will visit the heart through humaneness. Thus we shall realize once again to what a degree the farthest is the nearest. We also recognize each other through humaneness. Thus, in this hour of danger, let us labor for the most imperative.

79. It may be asked in what relation Our Teaching stands to the one already given by Us through Blavatsky. Answer that each century, after the manifestation of a detailed exposition, a conclusive culmination is given, which actually moves the world, along the line of humanness. Thus, Our Teaching includes the "Secret Doctrine" of Blavatsky. Similarly, Christianity was the culmination of the world wisdom of the classic epoch, and the Commandments of Moses were the culmination of that of ancient Egypt and Babylon. However, the significance of the ramiform Teachings must be understood. It is hoped that people not only read Our books but accept them without delay, for I speak briefly of that which must be remembered. When I speak of the need of fulfilling My Indications, I ask you to fulfill them with complete precision. I can see more clearly, and you must learn to follow the Indication, which has in view your own good. A man fell under a train merely because he stepped upon the rails, but he had been forewarned and should not have done so.

83. The dark forces have brought the planet into such a condition that no earthly solution can restore its conventional prosperity. None can regard the earthly standards of yesterday as suitable for tomorrow. Hence, humanity must understand anew the meaning of its transitory sojourn in an earthly state. Only through a fundamental defining of one's existence in the carnate form and through an understanding of the Subtle and Fiery Worlds can one strengthen one's own existence. One

should not think that the delusion of trading can even temporarily insure a secure existence. Life has been turned into trade, but who of the Teachers of Life has ever been a shopkeeper? You know the great symbol of driving the moneychangers out of the Temple; but is not Earth itself a Temple? Is not Maha Meru the foot of the Summit of Spirit? Thus one can indicate the predestined Summits to the inhabitants of Earth.

89. In schools one should not read only about heroes. Examples of the fate of a few anonymous waverers would be worthwhile. The bright flame of achievement would shine still more by comparison with the fate of the extinguishers.

112. It has been correctly observed that in order for the organism to adapt itself to a vegetable diet after a meat diet three years are needed. But if, for purely physical conditions, such a period is necessary, no less a period is required for the transformation of consciousness, unless karmic conditions induce special possibilities. To transform the consciousness means to enter a special world; it means to acquire a special evaluation of all that occurs; it means going forward without glancing back; it means leaving behind all complaints and acquiring good will. Does it not seem strange that alongside a period for a diet one must put the ethical concept of benevolence? But, fortunately, every physician will support us in this, because benevolence is the best expedient for the digestion. People like to have the spiritual foundations supported by dietetic advice.

121. Violence is the scourge of humanity. It springs from ignorance, for even a man who thinks but little feels terror in his heart when faced with the unnatural.

From every manifested terror let us turn to magnanimity. Although We shall not weary of reiterating about magnanimity, yet this is the last chance for many to realize it. Pay attention to the word LAST.

136. Any ribaldry and quarreling are already a tribute to darkness. The most deadly dagger is not at the belt but at the tip of the tongue. Sometime it will have to be understood that the

spoken and also that which is thought are indelible. Each one intending good can rejoice at this, and vice versa.

142. A demon decided to place a holy hermit in a helpless position. For this the demon stole some of the most sacred objects and offered them to the anchorite with the words, "Wilt thou accept these from me?" The demon hoped that the hermit would not accept the gifts, and thus would betray the holy objects; if, however, he did accept them, he would be entering into cooperation with the demon. When this horrible visitor had voiced his proposal, the hermit did neither one nor the other. He rose up in indignation and with all the force of his spirit commanded the demon to leave the objects on the ground, saying, "Dark spirit, thou wilt not retain these objects, thou wilt vanish, annihilated, for my command has been manifested from Above!" Thus must one rout the dark ones, and when one's confidence is fortified by Hierarchy, no dark force is able to keep back the flame of the spirit. Let us not consider these legends unnecessary. The demons are of many forms and each toiler of Light undergoes attacks.

143. A headache may have many causes, but it also may come from the non-acceptance somewhere of mental sendings; this can also be reflected as needle pricks in the heart. Hence, I am anxious that this harm should not take place. With some people a routine of negation is formed imperceptibly, and it becomes, as it were, a habit with them to feel offended. On the basis of these errors, people become impervious to the manifestations of mental sendings. In this state the most benign thought recoils from the obstruction of resentment. Moreover, the thought may return and only cause trouble to the sender. One should urge everyone not to do harm. Besides, a touch-me-not attitude is most petty and is nurtured by an undeveloped consciousness. Thus, in everyday life there exists a routine of resentment. It must be recognized and ejected as a most noxious insect. Petty earthly feelings are turned into a fiery Gehenna.

227. People must not keep anything rotten in their houses. The presence of fermentation or of stagnant water attracts undesirable entities. When the photographing of entities of the Subtle World becomes more advanced, it will be possible to record on film the difference between the surroundings of a bit

of cheese or meat and that of a fresh rose. Obviating logical arguments, one can actually see that the forms attracted by meat are repellent. These lovers of decomposition even accompany to the mouth itself the dish fancied by them. Also, before photographing auras one can gain experience by taking pictures of objects with their surroundings. As always, the experiment requires patience and perseverance. It should begin with indicative objects. Of the pure aromas, one must prefer the rose; it contains a very lasting oil. But it should not be forgotten that flowers should be gathered before decomposition has set in. I point out roses because they contain the greatest quantity of fiery energy. Thus, lovers of roses are near to fiery energy. The entities that feed on decomposition avoid the aromas of fiery energy. One must accept this indication in all simplicity, and just as information from a pharmacy.

246. You have read about the fact that for seventeen years daily earthquakes have been taking place; this scientific information is not entirely accurate. For eighteen years Earth has been continuously atremor. One must affirm all the details of the dates of the approaching fiery denouement. Indeed, in view of the growth of the waves of Earth's tremors, one should be alert and think whether all is in order. But the condition of the world is not helped by the seismograph needle. Even if at some time all the seismograph needles were to break, this would be of no help, and besides, what newspaper would publish anything about this breakage! In a word, events created by people have a greater significance than they think. Thus, count back the eighteen years and you will see a significant and highly abhorrent event.[1]

257. Suspicion is in itself a provocation. A provocation may be a conscious one, but in the case of suspicion the provocations are especially disorderly. Apart from all the vital complications, suspiciousness leads to susceptibility to infection. How many epidemics are multiplied merely by suspiciousness! Karmic embryos of disease are provoked by suspiciousness. The border line between fear and suspicion is almost indistinguishable. A guard must be alert but not suspicious.

---

[1]Note: This was written in 1933. —H.B.

Equilibrium is not created by suspiciousness. Courage seeks the cause but does not suspect. Therefore suspicion is primarily ignorance.

311. Advise the young scholar to collect everything regarding Fire from the most ancient teachings. Let the Puranas of India, the fragments of the Teachings of Egypt, Chaldea, China, Persia, and absolutely all teachings of the classic philosophy not be overlooked. Of course, the Bible, the Kabbalah, and the Teachings of Christ, all will yield plentiful material. Likewise, the assertions of the most recent times will add to the valuable definitions of Agni. Such a compilation has never been made. Yet can one advance toward the future without gathering the signs of millennia?

312. Evidence from the most recent researches should be valued. When people begin to soar into the highest strata and penetrate into subterranean caves, synthetic conclusions may be expected. Do not neglect observations on the effects of the lower strata of the atmosphere. In fact, one should take into consideration literally the whole of relativity, which can only enrich one's deductions. It is necessary that amidst all this relativity we find uses even for half-burned slag. Wherever Fire has been active, everything can provide valuable observations.

315. The Chinese method of healing by means of a puncture of the corresponding centers, of which you recently read, is not curing but only a temporary relief. The ancient Egyptians produced the same reaction by pressing upon the corresponding centers. And even nowadays cupping glasses and hot poultices are in the same category. Thus, throughout life one should eliminate irritation by means of corresponding complements. The Teaching of Old China also contained the process of healing by means of heightening the vitality. Precisely China has valued ginseng and a prolonged use of musk. Therefore, it is not to be wondered at if the latest medical research discovers aspects of the higher vitality. Likewise, one can notice the fieriness of the manifestations of vitality. May the best physicians learn how to discern the fiery origin of the vegetable and animal lifegivers. Such experiments should not be deferred; when fiery epidemics threaten, let us not forget that like cures like.

318. One should pay attention to impending events. One should realize that humanity is entering a period of continuous warfare. Such wars vary, but their sole basis is the same—hostility everywhere and in everything. No one reflects upon what a devastating conflagration is created when multitudes of people consolidate a circle of destruction around the entire planet. This is that very serpent which is more devastating than avalanches and glaciers. Do not think that this is a bugbear. No, each day brings evidences of destruction. The eternal skeleton does not slumber, but frivolity attempts to divert everyone's eyes from the conflagration.

319. Wars of arms, wars of trade, wars of unemployment, wars of knowledge, wars of religion—multiform are the wars, and earthly boundaries have already lost their significance! Planetary life is divided by innumerable boundaries.

321. One must persuade people to conserve their own treasures. The most miserly person on Earth is often a planetary squanderer. The New World, if and when it arrives, will manifest love for the treasures of nature, and they will provide the best emulsion of vital essence. Multitudes will have to spread out from the cities into nature, but surely not to sand dunes! In every part of the world oceans of sand have been formed. Similarly, the consciousness of mankind has crumbled into grains of malice. Every desert was once a flowering meadow. Not nature, but men themselves destroyed the flowers. Let thought about Fire compel people to ponder upon thrift.

344. At times it is useful to sit calmly, directing one's spirit to Infinity. It is like a shower from the far-off worlds. We ourselves must attract the currents, otherwise they may glide by without leaving a trace. Thought attracts positive currents like a magnet and repels negative ones like a shield.

358. Pythagoras forbade all raillery among his disciples, because it, above everything, disturbs solemnity. He who greets the sun with a hymn does not notice the small spots. In this command is contained the affirmation of the Beautiful. Let the dark ones retain for themselves the fate of mockery. Those who need jesters will leave no memory of themselves among the

wise. His insistence on the solemnity of hymns reveals Pythagoras as a Fire-bearer. Let us take an example from such Fire-bearers, who have traversed their assigned earthly path in beauty.

380. Since Hatha Yoga demands certain bodily exercises, the question may be raised as to whether such exercises are also needed for other Yogas? Neither Arhats nor Great Spiritual Toilers practiced these. Verily, theirs are the trials of the spirit, which not only subdue the body but take the place of all exercises of the flesh. Only the avowal of spirit can replace all else.

386. Among the prophylactics against cancer and other fiery ailments one may advise valerian. I often speak of this tonic and preventive remedy, but any prophylaxis must be systematic—every evening without fail, like the daily course of the sun.

399. Evolution is independent and voluntary, this is a fundamental law. It is not only the basic elements of karma but also the Fiery World which constitute a manifestation of conscious evolution. It is impossible to force people to evolve spiritually. A sleeping heart cannot be forced toward good. One can point out, one can set milestones, but to break the consciousness means to kill the root of the future tree. Millions of years may seem long, but neither years nor centuries exist. People have divided existence into seconds and have drowned themselves in zeros. Therefore the psychology of the Subtle World is so important, since there hours are not needed and only results are important. People are often indignant at the ordainments of the Teaching, exclaiming, "Why does not the book give the final formulas?" But such a demand proves an ignorance of the foundations. The Teaching gives the precise direction and kindles the fires along the entire path of labor. One can proceed by these beacons. One may find solutions already cosmically ripe. One may hear exact hints, but the spirit must by its own will combine them into a mosaic. To affirm the path is the Ordainment of the Great Architect. As in legends, we must put our ears to the ground lest we miss a single step or whisper. Though people read much they apply but little. Yet the dates are so close!

456. Walking on water or sitting upon water, like walking on fire, are remarkable proofs of thought-power. Let us recall, for example, how sitting upon water is achieved. True, the body has to be purified by a strict vegetable diet and by a transport of the spirit. But in addition one should know how to swim and to float upon the water, in order the better to protect oneself from the serpent of doubt. Selecting some shallow, quiet waters, the yogi prepares a light wooden support on which he sits, so constructed that the water reaches to his waist. Then he concentrates by means of the rhythm of pranayama and lifts his thought toward the supremely Ineffable. Thus several days can be spent, alternately resting and again drawing near to this spiritual exaltation. And when the thought frees itself from the earthly attraction the human body loses its weight. Thus the yogi rises upon the water and the wooden support floats away. But should the thought remain at the original level the position of the body will remain unchanged. In addition one may notice luminous emanations of the body, which, according to an ancient saying, link man to heaven. The only deciding factor in these experiments is the quality of thought. It is impossible for an impious man to sit upon the water, just as immunity from fire cannot be attained without a certain rhythm and exaltation. Who can determine how much time is required for a preliminary discipline of body and spirit sufficient to attain such an apotheosis of thought? It should be said that the degrees of patience, perseverance, and determination vary infinitely, and, besides, certain influences of cosmic conditions are also very necessary. Nor should one laugh on hearing that the conditions are more favorable around full moon.

484. In regard to the question of nutrition, it should be noted that it is necessary to have some raw vegetables or fruit each day; raw milk is likewise preferable if the cow is known, and also bread of a somewhat coarse flour. Thus one can obtain sufficient vitamins without increasing the obvious superfluity of food. Hence, one should not burden oneself with the thought of food, because such thought often obscures many valuable strivings. He who has found the balance between physical and spiritual demands already stands at the border of understanding the Higher World.

491. Mediocrity arises from the failure of man to realize his inherent forces. Mediocrity is contagious; it exists for generations; it kills the being on the threshold of life. In mediocrity is affirmed a general condition in which the personality and human achievements are annihilated. Constructiveness is especially abhorrent to mediocrity. In fact, to mediocrity the Fiery World is a most frightening bugbear.

561. It is better to go to sleep with a prayer than with a curse. It is better to begin the day with a blessing than in bitterness. It is better to partake of food with a smile than with dread. It is better to enter upon a task with joy than with depression. Thus have spoken all the mothers of the world; thus have heard all the children of the world. Without Yoga, the simple heart knows what is needed for advance. It can be defined in any terms, but the significance of a joyous and solemn foundation is preserved throughout all time. The Yoga of Fire must strengthen the basis of ascent. The Agni Yogi is first of all not a hypochondriac; he summons all those who are strong and joyous of spirit. When joy keeps its glow even under the most difficult circumstances, the Agni Yogi is filled with impregnable strength. There, beyond the most difficult ascent, the Fiery World begins. The manifestation of the Fiery World is immutable. A Yogi knows that nothing can stop him from attaining the Fiery World. Thus, the first prayer of a mother and the very splendor of the fiery worlds are on the same thread of the heart.

563. Today is a difficult day, therefore I shall narrate a tale. "A certain demon decided to tempt a pious woman. Dressing himself as a sadhu, the demon entered the hut of the woman, counting his beads. He asked for shelter, and the woman not only invited him in and set food before him but asked him to join her in prayer. The demon, the better to succeed, decided to accede to all her requests. They began to pray. Then the woman asked him to tell about the lives of the saints, and the demon began to recite like the best of sadhus. The woman rose to such ecstasy that she sprinkled the entire hut with holy water, and naturally sprinkled some over the demon himself. Then she proposed to the demon that they perform the pranayama together, and gradually she developed such power that finally

the demon was unable to leave the hut and remained to serve the pious woman and to learn the best prayers. A Rishi, passing by the hut, looked in, and seeing the demon in prayer joined him in praise to Brahma. Thus all three sat around the hearth, chanting the best prayers. Thus a simple woman, through her devotion, impelled a demon and a Rishi to sing in praise together. But in the Highest Dwelling Places this cooperation occasioned no horror, only smiles. Thus even a demon can be compelled to join in prayer."

564. Let us relate another tale about the heart. "Some people gathered together to boast of their prowess: some exhibited their muscular development; some boasted of taming wild beasts; one estimated strength by the hardness of his skull, another by his swiftness of foot—thus the various parts of the human body were extolled. But someone remembered the heart, which had remained unpraised. Then everyone began to think about how the strength of the heart could be estimated. Finally a newcomer said, 'You have discussed various types of competition, but you have forgotten one near to the human heart—a competition in magnanimity. Let your teeth, fists, and skull be at rest, and vie with each other in magnanimity. It will speed the path of the heart to the Fiery World.' It must be confessed that everyone became greatly concerned, for they did not know how to manifest magnanimity. And so the manifestation of love remained undiscussed, because even the gateway to it was not admitted to any place in the contest of prowess." Verily, if magnanimity is found, then love will kindle the fires of the heart.

582. Shamed be the land where teachers dwell in poverty and want. Shamed be those who know that their children are being taught by a man in want. Not to care for the teachers of its future generation is not only a disgrace to a nation but a mark of its ignorance. Can one entrust children to a depressed man? Can one ignore the emanation created by sorrow? Can one rest ignorant of the fact that a depressed spirit cannot inspire enthusiasm? Can one regard teaching as an insignificant profession? Can one expect an enlightened spirit in children if the school is a place of humiliation and affront? Can one perceive any construction during the gnashing of teeth? Can one

expect the fires of the heart when the spirit is silent? Thus I say, thus I repeat that the nation that has forgotten its teachers has forgotten its future. Let us not lose an hour in directing thought toward the joy of the future. And let us make sure that the teacher be the most valued member of the country's institutions. The time is coming when the spirit must be enlightened and made joyous through true knowledge. Fire is at the threshold!

592. Evil can be eradicated only by good. Such a truth is simple, and yet it remains not understood. The good in people is usually not operating and therefore remains inactive. They cannot imagine how good can expel evil, thus cutting short its existence. Good is the most active, vital, inexhaustible, invincible principle, but in its entire action it is devoid of cruelty. Therein, and also in its freedom from egoism and conceit, lies one of its most significant distinctions from evil. So if a religion and its emissaries display cruelty, it cannot be a religion that is a link with the Highest Good! How can one imagine a servant of religion as cruel? By his cruelty he would become the enemy of good. Moreover he would be indicating his ignorance with regard to the very covenant of religion. Good cannot sanction cruelty! But in affirming the sacred Teaching of active good one must ponder how to use one's entire time in the glorification of good. And such glorification will be not only a symbol, it will be the fire of the heart. If we want to advance we must apply active goodness. We must understand that we can replace a pit with a true temple. Step by step we must fill the abyss with strongholds of Light. We must put together the stones of good, over and above any personal moods. Let the small planet burn itself out, but our Father's house has many mansions. Each action for good is an eternal achievement. When the dross of evil shall have long since disintegrated, the sites of good will flourish.

619. People erroneously believe that poison gasses destroy only earthly life; there is a far greater danger in the death-inflicting gas fumes—they vitiate the strata of the atmosphere, in other words, disrupt the chemism of the luminaries. The gases not only endanger life but they can throw the planet out of equilibrium. Assuredly, if even the gas from dung fires is very harmful for the intellect, what of the exhausts from factories,

and, above all, what of war gases? This last invention is the crown of human hatred. A healthy generation cannot be born if evil is set in the foundation of life.

630. They will ask, "How can we best serve on Earth to effect the utmost benefit at present?" One must restore the health of Earth. By innumerable ways, one must carry out the world task of regeneration. One must bear in mind that people have destroyed the resources of Earth without mercy. They are ready to poison the earth and the air. They have laid waste to forests, these storehouses of prana. They have decimated animal life, forgetting that animal energy nourishes the earth. They believe that untried chemical compounds can take the place of prana and earthly emanations. They plunder the natural resources, unmindful that the balance must be maintained. They do not ponder over the cause of the catastrophy of Atlantis. They do not consider the fact that chemical ingredients must be tested over the course of a century, for a single generation cannot determine the symptoms of evolution or involution. People like to calculate races and sub-races, but the very simple idea of calculating the plundering of the planet never occurs to them. They think that by some act of mercy the weather will clear, and people will become prosperous! But the problem of restoring health does not enter their thoughts. Hence, let us love all creation!

631. The decline of the earthly garden is dangerous. No one thinks about the importance of the health of the planet. One thought about it—a single thought—would in itself produce a spatial impulse. One can grow to love the Origin of Origins and all the creations of the grandeur of thought.

632. In the acquisition of qualities one cannot keep to one system or one order of sequence. Whoever feels at heart the need of acquiring patience, let him set himself this task. Whoever strives to develop courage, let him gather this experience. One cannot forbid him who wishes to think of compassion or express himself in cooperation. Still worse are conventional coercive methods which force the disciple to strive for the quality farthest from him, which cannot yet be assimilated. With all the discipline of the Greek schools of philosophy, imposition on a pupil's free will was forbidden.

For example, all abusive words were forbidden by mutual agreement, without coercion, otherwise a man could send mentally still worse abuse. One should definitely indicate to the beginners the need for improving their qualities, but in the sequence of predilection. The fires of the heart kindle the centers according to the individuality. Thus, one should appreciate these fiery guideposts. It must be understood why we so insist upon a natural transformation of life. It is because otherwise the effects of deviation from the very nature of striving will result in a violation of all foundations.

663. How can one attain success? Remember, through joy—not through despair, but joy. Do not for an instant believe that We ponder the probability or improbability of success. The thought is, Does your joy suffice to quicken the ascent? We always counsel joy. It is necessary to realize and remember that you have succeeded when you rejoiced. Certainly this is not the frisking of a calf on the meadow, but the creative joy which transforms all difficulties. The play of the Mother of the World is in joy. She enfolds the enlightened ones in Her veil of joy. Rejoice amidst flowers; and in the midst of snow—equally redolent—also rejoice!

Fiery World vol. II

5. Let us remember the myth about the "Origin of Mountains." When the Planetary Creator toiled over the formation of the earth, He gave attention to fertile plains which could provide people with a quiet agriculture. But the Mother of the World said, "Verily, people will find bread and trade in the plains, but when gold will pollute the plains whither shall go the pure in spirit to gather strength? Either let them have wings, or let them have mountains, in order to escape from gold." And the Creator answered, "It is too early to give wings to people, they would carry death and destruction. But let us give them mountains. Even if some be afraid of them, for others they will be salvation." Thus there are two kinds of people—people of the plains and people of the mountains.

One may remember now these myths, which foretold the contamination of the planet. Indeed, why do people investigate so little chemism of the air? Even with earthly apparatus one may record the condensation of destructive substances. Of course not always can these currents be detected, just as is the case with the photographing of the manifestations of the Subtle World, which will not always be successful, but with patience much can be recorded. The Fiery World does not easily lend itself to earthly observations.

6. Let us recall the myth about the "Origin of Lightning." The Mother of the World said to the Creator, "When the Earth will be covered with dark veils of malice, how will the salutary drops of Bliss penetrate?" And the Creator answered, "Torrents of Fire may be gathered which can pierce the thickest layer of darkness." The Mother of the World said, "Verily, the sparks of Fire of Thy Spirit can give salvation, but who will collect and guard them for use when needed?" The Creator replied, "Trees and herbs will preserve My sparks, but when the leaves fall off, then let the deodar and its sisters preserve throughout the year their accumulations of Fire." Thus in various myths there has been reflected the link with the Higher World. Everywhere there has been stressed solicitude about humanity and all creatures. Likewise did the ancient priests carefully watch over the correct distribution of the creative Fire.

Nowadays man crosses fruits and plants without proper supervision, but one should observe through lengthy experiments how best to preserve the fiery substance. One must not lightmindedly interfere with the creativeness of Nature. The best counsels can be given from the Fiery World, but one should seek this Benefaction.

52. There are many convulsions in the planet. The volcanic belt is shifting considerably. If solar spots influence earthly matters, no less do poisonous gasses of an earthly shock have an effect. People do not sufficiently observe the effect of earthquakes upon human consciousness. Not only is the consciousness atremor near the centers of earthquakes, but also in space this effect is irradiated as a strong poisoning. Only the ignorant can say—"what have I to do with the gases in Chile or in Siberia?" Ignoramuses do not wish to think on a world scale,

but everyone who already thinks of the Fiery World understands the significance of subterranean gases and of rays from beyond.

59. Education in the primary schools and secondary schools must be the same for both sexes. It is inadmissible to impose upon a child some specialty, when it is not yet able to define its own aptitude. It is sufficient to begin in high school to map out programs according to student's abilities. Thus one may plan the education of children who cannot yet express their inherent capabilities. It is very important that the program should not differ for the two sexes. This alone will eliminate a very harmful attitude towards sex.

77. In order to stimulate the cognizance of beauty in schools, let there be introduced a study of the beauty of life. The history of arts and sciences will enter into this subject, for it must not only embrace conceptions of the past, but also contain indications of contemporary achievement. The instructor in this subject must be truly enlightened, in order to avoid bigotry, which contains in itself the seed of ignorance.

94. The heart in its full significance is a transmuter and a condenser. Often these processes happen to be so strong that human strength cannot suffice to contain and endure the tension. From antiquity has come the prayer about resigning one's spirit to God. One should understand truly this surrender of the spirit. If you feel an unbearable anguish in the heart, transfer it mentally to the Lord. Thus you may join your heart with the Inexhaustable Source—Hierarchy. Such action may be particularly needed when the tension of the entire planet is great. One must be prepared for the most diversified influences, both cosmic and human. The adherence of the heart to Hierarchy is a continuous action, but at present We are pointing out particular instances when it becomes necessary to strengthen the heart with the manifestation of Hierarchy with especial clarity of consciousness. Many will not understand how one can strengthen the heart by thought, because for them the heart is but a physical organ. But whoever has felt Our currents will understand the meaning of this bond. The World is living through such tension that it is timely to remind about the necessity of readiness for such communions. The Fiery World must be evoked in full consciousness. In case of need one may

even orally address the Lord. Upon all steps of Hierarchy there is the same transmission and communion. And how majestic is this Ladder of Immeasurable Help.

101. It is correct to remove from one's home all rotting substances. But besides decomposition of meat and water, equally harmful are decaying fruit and wilting flowers. When someone takes measures for the removal of dead flowers, one may observe that straight-knowledge removes lifeless plants not only in the name of beauty, but through knowledge of the law of the Subtle World. Since lower entities feed upon decomposition, then for lack of putrid products they are satisfied with plants. He can be commended whose spirit whispers the correct attitude toward all surroundings.

118. Labor may be of four kinds—toil with repulsion, which leads to decomposition; unconscious toil, which does not strengthen the spirit; toil devoted and loving, which yields a good harvest; and finally, toil which is not only conscious but also consecrated under the Light of Hierarchy. The ignorant may suppose that uninterrupted communion with Hierarchy can distract one from striving for the work itself, but, on the contrary, constant communion with Hierarchy lends a higher quality to one's labor. Only the eternal Source deepens the significance of perfectionment. This flaming measure of labor must be established. The very approach to the Fiery World demands realization of earthly labor as the most proximate step. Few of the workers can discern the quality of their own work, but if the worker were to strive to Hierarchy, he would immediately advance to a higher step. The ability to establish the sacred Hierarchy in one's heart is also an inner concentration, but such action comes through toil. By not wasting time upon oneself, it is possible in the midst of labor to become linked to Hierarchy. Let the Lord live in the heart. Let Him become as inalienable as the heart itself. Let the Name of the Lord be inhaled and exhaled with each breath. Let each rhythm of labor resound with the Name of the Lord. Thus should each one who thinks about the Fiery World know how to conduct himself. Can I lie before the Lord? Can I conceal anything from the Lord? Can I contemplate treason in the presence of the Lord

Himself? Thus let each reflection only strengthen and restrain one from the evil of faintheartedness and dark thoughts.

157. Certainly, cruelty must be eradicated; not only cruelty of actions but also cruelty of thoughts. The latter is worse than any action. It is imperative that the State take measures to prevent the inceptions of cruelty in infancy. Humanity must be purified of this most inhuman, dull and malicious darkness of low thinking, as of leprosy. Children are not cruel until they see the first cruel action, which reveals the current of dark chaos. Only a few are prepared to oppose the current of darkness. Such accumulation of consciousness is rare. One cannot presuppose such attainment in everyone; on the contrary, one should take measures befitting a lower step. Likewise, let us not repeat in a moribund manner the great Commandment, "Thou shalt not kill!" But let us ponder where is the greater killing, in the hand, in the word, or in the thought? One should reflect that the thought of people is ever ready for murder.

168. In general, food is not needed in the usual quantity. It is wisely said that eating is the chains of the devil. Many generations have been burdened by gluttony, therefore caution is required in applying counter-measures. In the final analysis, more people perish from over-eating than from hunger. But a gradual process is required always in overcoming atavism. It is impossible to abolish over-eating all at once, but it can be pointed out that all superfluous food is harmful.

202. Nowhere do people think about the Living Ethics. They think it possible to pass their lives in the usual way, yet with each day it becomes more evident that it is possible to save people only by means of faith, which surpasses all religions. There is not much of such faith, and let us not try to count in thousands where there are only tens. Unusual are such paths of realization of the Highest.

207. The greatest earthly cataclysms have resulted from under-sea ruptures. Let us not forget that while mountain peaks attain the height of 30,000 feet, submarine chasms even surpass this measure. They may be pictured as reaching a depth of 70,000 feet. The disappearances of lakes are not so dangerous, but a rising of the water level should be a matter of concern.

Several times the Earth has undergone the same fate, but people do not think on a planetary scale. Just now there may be observed a certain resemblance to past events. The lack of balance of fires and waters constitutes a subject for deep investigation. Some will ponder over it, and many will ridicule.

211. You have already seen that thousands of people may perish in a single hurricane. Is it possible that the manifestation of ominous storms does not impel humanity to reflect as to whence comes such imbalance that not only hurricanes and earthquakes, but even floods reach the highest dimensions? It is a fact that millions of people have already perished. But the consciousness continues to grow worse. It would be fair to ask humanity how many tens of millions of victims are required before a change of consciousness is recognized.

223. Above all else I am concerned with the imbalance of the world. Obsession is developing, and it threatens to become insanity. Many countries are governed by madmen in the fullest meaning of the word. Never before has this manifestation of mass obsession occurred. Why scientists do not pay attention to such a calamity is incomprehensible! People commit millions of murders. Is it possible that no one realizes that this is a hotbed of obsession!

244. Not only is the odor of the deodar pleasant, but it helps to invigorate breathing and expel dark entities. Many oils have a purifying property, but not all have an influence on the Subtle World. The deodar has a significance in the Subtle World, and it is usually connected with places of sojourn of the Rishi. They know that the deodar possesses the quality of driving away evil entities.

250. Despair is first of all ignorance. I am speaking not for encouragement, but for advancement. Many beautiful structures have been destroyed through unfitting despondency. It always attacks a man on the eve of complete attainment, when it seems as if someone has temporarily extinguished the fires; but the disciple does not know such terror.

292. In primitive religions the fear of God was taught first of all. Thus was suggested a feeling which usually ends in rebellion. Certainly, each one who contacts the Higher World

experiences a trembling, but this unavoidable sensation has nothing in common with fear. Fear is cessation of creative energy. Fear is ossification and submission to darkness. Whereas turning to the Higher World must evoke ecstasy and expansion of one's forces for the expression of the beautiful. Such qualities are born not of fear but through love. Therefore higher religion teaches not fear but love. Only by such a path can people become attached to the Higher World. The chains of fear are peculiar to slavery. But the creation of beauty is not slavery, but is reverence with love. Let us compare that done in fear with that done in love. The treasure of the spirit is not from the prison of fear; therefore let us counsel people to love and to be strengthened by the feeling of devotion. No one can defend a place that is fearful to him, but achievement is accomplished in the name of love. Apply this measure to the Gates of the Fiery World.

293. Not without reason did the ancient sages choose to occupy themselves with some art or handicraft. Each one had to acquire some manual skill. They had in mind a means of concentration. Each one, in his striving for perfectionment, thus intensified his will and attention. Even in the few objects which have come down to us, there can be seen a high quality of workmanship. Precisely at present, the time has again come to return to quality in manual work. It is impossible to place spiritual limitations within the confines of machines. It is necessary to take the time to produce a quality of workmanship that will revivify the imagination. Precisely quality and imagination are united on the steps of fiery attainment.

306. It may be asked—wherein lies the chief harm of black magic? Over and above personal injury must there also be cosmic damage? Precisely so. The lower conjurations create the utmost harm through the mixture of the elements and the invocation of portions of chaos. One must picture to oneself how in this manner entities of the lower strata obtain access into forbidden spheres and continue to work harm on a broad scale. That is why extensive measures are needed in order to safeguard the planet, which is sick enough as it is. Magic in general must be left alone.

307. Yet it is possible to weaken the harm of black magic to a considerable extent by conscious opposition to it. When one's heart transmits news about an attack, and the dark stars are revealed, one must calmly and fearlessly turn to Hierarchy. Many attacks are stopped immediately. But it would be a mistake to neglect the natural signs of the heart.

324. A messenger being overtaken by pursuers throws himself with his horse into the broadest part of the river. The pursuers stop in the hope that the messenger is drowning, but he instead rides out to the opposite shore. The pursuers, in their haste, rush to a narrow place, and drown in the current. Verily, where it is narrow, there it is dangerous. This consideration should be applied everywhere. Seeking the mirage of alleviation does not lead to achievement. The most difficult is the most accessible. People do not wish to understand that persistent quests awaken powerful energies. Therefore let us not strive for the narrow, let us prefer the broad principle.

327. It has already been said that blasphemy must be ejected, but one should recognize that each and every blasphemy is inadmissible. Sometimes people are freed from blasphemy only in a narrow circle of concepts, yet their tongues utter grave calumnies in regard to their neighbors. Who can tell what lofty heart channels may be touched by these evil revilements? Therefore blasphemy must be altogether excluded from life as an action unworthy and harmful.

335. It has been said that humanity must abandon luxury. Not without reason have people themselves so isolated this concept. Luxury is not beauty, not spirituality, not perfectionment, not construction, not benevolence, not compassion; no good concept can replace it. Luxury is destruction of resources and possibilities. Luxury is dissolution, for all structures without rhythm mean only disintegration. One can see clearly enough that the worldly luxury has already been shaken, but, as a cure, harmonious cooperation must be found in order to rid the world of the plague of luxury. Egoism will raise the objection that luxury is an earned abundance. It will also be said that luxury is regal. This will be slander. Luxury has always been a sign of decay and eclipse of the spirit. The chains of luxury are most terrible too

for the Subtle World. Needed there are advancement and continuous perfectionment of thought. The encumbrance of luxury will not help one to the next Gates.

343. Thought about impossibility definitely derives from the dark principle. Any depression of spirit must be abolished, because this path does not lead to Truth. Men of the most diverse nationalities identically express joy and sorrow. This means that the path to understanding lies open.

356. To realize that the Teaching transforms the consciousness will already be an essential comprehension, but in order to influence the consciousness one should repeatedly affirm the path of Hierarchy. One must accustom oneself to worthy conduct before the Image of the Hierarch. Thus I Say—it is needful to be girded with unceasing prayer. Such prayer is needed now, when the earth is shaken by terrors.

371. When we touch upon the true path we sense the power of joy. Our heart rejoices, feeling that our striving is the right one. One can be much grieved, wandering about outside of applicable reflections. But when the consciousness pictures truth, it is filled with joy. Such joy will be wise, for it is based on Hiero-inspiration. And such meditation will be useful on the pathways to the Fiery World.

396. Sleep affords communion with the Higher Spheres. Sleep proves that without such communion people are unable to exist. The explanation of sleep as bodily repose is a most primitive one. Without sleep people can usually go on but a very short time before their thinking falls into a most ailing state; hallucinations and torpor, and other signs of an unnatural existence appear. The organism strives for the life-giving exchange, and does not find the ordained way. As We said, sleep can be brief on the heights, where the currents of communion can be especially nourishing. People may remember about meetings in the higher Spheres or in the lower. The dense body can impede such essential communions, but sleep as such will be the gift of the eternal life. And such meditation will help on the path to the Fiery World.

442. Someone says that he wishes to attain cosmic consciousness; let him better think about purifying his heart. Let

154

him not so much imagine himself as conqueror of the Cosmos, but rather let him wish to cleanse his consciousness from dust. One cannot penetrate beyond the limits of the law without wishing to become transformed in the approach. Verily, the baker of bread, in both the spiritual and material sense, must not think only as to how to get his own fill.

457. Divide everything into four shares: the first—for the Highest; second—for the Common Weal; third—for your fellow-man; and fourth—for yourself. But the hour comes when only three parts remain, for the fourth will be swallowed up by the second. Such divisions are called fiery. Nothing but the heart can indicate the boundary lines between them. But let the sequence be flamingly inscribed.

Fiery World vol. III

7. I give this farewell bidding to the disciple: "Let thy prayer be—'Thee, O Lord, I shall serve in everything, always and everywhere. Let my path be marked by the attainment of selflessness'." When the disciple realizes in his heart the joy of the path, a path which knows no friction because all is transformed in the joy of Service, then it is possible to open before him the Great Gates. Amidst higher concepts the disciple must remember in his heart the records of Light. Amidst the frightening manifestations the disciple must remember about the records of darkness. There is inscribed upon the Shield of Light—"Lord, I come alone, I come in a manifested achievement, I shall reach the goal, I shall reach it!" And there is inscribed upon the Shield of Light honesty, devotion and self-abnegation. But fearful are the records of darkness. Let the hand of the disciple refrain from inscribing upon these permanent scrolls lie, hypocrisy, betrayal, selfhood.

75. The strongest index of achievement is self-renunciation. Indeed, it is necessary to understand this cosmic concept in all its beauty. Not only on the field of battle is the spirit adorned with the power of selflessness. To traverse the path of life impetuously, to cross all lives as upon a wire, to pass over all

abysses in song, is possible only for the selfless spirit. All structures which follow the cosmic designation are erected in fiery striving.

Let us look at the life of a hero of the spirit. From early years the spirit knows the Highest Guide. The manifestation of a sacred Guardian is its life's destiny. Physical and spiritual pre-eminence do not cloud the consciousness. Self-education is a manifestation of the synthesis. The realization of one's own superiority has given the spirit firmness and tolerance toward society. All manifested talents have been displayed in inspiration, to the wealthy and the poor; to the seekers and the enlightened ones. The hero of the spirit has known a Higher Protector, therefore he has given strength to others. The Higher Law has directed him to the rudder, and visibly or invisibly he has become a fiery hero. Thus has proceeded the mighty "Lion of the Desert."

Thus has been strengthened the great law of self-renunciation. Striving toward the higher powerful cooperation has given a direct contact with the cosmic forces and with the Highest Fiery Brotherhood. This direct link has been given only through a Higher Designation. When amidst the jungles of life the spirit knows the direction, then truly the worlds resound. On the path to the Fiery Worlds let us manifest understanding of true selflessness.

110. About the destination of man on the Earth. From times immemorial this question has occupied the minds of people. All religions have noted the affirmation about the destination of man who bears a kinship to Higher Force. Wherein then is revealed a likeness to Higher Force? Only in perfectionment of spirit may man be likened to Higher Force. The destination of man cannot be regarded as something accidental. Likewise it is impossible to regard all forms uniformly, because all spheres have their own forms and very precise correlations. We speak often about the bond between two Worlds, because it is imperative to get out of the charmed circle which has girdled the planet. It is necessary to find the exit. Thinking must be directed to the more subtle principles in order to discover points of contact. Reflecting upon the simplest processes, we shall reach the highest concepts. If we shall discover the subtle bond in all life

then indeed a striving toward the Higher World will not delay in coming. Since up to now it has been rather difficult to awaken the consciousness, at present it is necessary to push forward persistently all the foundations of the bond. All events, all affirmations, summon humanity to the achievement of transmutation of the fundamentals of a World outlook. It is especially needed to penetrate into the destination of man.

147. To know one's destination means to know that the spirit of man is an expression of Higher Forces. Only he who knows these strivings can understand how it is needful to harken sensitively to the voice of the Higher Forces. What a wonderful concept, that man has been created in the Image of God! Precisely this reveals Infinity, multiplying all forces and aspirations. How is it possible for man to deny Infinity and Immortality when before him is the great comparison of the Image of the Macrocosm with the microcosm? Surely, such an exhortation is a powerful call to perfectionment of the spirit. Reminding about the Prototype of God must lead man into New Paths, for it is impossible to scorn with impunity the higher destiny by an expression of denial. And the ogres who affirm a self-willed sojourn of man on the Earth will perish, together with all the enemies of Light. Thus let us manifest sensitiveness of striving for understanding of our destination.

172. The most difficult of all for humanity to understand is the beauty of achievement. Verily, achievement in life is a great motive power, for what can better awaken the consciousness than the beauty of achievement? What, then, can produce a striving upwards, and tear one away from the lower strata if not the spirit impelled to achievement? The direction of humanity manifestly is exactly the opposite, and is affirmed in the spheres which hold the spirit to the Earth for long periods of time. Therefore, each exalted feeling takes on such monstrous interpretations. Verily, life summons to fiery achievement, to great fiery Beauty. But man is torn away from his everyday life with such difficulty! Thus, on the path to the Fiery World let us strive for the achievement of Beauty.

194. Indeed, if humanity would not violate the manifestation of the First Causes, the foundations of Existence would retain that basis which manifests the beauty of life. Cosmic Right

brings understanding to the fact that a one-sided administration of the planet is plunging it into an abyss. Cosmic Right offers to humanity that Principle which can pierce the darkness. Cosmic Right reveals to the planet the unity of Principles which guides the entire Universe. Cosmic Right reveals the Feminine Principle as a manifested power. Cosmic Right reveals the greatness of the Feminine Principle, which manifests self-renunciation, and before which verily the great Arhats bow themselves. Verily, We reverence the great Feminine Principle. Verily, We reverence the giving Principle which bestows the life of Beauty and of the Heart.

216. Realization of responsibility for the spirit and for religion has been put by humanity in the last place. The tribunal of regulated society is concerned with preserving the physical body, making mangling of the body liable to prosecution. But existing laws and temples do not concern themselves with the millions who have been mangled in spirit. With justice has Ur. pointed out the stern responsibility which religions must bear. The uniting function of religion truly has not been awakened on the planet. That sacred power of the Earth, instead of uplifting, has been turned by mankind into production of that obvious disunity which is as a cleaving sword. And priests, and brahmins, and temple servitors all have distorted the cosmic ordainment. Verily, only affirmation of the true designation will impel the spirit to the higher understanding of the great Cosmic Right. Thus let us strive for the great responsibility for the spirit and for religion. So much must be purified in the Teachings of the World! The labor of strivingly purifying religions will result in a new consciousnsess. On the path to the Fiery World let us affirm the Bearers of Fiery Purification.

247. Life is brought into balance only through spiritual attainment. Spiritual ascent is the only way to individual attainment and to attainment of the Common Good. When humanity is engulfed in its desires and its engenderings, how can one attract energies out of the Subtle World and reconcile them with human actions and aspirations! An impetus toward attainment does not result in an accumulation of energies if the will does not act in affirmation of the origins of Good. It was spoken with reason about the distorted mirror. Precisely

humanity distorts each great concept in its warped mirror. Purification of consciousness and of the Teaching is the greatest problem of our time. Thus, on the path to the Fiery World let us remember the necessity of restoring the equilibrium of vital concepts.

264. In this time of world obstruction there is only the one path of regeneration of thinking. Precisely it is important to awaken the consciousness. Indeed, when the spirit can look back and know that yesterday's thinking has already passed, then takes place the transmutation bringing discernment. Indeed the expiring time can indicate to the spirit how all energies pass on and are reworked. But woe to those who wish to encounter the future by looking backward! For the spirit overburdened with yesterday's remains is laden with a massive weight. With such a burden one cannot ascend the Mountain, one cannot pass through the Gates of Light, one cannot become associated with the luminous Future. Thus, if the Church Fathers summon into the past, the Servants of Light summon into the future. Awakening of consciousness, clarification of the Teaching, and summons into the future will result in a great regeneration of thinking. On the path to the Fiery World, My Guiding Hand shifts energies.

285. The World is covered with the ulcers of human vices and defective engenderings. Incalculable are the human diseases of the spirit which infect the planet. One of the greatest ulcers is untruthfulness. When the World is crumbling away soap bubbles are no shield. When it is necessary to act in defense of such great affirmations as the Banner of the Lords, then it is inadmissible to resemble warriors carrying paper shields. It behooves us to give credit to the dark ones for their speedy actions and foresight, for each day can be considered the Day of Eternity. Therefore, in the days of the destruction and reconstruction of the World, it is important to affirm the principles of true constructiveness. Therefore, each damaging distortion will be considered as an obvious blow upon the Shield. Indeed, faint-heartedness and selfhood are the brothers of distortion. The practice of untruthfulness becomes a habit, and egoism displays its harmful effects. Therefore, when the

World is crumbling, it is well to ponder how to destroy all distortions.

309. Much has already been said about psychism, nevertheless this scourge of humanity is insufficiently understood. Psychism blunts each aspiration, and higher attainment remains inaccessible. The sphere of activity of a man engulfed by psychism is limited within a charmed circle in which all the energies which retard growth of the spirit find their fitting place. Psychism embraces the manifestation of the lowest energies, and the fires of the centers are extinguished by these precipitations. With psychism there is inevitably to be found disorder of the nervous system. In addition, the breaking away from vital functions closes the path to self-perfectionment. Creativeness is blunted, and there is established a passive state which makes a man an instrument for the influx of all kinds of forces. By reason of relaxation of the will, control is weakened, and by this the attraction of various lower entities is increased. He who wishes to approach the Fiery World must battle with these forces of evil.

310. The accumulations of countries are being weighed on the Cosmic Scales. The preponderance of the forces of destruction is unquestionable, but transmutation of the spirit and purification of space and of humanity will afford a new destiny. The reconstruction of the planet will touch upon all values, spiritual and material. Each center, manifesting its Karma, will produce a new tension. Humanity passes through a fiery cleansing. A new affirmation will be revealed upon the horizon of the planet. In truth, a fiery purgatory will reach all the ends of the World. On the Cosmic Scales, for the good of the Universe, are found both the sword and fiery transmutation. Thus, for the planet's good the Fiery World draws near.

314. The condition of the planet is so catastrophic that only the most intensive action will hold people back from savagery. Those who assume the Fiery Vigil of cosmic events can only keep guard over this saturation in unparalleled tension. In the defense of humanity it is necessary to contend with manifestations of imperfection, faint-heartedness and fear. The Karma of humanity consists of a mosaic of the most terrible atonements. Only the fiery guard of Hierarchy will save

humanity. On the path to the Fiery World let us assemble all the best swords of the spirit.

322. To reverence the Lord means to comprehend the Guiding Image. To reverence the Lord means to devote oneself to the Lord. To reverence the Lord means to turn one's gaze to the Highest. To reverence the Lord means to deliver one's heart to the Lord. To reverence the Lord means to serve the Hierarchy of Good. To reverence the Lord means to manifest understanding of the Service of Light in space. In sending thoughts of good beforehand, we already create those channels through which energies of Good can be collected and brought together. When the great reconstruction of the World is going on we must direct our affirmations to the assistance of the constructions of Light. Thus are new bridges created. On the path to the Fiery World let us reverence the Lord of Light.

334. The most frightful bane of humanity is its narrow world outlook. The best people think that the adoption of their horizon is the principal key to the salvation of the World, but their world outlook goes no farther than the boundaries of the physical world. Representatives of the church promise people salvation of the soul, but beyond the physical world they do not go. National leaders direct the thinking of their peoples toward reorganization, but further than the lower spheres they do not lead. Thus one can enumerate all the degrees of human leadership, and become horrified at the blind alley into which humanity has entered. Verily, only the reconstruction of the World and the regeneration of consciousness can awaken the energies needed for the maintenance of the planet. We untiringly repeat about the vital necessity of purifying the consciousness, for the last hour has come for the cleansing of that which has been created by mankind. Let us apprehend in the heart the Fiery Covenant to assist the reconstruction of the World.

337. Human intolerance toward everything high has converted people into degenerates. Upon all concepts and principles man has imposed his stigma. In each higher affirmation man has displayed his blasphemy. Not the World is cruel, but man. Not the World affirms injustice, but man; for man's choice of the path of isolation and selfhood has brought on a most threatening destiny. Intolerance toward everything

high and enlightened has become the disgrace of humanity. The purification of the consciousness is the great task on the path to the Fiery World.

347. In the future reconstruction of the World, on the higher spheres there will not be access for those who do not understand equilibrium. Long incarnations will be necessary, to study how to create cosmic equilibrium. Indeed, empires have fallen, nations have fallen, countries have been destroyed, all because the greatest question, that of equilibrium, has been reduced to nothing. Therefore it is so important to affirm the significance of the feminine principle. Precisely, not in the household measuring scale, but in that of the state. If the planet is retained, then future countries will flourish only through equilibrium. We will even admit a preponderance on the side of the feminine principle, because the conflict will be very intense. Indeed, Councils of Ministers will have to include women. Woman, who gives life to a people, must also have a voice in the making of its destiny. Woman must have the right of voice. If woman were accepted, as was ordained, the World would be quite differently impregnated. Thus, only affirmation of the law of Existence can restore the order of man.

424. It is asked—what most of all hinders every good beginning? Reply—precisely absence of magnanimity. No creative attainment, no cooperation, in fact no community is possible without magnanimity. One can observe how through magnanimity labor is made tenfold easier and, it would seem, nothing could be simpler during an inspired work than to wish only for the good and for success of one's neighbor! Joy is the result of manifested labor. Joy is a great helper.

523. The dispute about allopathy and homeopathy must also lead to synthesis. The wise physician knows where it is advantageous to apply one or the other principle. Even sweetened water may be applied with benefit. Let us not forget that spatial rays are highly allopathic and it is impossible to avoid the doses administered by Nature. The laboratory of the human organism is likewise highly allopathic. However, in such disputes let us be conciliatory.

162

587. It is always good to talk about the heart. It is timely to speak of that which is urgently needed. Precisely there where is heart is also Fire. The wayfarer does not sally forth without his flint, for he does not forget that he stands in need of it at night. Thus, without heart the night of the spirit approaches. Not so frightening are the impediments, but a stony heartlessness is terrible. No man is without heart, nor animal, nor plant, nor even stone. This means that heartlessness is no longer in the manifested World but in chaos.

AUM

16. Thought can move bodies and solid objects. Likewise must spatial thought react. For example one may point to experiments already performed many centuries ago. To the ceiling of the dwelling were attached many threads of different thicknesses and colors, and then, bringing the dwelling into a state of tranquillity, thoughts were sent out. The so-called harp of the spirit began to vibrate, and it could then be noted how certain thoughts affected threads of a definite color; then it was possible to observe the reaction of thoughts sent from afar. Of course, during such experiments one should know now to free oneself from one's own involuntary sendings. All may remember how at times slight objects begain to vibrate without apparent cause; for skeptics this is merely a draught of air like that in their own heads. The egotism of people makes them reluctant to concede the existence of anything above their own majesty.

20. Leave not Earth derelict. Realization of the distant worlds must broaden one's consciousness, but one must not turn away from earthly suffering. Otherwise everyone will take flight and abandon his hearth. It is necessary to co-measure so that there be no conflict between the heavenly and the earthly.

24. Besides the achievement of outward heroism, there may be a precious achievement which is unseen. In spirit the achiever attains the highest creativeness and thus becomes an assistant of the Creator. On Earth and above Earth, in the two

worlds thought is merged in one comprehensive flow, and such an attainment resounds for the salvation of humanity.

25. Why say *Aum*, when it is possible to say *prayer*? In substance they are the same, but because of its antiquity and refinement the sound *Aum* will be the stronger in its vibration. Let the resonance of the highest concept be pondered deeply. The word itself is vibration; such resonances are needed for the harmony of space.

Great Spiritual Toilers pray not for themselves.

29. No one should scoff at prayer. Even though it be primitive, nevertheless it is an indication of spirituality. It does not become man to revile the worthiest strivings of a brother. Man has no right to sneer at an offering to the Highest. Usually, base people particularly attack the prayers of others. For them, Aum and other prayers are only a source of inadmissible jests. Very often such base consciousness is encountered as the product of uncouth ignorance.

34. Prayer will never lack beauty; from near and far it will carry the same powerful mantram. Learn to love the beauty of the sound. The human voice is in itself a miracle. One can see how the voice carries effectively even without words. Everyone has heard choirs at a distance; though the words had been obliterated, yet the magic of the sound lived.

Thus, it is necessary always to remember how many miracles are inherent in man.

35. Prayer is exaltation and ecstacy. Self-seeking prayer is a more modern practice. How can man pray for himself? Does not the Higher Wisdom know what a man needs? Prayer is a conduit to the current of Benefaction. The current flows abundantly, but it is necessary to be united with it. One must find in one's own heart a concordance worthy to meet and welcome the highest and the most sacred treasure. Therefore, each prayer for self is incommensurate. Only when religions became instruments of state were they occupied with customary petitions for a fee. Prayer and payment—how incongruous! For this reason so many people have been repelled by the paid

service. The very joy of prayer of exaltation takes flight at the clang of metal.

38. The antithesis of prayer is profanity. It defiles and disturbs space. It is forbidden to have in the cities factories that produce poisonous gases; yet the consequences of blasphemy and foul speech are far more harmful. People are unwilling to free themselves from the most harmful substance which generates appalling disasters, not to mention the sicknesses caused by disturbances of the atmosphere. More terrifying than any diseases are the destructions of the strata near the planet. How many prayers and good thoughts are required to fill these abysses and ulcers in space! If arid deserts and cyclones are dangerous, the very same danger is courted when humanity ravages the regenerative forces surrounding it. For self-despoiled shells are like decomposing sepulchres.

Guard against profanity!

57. Prayer is a purifier. This definition should not be understood abstractly. Spiritual health is the primary basis of bodily health. Precisely prayer as a real link with the higher Source will be the best purifier of the organism against all diseases. Infection appears when the body permits the entrance of manifested messengers of evil. Each body is predisposed to many diseases, but spiritual strength is on guard to quell such uprisings. When the spirit can be properly nourished by the higher energies, it also protects the body against dangers.

Therefore, it can be affirmed that prayer is a purifier.

58. There are ignorant ones who assume that prayer is generally out of place in practical life. They should be asked what sort of business they consider incompatible with prayer—that which is evil and greedy? Certainly in evil there is no place for prayer, yet every good work is in need of prayer—that which reveals the Higher Forces.

Thus, in the New World one should affirm the true realities. We shall not retrogress if we keep in mind that which permanently and unalterably will be the law of Existence.

69. Prayer has no kinship with violence nor constraint. The first prayer of the child should not be ridiculed or reproved. A

boy once prayed, "O Lord, we are ready to help Thee." A passer-by was indignant and called the child presumptuous, and in this way the first feeling of unselfishness was defamed. A little girl prayed about her mother and her cow, and her prayer was ridiculed. Thus her memory retained only something ludicrous, whereas such solicitude was really touching.

Likewise, using the name of God for intimidation is a great blasphemy. Forbiddance to pray in one's own words is in itself an intrusion into the young consciousness. Perhaps the child remembers something very important and extends his thought upward. Who, then, can intrude to smother such a luminous impulse? The first instruction about prayer will be a directive upon the whole path of life.

71. Prayer is good at any time, yet there are two periods of change of currents when turning to the Higher World is especially desirable—at sunrise and after sunset. Besides, upon going to sleep it is befitting to invoke the Higher World.

Sleep is not understood by science. The idea of rest is primitive. If each action is preceded by a spiritual act, then such an extraordinary state as that of sleep must be especially noted. For almost half their lives people entrust themselves to an invisible world. It is necessary to purify one's consciousness before entrance into the sacred Gates. Thought about the Higher World, thought about the Guardians, already lights up the drooping consciousness; hence, there may be more desirable meetings, and attacks may be warded off. Only the heart's thought about the Higher World provides an impenetrable armor.

Thus, let us be conscious of all that is most beautiful and needed on the lengthy journey.

87. Lenience is one of the qualities of the Higher World, therefore each one in turn must show this quality wherever there is a spark of good. Let people not weary of seeking this power of Grace. Thus in eternal vigil one may take upon oneself the service of the Higher World. One must not pride oneself on such distinction; no particular pride is fitting, but a special joy is permitted.

104. Meditation in quiet about the Higher World will be equal to the best remedy. It is possible thus to sense the relativity of that which exists. Such measure will not be a limitation, on the contrary it will strengthen the flight of thought. When confusion takes possession of the world, propound the most simple.

Earthly existence cannot be final, and in such a transitory state one may only prepare that which is most needed for the future flight, in other words—sharpen thought. Wings grow only through thought.

174. Humanity is wiping out the distinction between tribes, therefore one should speak with special caution about tribes. Even those tribes that are still distinct in appearance and language are not basically and essentially isolated from each other. In conventional terms the subdivision is clear, but not in the matter of blood. An admixture is taking place which is so characteristic during a change of race. It is more appropriate to speak about humanity as a whole than to speak conventionally about the interlacing of the branches.

It is significant to observe the oneness of the transmitted foundations. One should not forget the individualistic expression of each man, rarely will it be a tribal one. The history of each state shows how many wayfarers have crossed its land. Honest study leads one to contemplate mankind as a whole.

187. A man striving toward the Higher World will commit no bad deeds. The name alone—the Higher World, already indicates that everything connected with it is lofty. People may call such striving by different names, but its essence is one, and its activity is always useful to humanity. I do not speak of outer activity, but of the heart's fire which adorns each task with a radiant quality.

190. For him who wishes an easy life it is better not to live. Let him not think about the Higher World who willfully demands rewards for his merits. Whoever reckons wealth in the material world is a pauper in the Higher World.

211. It is necessary for people to free themselves from any arrogance in relation to all that is unknown to them. Thus, one can observe continually that the ignorant ones express themselves offensively about everything inaccessible to them. It is indispensable that the foremost scholars make themselves worthy examples of broadmindedness. Evolution is completely excluded where people do not recognize the possibilities of infinite cognition. I repeat, the success of perfection begins with self-perfection.

Each one who wishes to enlist in the Great Service must free himself from arrogance.

223. No one should call a psychic influence "sorcery." Such an ignorant opinion belongs to times long past. On the contrary, investigation of psychic energy is true progress.

245. Thinkers are subjected to many persecutions. But let the oppressed ones answer, "Though you persecute us, our thoughts are already sown, and nothing can erase thought in space." There is no point in exiling the thinker, his heritage is indestructible throughout all the worlds. Not only is thought indestructible but it even grows in space. The very departure of the thinker from the physical world only opens a broader domain for his thinking. Murderers and poisoners show little acumen; aiming to free themselves of the sowings of the thinker, by their very act they but strengthen him.

258. If scholars are told of magnetized water, they accept such an expression; but if you speak about enchanted or bewitched water, you will be classed with the ignorant. Whereas, the distinction is only in name, for in essence the same energy is applied.

It is time for science to broaden its horizon, unhampered by casual designations. All the dramas of life arise precisely from denominations. One should accustom oneself from childhood to ascertain the essential nature of things.

266. There is so much intolerance and brutality in humanity that it is not difficult to arrive at a conclusion as to its degree of ignorance. Such a degree of ignorance forces one to reiterate the fundamentals. Of what avail is man's literacy if he remain only

a beast! Animals too have learned to understand certain signs, yet they are still animals eager for bloodshed.

Therefore, it is necessary to tell of the shame of ignorance with special brevity and speed.

303. Man should be told, "Do not weaken yourself; discontent, doubt, self-pity, all consume the psychic energy." The manifestation of enshrouded toil—what a frightful spectacle! One should compare the fruits of luminous labor with those of a toil enshrouded by man when he has robbed himself.

I deem that science should also aid in this procedure. Apparatus already exist for the measuring of blood pressure; there will also be apparatus for comparing the organism in its overburdened or inspired state. It can be proven that a man who is unmolested by the influence of the three vipers mentioned above works ten times better; besides he preserves an immunity against all illnesses. Thus, again it is possible to be convinced graphically that the psychic principle prevails over the physical.

It is evident, especially at present, how much harm humanity is inflicting upon itself. Each thought is either a stone in the construction or poison in the heart. It need not be thought that, when speaking about self-poisoning, We have in mind anything new—this truth is as old as the world! But when the vessel is approaching shipwreck, all forces should be summoned to the common task.

322. The rhythm of labor is the adornment of the world. Labor may be regarded as a victory over everyday routine. Each hard-working man is a benefactor of humanity. To imagine Earth without workers is to see a reversion to chaos. Invincible tenacity is forged by labor; precisely everyday work is the accumulation of the treasure. The true toiler loves his labor and understands the significance of tension.

Work has already been called prayer. The highest unity and quality of labor arises from its rhythm. The best quality of work brings forth the rhythm of the Beautiful. Each labor contains within itself the concept of the Beautiful.

Labor, prayer, beauty—all are facets of the great crystal of Existence.

325. Among secret things, especially undiscoverable remains the knowledge as to who reaps the most benefit from the good sent forth. No one knows whom his goodness has helped. It may be assumed that a thought of good reaches a definite person, but this is only a supposition. It may be that this thought has greatly aided someone unknown to us. Such a thought is a messenger of good, and the rescued man may not know his savior; so his gratitude is turned toward the Higher World. When he wishes to express his enraptured gratefulness, he looks upward into the eternal Furnace of creative thought.

326. Anonymous thoughts also receive secret gratitude. Each thought of good receives the best gratitude. It is not for us to judge where the song of gratitude will arise. Gratitude need not be defined. The most beautiful song of gratitude resounds in a moment of joy; but the thought of such joy has been sent by someone.

Let us say gratefully—Aum!

411. If you wish to make a present of a book, I advise you to send it after having read it through. In olden times a book which had been read by the giver was highly esteemed. It was understood that in the process of reading a particular force was accumulated upon the book. Thus, observe all the possibilities of interchange of energy.

415. The Mother of the World! It would seem that in one sounding of these words the meaning of the grandeur of the concept would be made clear, but life shows otherwise.

Poets and singers frequently glorify woman, but governments are unable to recognize simple equality of rights. It will be a shameful page of history which will record that even now equal rights have not yet been established. Woman's upbringing and education are not on a level with man's, and motherhood itself is not protected.

Whoever is first in carrying out such an action of universal import will be proceeding in harmony with evolution.

416. Woman herself must set an example in unity. We know how seldom such harmony is attained. But if the one real motivation be emphasized, then it becomes impossible to remain

deaf just by reason of absurd customs. Indeed, many of them have a historical basis, but these obstructions must be destroyed.

By their own hands women of all races and beliefs will help to mold the steps of evolution. There should be no delay!

417. You will encounter two types of opponents of equal rights—one, an admirer of the rule of the harem, who says that the age-old customs should not be disturbed; the other, indignant at the past, will demand supremacy for herself in everything. Both will be remote from evolution.

It is impermissible to drag past offenses into the future. It is impermissible also to preserve the ossification of an outworn way of life. It is impermissible to erect obstacles to free cognition. Affirmation of true equality of rights might better be called full rights. The obligations attending the recognition of full equality will liberate life from coarse customs, from foul speech, from falsehood, from dusty routine. But the new evolution must be begin early in life if thoughts about it have not flashed out independently.

One may perceive that at present there are many women who perfectly understand the significance of full rights. They may be relied upon throughout the world.

418. Universally full rights for all humanity should be a sign of the times. Public opinion must imperatively demand justice. Such fullness of rights must be manifested as a natural law in world relationship. Full rights are the most indispensable condition.

People pride themselves on the abolition of slavery, but has it actually been eliminated everywhere? Can the inhabitants of Earth sleep in peace while somewhere human dignity is abased to a beastlike condition? Can people boast of enlightenment when they know that full rights do not exist?

Thus, one should not regard the matter of full rights as having been already justly solved.

419. In establishing full rights it is necessary to avoid making it appear as something extraordinary. It is a natural condition and must be accepted calmly. In spirit one may

deplore the fact that such a natural condition was not reached sooner. But it is no cause for proud boasting when something is done which nature itself preordained.

420. Fullness of rights involves full obligation. Lacking such understanding, full rights will change into arbitrariness. Among women can be found that conscientiousness which will provide the quality of evolution.

Without an innate striving for quality it is impossible to acquire the feeling for perfectment.

421. Woman may be judge as well as legal adviser, for injustice will be diminished when the tribunals themselves shall repel the malign principle. Such a distinction will transform the whole way of life.

When I say, "You, women, can comprehend cooperation," I thereby wish to evoke the slumbering fires from the depths of your hearts.

424. Much opposition will be shown to cooperation. Some, through selfishness, will not wish to accept it altogether; others will make use of it for personal gains, but will deny its existence; a third group will unite the concept of cooperation with the overthrow of all order.

There will be a great number of objections; therefore the implantation of collaboration becomes one of the most difficult tasks. An abyss of atavism will appear; the most absurd examples from outworn ages will be adduced; crimes will be enumerated which were the result of dishonest cooperation. Too often obstacles have been set up and the new conditions of life forgotten. The trend toward infatuation with mechanization can be rationally solved by cooperation.

Besides, cooperation must not be limited only to certain aspects of labor. Cooperation must be accepted as the foundation of Existence. Only through the broadest cooperation is it possible to find the true relationship between the state and national labor. Otherwise the ruinous indebtedness of the state will increase. The solution of such a problem by means of war will be a sign of barbarism. One must think not about the destruction of nations, but about the improvement of the planet!

When psychic energy occupies its due position, when woman enters as the protectress of culture, when cooperation is made the basis of the structure—then all life will become transformed. Knowledge and creativeness will occupy their manifest position. I say manifest in this sense, that even amid remote ages may be found examples of understanding of the significance of science and art.

Cooperation reveals easy paths toward perfection.

425. The questions of self-perfection and of national health are closely connected. Let us summon woman to one and to the other. Both tasks are in need not so much of governmental as of family enjoinment. One cannot command purity of thought; one cannot even command purity of speech. One cannot command a healthful cleanliness of the home. Only enlightenment affirms sanity of spirit and body.

428. Why is the participation of woman so necessary in experiments with psychic energy? Why is woman's care for flowers so beneficial? Why is woman's touch so curative in cases of illness?

A great number of manifestations can be named wherein precisely woman can lend a special tension of psychic energy. But due attention has not been paid to such special qualities of women. It is rarely understood among physicians why the participation of a woman in operations can be particularly useful. The eternal Feminine Principle has not yet found its just interpretation.

Scientists do not admit that the mere presence of certain people is equal to the strongest apparatus. Experiments are not performed that could note graphically the different reactions which result from different people. Indescribably useful is each experiment with psychic energy.

454. Gratitude is a great motive force. No one solicits gratitude, but great is the quality of this power. Gratitude acts as a purifier, and whatever has been purified is already more easily moved. Thus, gratitude is a means of hastening the path.

Some believe that by a transport of gratitude they lower themselves. What ignorance! Gratitude only exalts, purifies; it attracts new energies. Even a machine works better without dust.

584. A disciple asked his Teacher, "Tell me, how shall I apply the Teaching in life?" The Teacher advised him, "To begin with, become kinder. Do not consider good as a supernatural gift. Let it be the foundation of your hearth; upon it build your fire, and on such a ground the flame will not be scorching." Thus asked the disciples, and the Teacher was amazed that after all the Teaching a question as to how to begin was necessary.

Not tales but life itself reveals these cases of incommensurateness. The disciple must feel in his heart which quality is nearer to him.

"By whatever Paths ye come to Me, I shall meet ye."

587. There are two kinds of people—the first prefer to exploit the labor of others, while the second like to attain by themselves. Pay attention to the second, among them you find investigators and co-workers. Help them, for such people are especially reticent and impressionable.

New methods of observation ought not to be condemned. Many initial researches have been savagely wrecked by the ignorant. Safeguard the manifested sensitive seekers against the attempts of the hangman. Each one, within his own horizon, can do so much that is useful and unselfish.

Let us be selfless.

593. Think of yourselves not as inhabitants of Earth, but of the Universe. In this way you will assume a greater responsibility. Likewise, you will apprehend how strenuous is the battle for each victory in the realm of Infinity. Do not think that by placing upon yourselves a great responsibility you fall into arrogance. The quality of arrogance befits ignorance. Responsibility is a duty of oneself and to the Highest. Thought about duty will in itself be constructive striving, but for such a path one must cultivate oneself each hour.

He cannot be called a man who does not know how to think about collaborating with the higher energies. How is lofty Communion possible for him if his heart is closed to inspiration!

Learn to understand words in their full significance, otherwise such a lofty concept as inspiration is reduced to an empty sound. As I summon you for the journey, I am anxious that you do not forget, as a result of hustle and bustle, that which is most needed. Frequently, hurried travelers burden themselves with needless things and forget the key to the most necessary coffer.

Brotherhood

17. Brotherhood must be looked upon as an institution wherein the members work not by the day but by the task. One must love the labor in order to prefer the task work. It must be realized that the tasks are infinite and the process of perfectment is also unending. Whoever is afraid cannot grow to love labor.

You have sometimes listened to the beautiful singing of workers. Verily, work can be accompanied by both joy and inspired thought. But one must test oneself for everything.

21. Any food containing blood is harmful for the development of subtle energy. If humanity would only refrain from devouring dead bodies, then evolution could be accelerated. Meat lovers have tried to remove the blood, but they have not been able to obtain the desired results. Meat, even with the blood removed, cannot be fully freed from the emanations of this powerful substance. The sun's rays to a certain extent remove these emanations, but their dispersion into space also causes no small harm. Try to carry out a psychic energy experiment near a slaughterhouse and you will receive signs of acute madness, not to mention the entities which attach themselves to the exposed blood. Not without foundation has blood been called sacred.

There can thus be observed different kinds of people. It is possible to convince oneself particularly as to how strong atavism is. The desire for food containing blood is augmented by atavism, because the many preceding generations were saturated with blood. Unfortunately, governments pay no attention to improving the health of the population. State medicine and hygiene stand at a low level. Medical supervision is no higher than that of the police. No new thought penetrates into these outworn institutions. They can only prosecute, they cannot help.

Hence, on the path to Brotherhood there should be no slaughterhouses.

22. Yet there are people who speak much against bloodshed but are themselves not averse to eating meat. There are many contradictions contained in man. Only the perfecting of psychic energy can promote the harmonization of life. Contradiction is nothing but disorder. Different strata have corresponding contents. But a tempest can stir up waves, and not quickly thereafter is the right current again established.

24. Hypocrisy, bigotry, and superstition are three of the dark qualities which must be rejected on the path to Brotherhood. Let each one reflect whence have been born these minions of ignorance. Whole books can be written about such paths of darkness. One should ponder upon how these pernicious corrupters have grown up. They grow imperceptibly. But there has never been a time when they were more numerous than at present. Notwithstanding the spiritualization of science, and in spite of conditions of rational investigation of the manifestations of the Subtle World, still the growth of crimes due to ignorance is unprecedented. People cannot understand that spatial thought can free them from their shackles.

Consider the dark times as passing—knowledge shames the ignorant.

56. Patience, patience, patience—let this not be an empty sound, let it protect one on all paths. When it seems that all forces have been exhausted, such an illusion is most dangerous. The forces are inexhaustible, but people themselves try to cut short their flow.

Also, the path to Brotherhood requires much patience. The same power of thought must be applied in order to draw close to the consciousness of the three worlds.

57. The true family is the prototype of communal life. It can personify cooperation and Hierarchy and all the conditions of Brotherhood. But such families are extremely rare, and therefore it is impossible to say to everyone that the family is the symbol of Brotherhood. It might be replied, "Is not the family a symbol of hostility?" So much have people become accustomed not to respect the home. Therefore, as to the question of upbringing, let us pay special attention to the life in the home. It is impossible to think about building the state without building the home.

What conception of Brotherhood can the people have who do not understand the dignity of state and home? No specific decree can restore the feeling of dignity if it has been obliterated. It is necessary to begin its implantation by education, by recognition of the value of broad knowledge and of exact scientific studies. Only thus can people again remember humaneness.

Upon the step of humaneness will the understanding of Brotherhood be established.

58. The very austerity of labor can acquire a beautiful meaning by the elimination of all coarsening effects and the introduction of the concept of cooperation. It must be remembered that coarseness is contrary to all laws of nature. Every coarse action creates such a hideous vortex that if people could but see it they would certainly be more careful in their conduct. The karma of coarseness is extremely heavy.

With broadening of consciousness people became especially sensitive to any and every coarseness. Thus, one may be assured that coarseness is most inadmissible.

80. Usually, when people return to a former place they experience a certain sadness. They feel that something has not been accomplished. And so it is. In Infinity there must always be sensed something preordained.

86. Mercy is not an easy concept, and only the very far-sighted can scrutinize the effects of it. When magnanimity prompts, "Let live!" this verdict will not be difficult. Perhaps, precisely in this hour destruction might have been approaching, but the farsighted one understood that the positive is greater than the negative. For the near-sighted such mercy is unfitting, but for the far-sighted it is as an arrow into the target.

92. Detested labor is not only a misery for the unsuccessful worker but it poisons the whole surrounding atmosphere. The discontent of the worker does not permit him to find joy and to improve the quality. Moreover, imperil born of irritation redoubles gloomy thoughts, with effects fatal to creativeness. But the definite question may arise as to what is to be done if not everyone can find work corresponding to his vocation. Undoubtedly, many people cannot apply themselves in the way they would like. There exists a remedy for lifting such a blight. Scientific attainments show that above the everyday routine there is a beautiful domain accessible to all—the realization of psychic energy. In experiments with it one may be convinced that farmers often possess a goodly store of the energy. Likewise, many other fields of labor aid the conservation of energy. Therefore, amid the most diverse labors one may find uplifting strength.

93. All is possible; only depression of spirit can whisper about impossibility. Each step of science does not limit; it provides a new possibility. If something appears impossible from the earthly point of view, it may be entirely feasible through application of subtle energies. The face of a man changes with the source of light. Lighting can alter to the point of non-recognition the facial features and can reveal a quite unusual expression. But there are so many rays and currents, of diverse influence, and they can transform that which exists!

Is it not encouraging to realize that all is possible?

110. If the surpassing feeling of Brotherhood is difficult in the earthly condition, nevertheless Brotherhood is entirely accessible to each aspiring mind. There is no need to make something complicated of it, if you are able to wish for your neighbor nothing that you do not wish for yourself. Thus,

every day, in every task, in every thought, one may be affirmed in the realization of Brotherhood.

114. Let us also not forget another quality indispensable on the path—non-attachment to property. Avarice in general is nowhere fitting; this quality holds one back to the lower spheres. The attachment of a miser is an insurmountable obstacle. While it is not easy to renounce property, avarice is indeed the most grave condition of plunging into the abyss.

115. One may make the mistake of assuming that the majority of people know how to read books. Such ability has to be cultivated. When people accept the book, it does not mean that they know how to read it properly. It can be seen how relatively they interpret what has been read, and how far removed their understanding often is from the writer's thought. I affirm that books are too little comprehended, yet the manifestation of the primary energy can be an excellent guide. It frequently helps one to find a needed book and to select from it what is desired. One has but to be attentive. But this quality also must be cultivated in oneself.

119. It may be noticed that patience is developed to the extreme in certain people while others are totally lacking in this quality. What is the reason for this? Such a basic quality cannot be a matter of chance. Know that the possessor of patience has build it up in many lives. A patient man is a worker of vast experience. Only in great labors does a man cognize the worthlessness of irritation. Before the Great Image he perceives the complete insignificance of transitory manifestations. Without many testings it is impossible to appraise and distinguish the qualities of manifestations in life. One should not assume that patience is a distinction conferred without reason; on the contrary, it belongs to the qualities that have been earned with special difficulty, both in the earthly and in the subtle sojourn. Hence, the patient man is rich in experience while the impatient one is a novice in life. Thus let us remember, for the Path.

126. Never before have we held discourses under such tension. Never has Earth been so enshrouded in brown gas. Never has the planet been so flooded with hatred. It is

unthinkable not to sense the convulsions of nations; therefore, when I speak about care toward health I have in mind the unusual state of affairs throughout the world. It is regrettable that the nations do not think about the condition of the world. Much energy is being wasted. Do not think that the special tensions come only from private circumstances; it vibrates in conformity with the conditions in the world. The psychic energy is tensed, ready for both reception and repulsion. The spirit senses thoughts manifested in the Subtle World.

130. "Brotherhood on Earth is impossible!" Thus exclaim those filled with selfhood. "Brotherhood on Earth is impossible," say the dark destroyers. "Brotherhood on Earth is impossible," whisper the weak-willed. Thus do many voices try to deny the fundamentals of Be-ness. Yet, so many true Brotherhoods have existed in different epochs, and nothing was able to cut short their existence. If people do not see something, then for them it does not exist. Such ignorance can be traced from ancient times up to this day. Nothing can force a man to see if he does not wish to see. It is time to understand that it is not only the visible that exists but that the world is filled with invisible realities.

148. People are vainly seeking new remedies and medicaments without making use of the old ones. Even milk and honey are not sufficiently in use. Whereas, what can be more beneficial than vegetable products reworked through a succeeding evolution? Milk and honey are to be had in infinite variety, and they constitute the best prophylaxis when employed rationally and scientifically. The point is not simply to drink milk and eat honey; first of all, one must consider what kind of milk and what kind of honey. It is right to assume that the best honey will be from places that are replete with curative herbs. It may be understood that bees bring together not mere chance combinations of their extractions. Nature lore about bees has importance in the way of directing attention to the particular quality of the honey.

Moreover, many vegetable products require investigation. People regard things so primitively that they are content with the expressions "good and bad," "fresh and spoiled;" besides, they are elated by the large size of a product, forgetting that artificial enlargement diminishes the qualitative value. Even such primitive considerations are lost sight of. In the development of vitality, its essence ought to be derived from all the kingdoms of nature.

172. Inexperienced physicians try to drive a disease inward in order even temporarily to evade dangerous symptoms—thus are established hotbeds of maladies. But the experienced physician tries to draw out the germ of the disease in order to eradicate it in good time. The same method ought to be applied in all sicknesses. It is better that a crisis be lived through than that a destructive collapse seize the whole organism. It is possible to live through a crisis, and such shock may call new forces into life. Whereas disintegration and rot but infect all the surroundings. Thus, let us understand it in forty ways.

175. Great Service has called forth everywhere much misunderstanding. To people it usually has the aspect of something unattainable. They hope that responsibility for such Service will pass them by. But let us reflect upon certain great Servitors. Let us see if They were unapproachable supermen. Pythagoras and Plato and Boehme and Paracelsus and Thomas Vaughan were men who bore their lamps amidst their fellowmen in life under a hail of nonunderstanding and abuse. Anyone could approach them, but only a few were able to discern the superearthly radiance behind the earthly face. It is possible to name great Servitors of East and West, North and South. It is possible to peruse their biographies; yet everywhere we feel that the superearthly radiance appears rarely in the course of centuries. One should learn from reality.

Let us not link ourselves with the vilifiers of Plato and the persecutors of Confucius. They were oppressed by citizens who were considered the pride of the country. Thus has the world raised its hand against the great Servitors. Be assured that the Brotherhood formed by Pythagoras appeared dangerous in the eyes of the city guard. Paracelsus was a target for mockery and malignance. Thomas Vaughan seemed to be an outcast, and few wished to meet with him. Thus was the reign of darkness manifested. Of course darkness, too, has its own laws. The dark ones watch intently a "dangerous" Great Service.

Let us apply examples of the past to all days of life.

180. Let us refer, with regret, to the generally accepted idea of comfort and security. In it is contained torpor and vacuity. We learn to welcome all inceptions of thought, and We always esteem the pressure of a forward striving. A multitude of examples may be cited from physics and mechanics showing pressure as a motive force. For many, it is not easy to agree that pressure is but the gateway to progress. But if humanity will recognize this truth, in so doing it will also understand the meaning of progress. From the point of such cognition it is not far to Brotherhood.

200. He who appeals for better quality is already on the path.

201. The best curative products are often neglected. Milk and honey are considered nutritious products, yet they have been entirely forgotten as regulators of the nervous system. When used in their pure form, they contain the precious primary energy. Precisely this quality in them must be preserved. Whereas, the sterilization of milk and the special processing of honey deprive them of their most valuable property. There remains the nutritive importance, but their basic value dissappears.

Indeed, it is indispensable that the products be used in their pure state. Thus, the animals and bees must be kept under healthful conditions, but all artificial purifications destroy their direct usefulness.

The ancient knowledge protected cows as sacred animals, and it wove an attractive legend about bees. But in time people lost the conscious regard for the remedies as first given to them. In the old manuals of healing, each remedy was looked upon from the standpoints of both usefulness and harmfulness. But such valuable substances as milk, honey, and musk carry no injury when they are pure. It is possible to point out many useful remedies in the plant world also, but the majority of them are best in the pure state, when the basic energy inherent in them, over and above so-called vitamins, has not been lost. The juice of carrots or radishes, or of strawberries, is best in the raw, pure state. Hence, it may be understood why the ancient Rishis subsisted on these wholesome products.

235. Hatred of humanity is reaching out for radical methods of destruction—by gases and poisoning. Let scientists make it clear that these gases do not disappear immediately but precipitate for a long time. Let the inventors of gases settle down in a house the walls of which have been rubbed with arsenic or corrosive sublimate, or other emanative poisons. By experience on themselves, on their eyes, skin and lungs, let them be convinced as to how long the emanating poisons continue to act. Moreover, in a large number of poisons their preparation works injury at great distances. Only criminal stupidity thinks that the damage will be done only to the enemy.

Likewise poisonous are the gases which irritate the mucous membranes. It cannot be permissible to poison a people, condemning it to maladies which make their appearance only after a passage of time. So-called enlightened rulers infect wide spaces and soothe themselves with the thought that the poisoning is harmless. Let them try living in a house which has been poisoned!

Among all the scientific discoveries gases and poisons will remain a disgraceful stain.

238. Many teachings enjoin abstinence from any killing. Indeed, what has been let unspoken is the question of the killing of the tiniest invisible creatures. Of course, what was considered was premeditated killing through evil will; otherwise with every breath man would be a murderer. The consciousness can whisper where the boundary line is. The heart can sense and can keep a man from killing.

If a bough has been senselessly broken let us nevertheless carry it to the temple, that is to say, let us be compassionate. The same feeling prompts one to guard against killing.

248. People are astonished at the quantity of crimes, but they forget about the incomparably larger number of evil deeds that are never detected. One may be horrified by the countless mental crimes which have not been legislated against, and yet they are destroying the lives of people and the life of the whole

planet. One should reflect sometimes how much the fertility of the planet is diminishing, in spite of all the artificial measures taken at times by governments. It is possible to plant a grove of trees and, at the same time, poison and destroy entire forests. People marvel at the remains of primeval forest giants, but they do not ponder whether such giants can grow up nowadays. People strip away the virgin covering of the planet and then are astounded at the spread of sandy wastes. Upon recounting all the species on the planet one may be surprised at how little they are improved. Let us not consider certain peculiar cross-breedings that, like dropsy, can swell the size of certain vegetables. Such experiments have no influence on the general condition of the planet.

250. Is a deluge possible which can wash away entire regions? Can there be an earthquake which destroys whole countries? Can there be a whirlwind sweeping away cities? Can there be a fall of enormous meteors? All these are possible, and the swing of the pendulum can be increased. Does the quality of human thought have no significance? Thus let people reflect about the essence of things. It is very near to thought, and many thoughts are directed here from other worlds. Let us not blame sunspots alone.

A single thought about Brotherhood is already salutary.

251. Threat and violence are not of Our domain. Compassion and warning will be the province of Brotherhood. One would have to be of a cruel nature to take a warning for a threat. People judge according to themselves; they try to insert their own meaning into each word they hear. It is instructive to give to a most diverse group of people the same simple text for interpretation. It is astonishing how differently the contents may be explained. Not only basic traits of character but also casual moods are reflected, causing the contents to be misconstrued. Thus, it may be confirmed that the evil see evil, whereas the good see good. The same truth carries through in all branches of knowledge. Only very keen eyes distinguish where is reality and where the mirage of a casual mood.

When man dreams about Brotherhood, let him first of all cleanse his eyes from the layer of accumulated dust.

273. A wise philosopher, having been sold into slavery, exclaimed, "Thanks! Evidently I can pay back some old debts." An emperor, nicknamed the Golden, was terrified, "Luxury pursues me. When will I be able to pay off my debts?" Thus have wise people thought about the quickest payment of their debts. They understood that former lives surely do not elapse without incurring indebtedness. But a man with much income must make haste in settling his accounts.

282. In the Brotherhood each one works as much as he can. Each one helps in accordance with the measure of his forces; each one does not condemn in his heart; each one affirms knowledge according to his experience; each one lets no time escape, for it is irrecoverable; each one is ready to lend his strength to a Brother; each one displays his best quality; each one rejoices at the success of a Brother. Are these principles too difficult? Are they supernatural? Are they beyond human strength? Do they require superknowledge? Is it possible that only heroes can understand unity? Precisely for the sake of comprehension examples have been given of the better people becoming physicians, cobblers, weavers, butchers, in order to infix better thinking through different kinds of labor.

Over and above man's work stands the manifestation of woman. She leads, she inspires, she guides on all paths, and she displays an example of synthesis. It is astonishing how quickly she enters any domain. From Earth up to the far-off worlds she succeeds in weaving wings of Light. She knows how to preserve the Chalice in different atmospheres. When We speak about cooperation, We always point to the achievement of woman. The domain of Brotherhood is the field of cooperation.

354. Lunar reactions and the influence of sunspots long ago attracted the attention of the best scholars. But why do other, no less significant, manifestations remain neglected? Lunar manifestations such as somnambulism are extremely crude compared with the action of many rays and currents. Even those having refined organisms assimilate only with difficulty the fact that their inner sensations depend first of all upon spatial currents.

Among scientific discoveries, the statement that sunspots promote wars sounds strange. From the standpoint of scientific analysis would it not be better to say that sunspots engender human madness? Such a definition is far nearer the truth, for this chemism actually reacts upon the nervous system. In this let us not forget that such a chemical reaction is quite prolonged. It would be incautious to consider that a lessening of sunspots immediately does away with the chemism in space.

Likewise, the results of poison gases go on acting for a long time. It is senseless to think that it is possible to open a window and the poisons will evaporate. They are absorbed in the soil, in fabrics, and they unquestionably act upon the internal organs. Moreover, such reactions are so little felt that only future effects will attract attention. There is much poisoning!

440. If catastrophe threatens Earth, is it not absurd to write something down, to study, and to conserve? Only from an earthly point of view is it possible to arrive at such a premise. If no Subtle World exists, then from the earthly point of view it is not worth-while to be concerned. But We are speaking about life, not about a handful of earth.

442. Without any instructions people know how to care for a beloved object. They will resourcefully discover how to keep it in concealment. They will exert themselves not to break or damage a beloved thing. Someone has said that people are most competent at preserving stones and metals, less so with plants, still less with animals, and least of all with man. You can judge for yourself how just is such an understanding. Man is a most subtle organism, and yet the most cruel treatment falls to his lot. Let us not close our eyes to the fact that the so-called abolishment of corporal punishment is merely a screen for still greater cruelty. When will the abolition of spiritual persecutions finally come! When will people realize that the highest degree of torture is torment of the spirit! As long as they are not conscious of the Subtle World, humaneness will not be realized. Let us not be surprised that some people require the division of the higher worlds into many degrees. Rather, let people, including those who demand the most, understand at least the Subtle World, so that they may know how to enter it worthily. The

division will be grasped afterwards when at least the first degree of Infinity shall have been comprehended.

459. Thirst is slaked by water. Thirst for knowledge is slaked by the path of approach to the Higher World. Many scholars suffer their whole lives from indescribable anguish, because they alienate themselves from cognition of the Higher World. The anguish of the wrong path is most cruel, most devouring! In the end such a man finally abrogates his progress and is in torture without understanding his own error. Much malice is engendered by such beings. They are ready to persecute even the least manifestation of Light.

502. Can there be any judgment concerning peace among those who are full of coarseness and cruelty? One should observe such peacemakers in their daily home life. One should hear how they discuss their own affairs and those of others. One ought to become acquainted with their jokes and slanders in order to understand their complete unfitness in the matter of peace. But no one is concerned with the moral level of those who sit in judgment on the destinies of whole nations. No one will reflect that nothing clean comes out of dirt.

504. Where, then, in earthly existence should one seek the flashes of Brotherhood? Signs of it may be found among very simple workers who have come to love their work. Labor, love, and brotherhood dwell together.

510. In ancient epochs the meaning of life was understood more profoundly than at present. All the remarkable contemporary discoveries not only have not focused attention upon the fundamental meaning of life but they have often led away the thought even into the realm of mechanics. Efforts must be exerted to direct thought to the very basis of existence. The level of thinking of ancient philosophers should be compared with the trend of the reasonings of contemporary scientists. Aside from knowledge of many scientific discoveries, the philosophers of antiquity often knew how to present very profound formulas of life. It is essential that the art of thinking again rise above the external conditions, which are subordinate factors of existence.

525. The Atlanteans had mastered aviation, they knew how to crossbreed plants, they employed powerful energies, they knew secrets of metals, they excelled in deadly implementations of war. Are not these achievements reminiscent of some other ages?

578. With what can one block the path of evil? Only with labor on Earth. Thought and work directed to the Common Good will be a strong weapon against evil. People frequently begin to verbally curse evil, but the disparagement is so ugly that it is impossible to fight it also by means of ugliness. Such weapons are worthless. Work and lofty thought will be the arms of victory—such is the path of Brotherhood.

585. Each instant, someone somewhere is undergoing terrible misfortune. Let us not forget these perishing ones; let us send them thoughts of help. Perhaps people do not realize that afflictions are forever taking place, without end. In the Brotherhood they are known, and benevolent arrows are sent. Even if you cannot determine precisely the place of its destination, nevertheless send your salutary thought into space. It will find the right course and will be joined magnetically with Our Help. Beauty is found when, from diverse quarters of the world, thoughts of salvation come flying—in this each one will emulate the Brotherhood.

593. The peoples of Asia have preserved the memory of the Brotherhood; each in its own way, in its own toungue, with its own possibilities has preserved in the depths of its heart a dream about an actual Refuge. The heart will not relinquish its dream about the Community of salvation, but will remember amidst sorrows that somewhere beyond the mountain peaks dwell the Protectors of the peoples. The very thought about them purifies the thinking and fills one with vigor. Thus, let us honor those who do not relinquish their best treasure.

596. A city of science will always be the dream of enlightened people. No one would presume to raise objections to an abode of scientists, where in peace and wise communion truths would be brought to light. Each learned worker would have the best equipment at his disposal. One can picture what discoveries would issue from general concordance and

cooperation of all the branches of science! No one would consider the idea of such a city utopian. If only the means and good will could be found! But if one were to say that a certain Abode of Knowledge does exist, a multitude of doubts and denials would come tumbling out. And if to the word *science* one were to add the word *Brotherhood*, it will certainly be said that such a chemical combination is impossible. But who has said that science and Brotherhood are incompatible?

597. Precisely, Brotherhood is founded on knowledge. True science lives through brotherly communion—such is the Covenant of Brotherhood.

599. As bees collect honey so you, too, should collect knowledge. It will be asked, What is new in this advice? Its newness is in that one should collect knowledge from everywhere. Until now knowledge had fixed limits, and entire domains of it were kept under prohibition, suspicion, and in neglect. People have not had the courage to overcome prejudices. They have forgotten that a scholar, first of all, must be open to all that exists. There are no forbidden domains for a scholar. He does not belittle any manifestation of nature, for he understands that the cause and effect of each manifestation have a profound significance.

Brotherhood teaches unprejudiced cognition.

601. Likewise, let us welcome those schoolteachers who can find an hour to talk to their pupils about the dignity and responsibility of man, about the primary energy, and about the treasures belonging to all peoples. Such preceptors will indeed make more manifest the path of labor and achievement. They will find harmony between the preeminence of the spirit and the health of the body. They will introduce the book of knowledge into each dwelling. The life of such teachers is hard. Let there live in them the life-giving dream about the Brotherhood.

Chapter 6

Alice A. Bailey

The third remarkable woman is Alice A. Bailey. She, too, like Blavatsky and Roerich, had direct contact both personally and telepathically with the Masters of Wisdom.

All three had extraordinary capacities for heavy labor, inner striving, and the necessary abilities to express these activities in teaching and writing. They are thus inspirations to all of us, helping enlighten humanity by their examples of inner striving and outer service. Their great expression of love and compassion toward struggling humanity in the course of their great service makes each of them unique and truly remarkable women.

Alice Bailey was born Alice Ann La Trobe-Bateman on June 16, 1880 in Manchester, England. She died in New York City on December 15, 1949. Her ancestors included Hollinshed, "the chronicler," of English literary fame, Charles La Trobe, one of the first governors of Australia, and others who had been traced back in English history to the time of the Crusades.

Yet despite being born in a wealthy, aristocratic family, she had an unhappy childhood.

"I cannot remember the time when I was not thinking and puzzling and asking questions and rebelling and hoping. Yet I was 35 years old before I really discovered that I had a mind and that it was something I could use. Up to that time, I had been a bundle of emotions and feelings; my mind—what there was of it—had used me and not been used by me... During those early years I was surrounded by beauty; my life was full of variety and I met many interesting people. I never knew what it was to want anything. I was brought up in the usual luxury of my day and class; I was watched over with the greatest care—but within myself I hated it all."[1]

But on June 30, 1895, at the age of 15, a memorable event occurred for her, one she never forgot:

"I had been for months in the throws of adolescent miseries. Life was not worth living. There was nothing but sorrow and trouble on every hand. I had not asked to come into the world but here I was... Nobody loved me and I knew I had a hateful disposition and so was not surprised that life was difficult. There was no future ahead of me, except marriage and the humdrum life of my caste and set. I hated everybody (except two or three people)... I had been taught the narrowest kind of Christianity; unless people thought as I did, they could not be saved. The Church of England was divided into the High Church party which was almost Anglo-Catholic; and the Low Church party which believed in a hell for those who did not accept certain tenets and a heaven for those who did. I belonged for six months of the year to one party and for six months of the year (when I was not in Scotland under the influence of my aunt) to the other. I was torn between the beauties of ritual and the narrowness of dogma. Missionary work was dinned into my consciousness by both groups. The world was divided into those who were Christians and worked hard to save souls, and those who were heathen and bowed down to images of stone and worshipped them. The Buddha was a stone image; and it never dawned on me then that the images of Buddha were on a par with the statues and the images of the Christ in the Christian churches, with which I was so familiar on the continent of Europe. I was in a complete fog. And then—in the height of my unhappiness and in the very middle of my dilemma and questioning—one of the Masters of the Wisdom came to me.

"At the time of that happening and for many years after, I had not the remotest idea Who He was. I was scared stiff at the occurrence...

---

[1]Alice A. Bailey, The Unfinished Autobiography, Lucis Publishing Company, New York, 1951, p. 12

"It was Sunday morning. The previous Sunday I had heard a sermon which had aroused all my inspiration. This Sunday, for some reason, I had not gone to church ... there was no one in the house but myself and the servants. I was sitting in the drawing room reading. The door opened and in walked a tall man dressed in European clothes (very well cut, I remember) but with a turban on his head. He came in and sat down beside me. I was so petrified at the sight of the turban that I could not make a sound or ask what he was doing there. Then he started to talk. He told me there was some work that it was planned that I could do in the world but that it would entail my changing my disposition very considerably; I would have to give up being such an unpleasant little girl and must try and get some measure of self-control. My future usefulness to Him and to the world was dependent upon how I handled myself and the changes I could manage to make. He said that if I could achieve real self-control I could then be trusted and that I would travel all over the world and visit many countries, 'doing your master's work all the time.' He emphasized that it all depended upon me and what I could do and should do immediately. He added that He would be in touch with me at intervals of several years apart.

"The interview was very brief. I said nothing but simply listened whilst He talked quite emphatically. Having said what He had come to say, He got up and walked out, after pausing at the door for a minute to give me a look which to this day I remember very distinctly."[2]

After she had recovered from the shock of this electrifying experience, she decided to be a nicer person and to learn to control her temper.

"I tried not to be so cross and to control my tongue and for some time became so objectionably good that my family got disturbed; they wondered if I was ill and almost begged me to resume my explosive displays. I was smug and sweet and sentimental."[3]

---

[2]IBID pp. 34-36
[3]IBID pp. 36-37

"Then in 1915 I discovered who He was and that other people knew him...

"I found that this visitor was the Master K.H., the Master Koot Hoomi, a Master Who is very close to the Christ, Who is on the teaching line and Who is an outstanding exponent of the love-wisdom of which the Christ is the full expression...

"The value [of this experience] is to be found ... in the fact that everything that He told me came true (after I tried hard to meet requirements) and because I discovered that He was not the Master Jesus, as I had naturally supposed, ... Anyway, the Master K.H. is my Master, beloved and real. I have worked for Him ever since I was fifteen years old and I am now one of the senior disciples of His group, or—as it is called esoterically—in His Ashram.

"I make these statements with a definite purpose in mind. So much nonsense has been talked along these lines and so many claims made by those who have not the experience and the mental and spiritual orientation required, that true disciples are ashamed to mention their work and position.

"I want to make it easier for such disciples in the future and to 'debunk' the nonsense put out by many esoteric (so-called) schools of thought. The claim of discipleship is ever permissible; it gives nothing away and only carries weight if backed by a life of service. The claim that one is an initiate of a certain status is never permissible, except among those of the same rating and then it is not necessary. The world is full of disciples. Let them acknowledge it. Let them stand together in the bonds of discipleship and make it easier for others to do the same. Thus will the existence of the Masters be proved and proved in the right way—through the lives and the testimonies of those They train."[4]

Her love and compassion for these hard-working disciples of the world was the motive for her writing her Unfinished Autobiography in which she says:

---

[4] IBID pp. 37-38

"...I would really render a service if I could show people how I became what I am from what I was. It might be useful to know how a rabid, orthodox Christian worker could become a well-known occult teacher. People might learn much by discovering how a theologically minded Bible student could come to the firm conviction that the teachings of the East and of the West must be fused and blended before the true and universal religion—for which the world waits—could appear on earth. There is value in knowing that the love of God antedates Christianity and recognises no boundaries. This was the first and most difficult lesson I had to learn and it took me a long time. It takes all fundamentalists much time to learn that God is love. They assert it but do not believe it in practice, God's practice I mean.

"I would like, among other things, to show how the world of human beings opened up to a very class-conscious English woman and how the world of spiritual values with its direct, inner, spiritual government became a proven fact to an exceedingly narrow-minded Christian. I glory in the name of Christian but I now belong to the inclusive kind and not the exclusive.

"One of the things that I seek to bring out in this story is the fact of this inner direction of world affairs and to familiarise more people with the paralleling fact of the existence of Those Who are responsible (behind the scenes) for the spiritual guidance of humanity, and for the task of leading mankind out of darkness into Light, from the unreal to the Real and from death to Immortality.

"I want to make the Disciples of the Christ who are the Masters of the Wisdom, real to people, as real as They are to me and many thousands in the world. I do not mean a hypothetical reality (if we may use such a phrase) or as a subject of faith and belief. I want to show Them as They are—Disciples of the Christ, living men, and ever present factors in human affairs. Those are the things which are of moment and not the earthly experiences, the happenings and events in the life of one of Their workers.

"I have lived many incarnations in one. I have moved forward steadily but with exceeding difficulty (psychological and material) into an ever widening field of usefulness. I want to show that in each cycle of experience, I did sincerely try to follow a leading, coming from within, and that when I did, it always meant a step forward in understanding and a greater ability, therefore, to help. The result of this apparently blind moving forward (as when I married and came to the U.S.A.) was extended opportunity. I have played many parts in my life. I was an unhappy, exceedingly disagreeable, little girl, a society girl in the gay nineties (which I didn't find so gay) and then an evangelist of the 'Billy Sunday' type and a social worker. Again—not so gay, except that I was young and tremendously interested in everything. Later, I married Walter Evans and found myself functioning as the wife of a rector of the Protestant Episcopal Church in California and the mother of three girls.

"This varied experience of living and working in Great Britain, Europe, Asia and America led to basic changes in my attitudes to life and people. To remain static in a point of view strikes me as unintelligent. It means that there comes a point in one's development when one ceases to learn, when one fails to extract the meaning out of events, schools of thought and circumstance, and when one remains mentally quiescent in the face of life. That is disaster. That is evil. That, surely, is what hell must mean. The awfulness of hell (in which I do not believe from the orthodox point of view) must lie in 'everlasting' sameness, in a forced inability to change conditions.

"I became next an occult student, a writer of books which have had a wide and constant circulation and which have been translated into many languages. I found myself the head of an esoteric school—all unwittingly and without any planned intention—and the organiser, with Foster Bailey, of an International Goodwill Movement (not a peace movement) which proved so successful that we had centres in nineteen countries when the war broke out in 1939.

"I have not, therefore, been useless where world service is concerned but I do not, and cannot, claim that my success has been due to my personal efforts alone. I have always been blessed with marvellous friends and helpers who—down the years—have remained my friends, no matter what I did to them. I have had many such friends and a few—a very surprisingly few—enemies. These latter have done me no real harm, perhaps because I could never dislike them and could always understand why they disliked me. My husband, Foster Bailey, has for over twenty-five years made all my work possible. Without him I feel I could have accomplished very little. Where there is deep and abiding love and understanding, respect and unbroken comradeship, one is rich indeed. He has been to me a tower of strength and 'the shadow of a great rock in a thirsty land.' There are things which are damaged by expression in words and which sound meaningless and futile when written down. Our relationship is one of them. For many lives we must have lived and worked together and we both look forward to many more. I have no more to say on this subject. What, I often ask myself, could I have done without the understanding friendship, affection and staunch cooperation of my many friends and co-workers who for years have stood by me? I cannot list them but they are the people who are essentially responsible for the success of the work we—as a group—have done.

"The reason for this autobiography is therefore a threefold one, for there are three things upon which I want to lay the emphasis, and which I hope will emerge into clarity.

"First of all, the fact of the Masters of Wisdom, Who work under the guidance of the Christ. I want to make clearer the nature of Their work. I want to present Them to the world as I personally know Them, because, in the years that are coming, more and more people will testify to Their existence, and I would like to make the way easier for them. This I will enlarge upon later and show how I personally came to know of Their existence. In everyone's life there are certain convincing factors which make living possible. Nothing can alter one's inner conviction. To me, the Masters are such a factor and this knowledge has formed a stabilising point in my life.

"The second thing which I would like to do is to indicate some of the new trends in the world today which are definitely influencing mankind and raising the human consciousness. I want to point to some of the newer ideas which are coming out into the world of human thought from the inner group of

Masters and which are ushering in a new civilisation and culture and—incidentally from the angle of eternity—destroying many old and beloved forms. In my life I have seen, as have all thinking people, the disappearance of much that was worthless in the field of religion, of education and of the social order. And that is very good.

"Looking back, I can imagine nothing more appalling than the perpetuation of the Victorian era, for instance, with its ugliness, its smugness, and the excessive comfort of the upper class (so-called) and the frightful condition under which the labouring classes struggled. It was in that well-padded, sleek and comfortable world I lived when a girl. I can imagine nothing more blighting to the human spirit than the theology of the past with the emphasis upon a God who saves a smug few and condemns the majority to perdition. I can imagine nothing more conducive to unrest, class war, hate and degradation than the economic situation of the world, then and for many decades—a situation largely responsible for the present world war (1914-1945).

"Thank God, we are on our way to better things. The group who have shared our work—along with many other groups, responding to the same inspiration of love of humanity—will have done our tiny part in bringing about much needed changes. The world trend towards federation, towards understanding and cooperation, and towards those things which will benefit all and not just a chosen few is of encouraging importance. We are on our way towards brotherhood.

"The third thing which I would like to do is to show how wonderful human beings are. I have lived on three continents and in many nations. I have known the very rich and the very poor, intimately and from the angle of close friendship; the very highest in the world have been my friends and the very lowest; and in all classes, nations and races I have found the same humanity, the same beauty of thought, the same self-sacrifice and the same love of others, the same sins and weaknesses, the same pride and selfishness, the same aspiration and spiritual objectives and the same desire to serve. If I can manage to bring this out with clarity and force, that alone will justify this book.

"In the long range of human history and placed along with the world's great Figures, who is Alice Ann Bailey? A quite unimportant woman who was forced (usually against her will) by circumstances, by an actively intruding conscience, and by a knowledge of what her Master wanted done, to undertake certain tasks. A woman who was always scared of life (perhaps partly due to an oversheltered childhood); who is naturally so shy that even today, if she has to go to a luncheon party, has to muster the courage to ring the bell; who is very domestic and loves to cook and wash (and God knows has done her full share of it) and who hates publicity. I have never been robust but have enormous vitality. All through my life I have been forced to spend weeks and sometimes months in bed. For the last eight years I have been kept alive by medical science, but—and this is one thing about which I could say I am proud—I have kept going on, in spite of it all. I have found life very, very good even when having what most people regard as the worst possible time. There has always been so much to do, so many people to know. I have only one basic grumble and that is that I have always been so tired. In an old churchyard in England there is a tombstone which has on it words which I can fully understand.

> Here lies a poor woman who always was tired.
> She lived in a world where too much was required.
> Weep not for me, friends; the land where I am going
> There'll be no more dusting or sweeping or sewing.
> Weep not for me, friends, though death us may sever.
> I am going to do nothing for ever and ever.

"Now that really would be hell and I don't want to go there. I want to take a new and more adequate body and come back to gather up the old threads, find the same group of workers and go on with the job. If the story of my life encourages another ordinary person to push forward, this book will be worth while; if it leads some person with aspiration to launch out in obedience to spiritual impulse, something will have been gained and if I can give strength and courage and a sense of reality to other workers and disciples that will be good.

"You can see, therefore, that as a life story mine does not matter much. As a means, however, of proving certain facts which I know to be essential to the future happiness and progress of humanity—the fact of the Masters, the unfolding future for which the world war (just ended) is but a preparatory stage, and the possibility of telepathic and direct spiritual contacts and knowledge—what I say may prove to be of service. Many isolated mystics, disciples and aspiring men and women down the ages have known all these things. The time has now come when the masses of men everywhere must know them too.

"Between you and me, people's profound interest in themselves and in their souls and all the intricacies of related experiences almost staggers me. I want to shake them and say, 'Come outside and find your soul in other people and so discover your own.' What is going on in people's minds and hearts and what is happening in the world of men is the fundamental interest. The broad sweeps of human progress from the primeval age to the dawn of the impending new civilization is of interest and all of spiritual import. The self-disclosures of the mystic of medieval times have their place but it lies in the past; the achievements of modern science (though not man's use of these revelations) are a major modern spiritual factor; the struggle that is going on between political ideologies, between capital and labour and the breakdown of our past educational systems are all indicative of a divine and spiritual ferment which is leavening humanity. And yet the mystic way of introspection and of divine union must precede the occult way of intellectual realisation and divine perception. It always has in the life of the individual and of humanity as a whole. The mystic and the occult way, the way of the heart and the head, must fuse and blend and then humanity will know God and not just 'feel after Him if haply they may find Him.'

"This personal knowledge of God will, however, come by living normally and as beautifully as possible, by serving and by being interested in others and thus being decentralised. It will come by recognising the good life and the good in all peoples, by happiness and an intelligent appreciation of opportunity—one's own as well as other people's. It comes through full and complete living."[5]

When she was 22, Alice started on a career as an evangelist among British troops in Ireland. Her mental outlook was that of a dyed-in-the-wool fundamentalist "completely convinced that certain fundamental, theological doctrines, as expressed by leading churchmen, were summations of divine truth."[6]

After overcoming great shyness, and no little stage fright, she became a good speaker and learned to like speaking in public. She also learned how to gently but effectively handle soldiers who appeared at her gospel services in a drunken state. She discovered that, like lion tamers use, a strong chair came in handy to keep a safe distance from the affectionate type drunks and herself!

During the days, besides composing her sermons, she spent her time baking buns, frying eggs, and making cocoa for the soldiers.

One day, her supervisor got a letter from India stating that the head of this work there in India was not well and needed to be replaced. She relates that with her usual smug, religious reaction, she said: "If God means me to go, He will send the money."[7]

Two or three days later, an envelope arrived with no indication of the sender. Inside, there was no letter, but there was a bank draft for five hundred pounds and written across it, "For the work in India".

Her first responsible assignment in India was in Quetta. The troops there had taken over the Soldiers' Home, which was to be her responsibility, and gotten out of hand.

"About twenty of them would come down from barracks together. They would go into the coffee-shop, order cocoa and fried eggs and then spend the rest of the evening slinging jugs of

[5] IBID pp. 1-8
[6] IBID p. 50
[7] IBID p. 64

cocoa and fried eggs at the wall... The mess was abominable and their attitude worse."[8]

Although she was terrified and didn't know what to do at first, she looked the situation over for several days finding that her presence made things even worse. Rumor had it that she was a "hard boiled young thing" and would likely report them to the authorities which made them even more wild.

"When I had at last discovered just who they were and who were the ring-leaders, I sent an orderly up to the barracks one morning to ask those of them who were not on duty to come down to the Soldiers Home at a certain hour. For some reason, none of them was on duty and sheer curiosity brought them all out. When they arrived, I loaded them into native carriages (gharris), put in all the makings for a picnic and drove to a place that in those days was called Woodcock Spinney. It was a lovely, hot, clear day and the fact that the place was then infested with snakes (kraits, deadly and small) did not seem to bother us. There we made tea and told silly stories; we asked riddles and never once did we talk religion and never once did I refer to their iniquities and then, as evening came on, we went home. I had said not a word of censure, of criticism, of request or pleading. They were certainly a bunch of mystified men. All through the evening I said nothing and, still bewildered, they went back to barracks. The next afternoon one of our coffee-shop managers sought me out and asked me if I would mind coming to the coffee-shop for a minute. There I found all these men cleaning the walls and painting them, scrubbing the floors and making the place much nicer than it had ever been before. The question in my mind is: was I too terrified to bring the matter up or was I just clever? The episode happened: I did not intentionally plan it.

"I learnt a great lesson at that time. I proved to myself, with much surprise, that understanding and love will work with individuals when condemnation and accusations will fail. I never had any more trouble with that gang. One of them is still

---

[8]IBID p. 73

my friend although I have lost sight of all the rest during the forty years which have elapsed since then.

"This man came to see me when I was in London in 1934 and we talked of those far away times. He is doing well. I made, however, a disturbing discovery. These men had been won over to better things, not by my eloquent preaching or by any emphasis upon the theological precept that the blood of Jesus could save them, but simply by loving understanding. I had not believed that that was possible. I had yet to learn that love is the keynote of Christ's teaching and that it is His love and life that saves and not any violent theological pronouncements over the fear of hell."[9]

Her organizational abilities began developing during this time. She conducted an average of fifteen meetings a week, conferred with the various managers, wrote the correspondence, calculated the amounts, and supervised the feeding of five or six hundred men in each coffee shop every evening. She spent her afternoons in the hospital wards where there were no women nurses and was called in by chaplains of all denominations to sit with boys who were dying. She would be holding their hand while they passed over on to the other side.

"I learnt one important thing ... nature or God takes care of people at these times and they usually die quite unafraid and are often glad to go. Or else they are in a coma and physically conscious of nothing. ...Death is not so awful when you are face to face with it. It often seemed to me like a kind of friend and I never had the slightest feeling that something real and vital was coming to an end. I knew nothing of psychic research or the law of re-birth and yet, even in those orthodox days, I was sure it was a question of passing on to the other work. Subconsciously I really never did believe in hell, and a lot of the men orthodox from the Christian point of view, ought to have gone there."[10]

The next phase of her education came from her old personal bearer, a native called Bugaloo when she had gone to open the

[9] IBID pp. 74-75
[10] IBID p. 78

204

Soldiers Home in Umballa. Bugaloo was an old gentleman with a long white beard who looked after her constantly, kept her out of trouble with the natives, and cared for her as solicitously as if he were her father.

"I was standing one day on the verandah of our quarters in Mumballa, looking out on the road in front of the compound and at the countless hordes and throngs of Indians—Hindus, Mohammedans, Pathans, Sikhs, Gurkas, Rajputs and the babus, sweepers, men, women and children who passed ceaselessly along the road. They plodded silently—coming from somewhere, going somewhere, thinking of something, and their name is legion. Suddenly old Bugaloo came up to me and put his hand on my arm (a thing no Indian servant ever does) and gave it a little shake to attract my attention. Then he said in his curious English, 'Missy Baba, listen. Millions of people here. Millions, all the time long before you English came. Same God loves me as loves you.' I have since often wondered who he was and have asked myself whether my Master K.H. had used him to break the shell of formalism in me. This old bearer looked and acted like a saint and probably was a disciple. Again I was faced with the same problem ... the problem of the love of God. What had God done about the millions of people down the ages, throughout the entire world, before Christ came? Had they all died unsaved and gone to hell? I knew the trite argument that Christ, during the three days whilst His body was in the tomb went and 'preached to the spirits in prison,' i.e. in hell, but that didn't seem fair. Why give them only one small chance lasting three days, after thousands of years in hell, because they happened to live before Christ came? You can see, therefore, how little by little these interior questions were thundering in my spiritual ears."[11]

In 1906, her physical health began to break down. The overwork and responsibilities she faced in her self-appointed task of "saving souls" was the principal reason. But close behind that was the increasing psychical conflicts she had about the value of her work. She said:

---

[11]IBID p. 83

"The only fact I have never questioned and of which I am eternally sure is the fact of Christ Himself. I do know Whom I have believed. That fact has stood the test and is no longer on the basis of belief but of knowledge. Christ Is. He stands—'the Master of All the Masters and the Teacher alike of angels and of men.'"[12]

But her actual teaching, conventional, fundamental, and rigid, was raising great doubts in her mind as to its real value to anyone; especially when she gave a lecture on hell and damnation and lost her whole audience, except for a small group of soldiers known as "bible thumpers" by the vast majority, who had walked out on her. The last reason was that she had fallen in love with a soldier, a private named Walter Evans.

She returned home and was assured by a leading London neurologist that she was sound and would be cured by his prescription; six months of bedrest and to keep busy with sewing, which she had always enjoyed. She recovered and after arrangements were made, she married Walter Evans. They traveled to Cincinnati, Ohio where her husband completed a course at the Lane Theological Seminar, became an Episcopal minister, and Alice had her first child, Dorothy. Evans was given a charge under the Bishop of San Joaquin in California and they then moved there. It was at this time that her husband's temper got out of bounds. Her second daughter, Mildred, was born at this time, August, 1912, but it did nothing to nullify Evans' rage. Eventually the congregation found out about Evans and the Bishop, who was compassionate toward Alice, offered Evans another parish, hoping that a fresh start would calm him down. Her third and last child, another daughter, whom they named Ellison, was born. She was in a delicate condition due to Evans' throwing Alice down a flight of stairs before Ellison was born. Finally they parted for good. Evans was sent to a charge in Montana with the understanding that part of his stipend would be sent to his wife. Alice and her three children moved to a tiny three-roomed cottage in Pacific Grove, California. Little of the stipend ever reached her and she, a high-born British woman, with almost no practical skills,

---

[12]IBID p. 86

had to find a job to support herself and her three daughters. She found a job in a sardine cannery. She found out that she couldn't make enough money in the labelling department, labelling the large, oval cans of Del Monte sardines, so she transferred to the packing department to pack the sardines in cans.

"It was a much rougher group of factory hands—rather tough women, Mexicans and the type of man I had never met before—even in social work. When I first went into this department they made it hard for me by poking fun at me. I didn't belong, apparently. I was obviously too good and, of course, exceedingly proper and they did not know what to make of me. A gang of them used to collect near the gate of the factory and when I hove in sight they'd start singing, 'Nearer my God to Thee.' I didn't like it at first and used to shudder at the thought of going through the gate but, after all, I'd had a lot of experience in handling men and little by little I won them, so that I really had a good time. I never lacked for fish to pack. A clean newspaper would find its way mysteriously on to my stool. They watched out for me in all kinds of ways and I would like again to point out that this had nothing, whatsoever, to do with me. I did not know the names of these men and women. I had never done them a kindness in my life, but they were just straight good to me and I have never forgotten it. I learnt to like them very much and we grew to be good friends. I never, however, learnt to like the sardines. I made up my mind that if I was going to be a packer I would make it financially worth while. I wanted money for the children, so I brought my mind to bear on the problem of packing. I watched the other packers. I studied every movement so that there would be no waste effort and in three weeks' time I was the show packer in the factory. I handled an average of ten thousand sardines a day and packed hundreds of cans. Visitors to the factory were brought to watch me and then I paid the price of my good work and had to listen to comments such as, 'What's a woman like this doing in a factory?' and 'She must have done something to have brought herself down to this kind of work.' 'Better not be taken in by appearances, she's probably a bad egg.' I am quoting literally. I remember once the foreman of the factory was standing by listening to a group talking about me in this way and watching me squirm. The comments had been particularly rude and my hands were literally shaking with fury. After they had passed on he came up to me and said, with the kindest expression on his face, 'Never you mind, Mrs. Evans, we here call you "the diamond lost in the mud."' I found that full compensation for all that had been said. Is it to be wondered at that I have an unalterable and unshakable faith in the beauty and divinity of humanity? If these had been people who were under obligation to me, the story would be different, but all this expressed the spontaneous kindness of the human soul to people in similar difficulties to their own. The poor are usually kind to the poor."[13]

She entered a new cycle when she turned thirty-five. She met two English women living in Pacific Grove, California who had similar social backgrounds to her own and who introduced her to Theosophy and Helene P. Blavatsky's The Secret Doctrine. Here she met others, two very old ladies, who had been personal students of Blavatsky, and who answered her many questions about the intricacies of The Secret Doctrine. She found that now she was getting answers that were beginning to satisfy her questioning mind and disturbed heart.

"I discovered, first of all, that there is a great and divine Plan. I found that this universe of ours is not a 'fortuitous concurrence of atoms' but that it is the working out of a great design or pattern which will be all to the glory of God. I found that race after race of human beings had appeared and disappeared upon our planet and that each civilisation and culture had seen humanity step forward a little further upon the path of return to God. I discovered, for a second thing, that there are Those Who are responsible for the working out of that Plan and Who, step by step and stage by stage, have led mankind on down the centuries. I made the amazing discovery, amazing to me because I knew so little, that the teaching about this Path or this Plan was uniform, whether it was presented in the Occident or in the Orient, or whether it had emerged prior to the coming of Christ or afterwards. I found that the Head of this Hierarchy of spiritual Leaders was the Christ and when this dawned on

---

[13]IBID pp. 129-130

me, I felt that He had been given back to me in a nearer and more intimate way. I found that He was 'the Master of all the Masters and the Teacher alike of angels and of men.' I found that the Masters of the Wisdom were His pupils and disciples, just as people like myself were pupils of some Master. I learnt that when I, in my orthodox days, talked about Christ and His Church I was really speaking of Christ and the planetary Hierarchy. I found that the esoteric presentation of truth in no way belittled Christ. He was, indeed, the Son of God, the First Born in a great family of brothers, as St. Paul had told us, and a guarantee to us of our own divinity.

"The third teaching which I came across and which pulled me up short for a long time was the dual belief in the law of re-birth and the law of cause and effect, called Karma and Reincarnation...

"With the discovery that there was a law of re-birth I found many of my problems, personal and individual, were capable of solution. Many who come to a study of the Ageless Wisdom find it difficult at first to accept the fact of the Law of Re-birth. It seems so revolutionary; it is apt to evoke a spirit of weariness and of spiritual fatigue. One life seems hard enough without contemplating many lives, both behind us and before us. Yet, if one studies the alternatives of the theory, it seems possibly the best and the most tenable. There are only two other theories which really warrant attention. One is the 'mechanical' alternative, which considers man as purely material, soulless and ephemeral so that (when he dies) he dissolves again into the dust from which he came; thought, under this theory, is simply a secretion of the brain and its activity, just as other organs produce their peculiar phenomenal secretion and there is, therefore, no purpose or reason for man's existence at all. This I could not accept, nor is it widely accepted anywhere.

"Then there is the 'one creation' theory of the orthodox Christian, which I had held without any speculation as to its truth. This posits an inscrutable God Who sends human souls into incarnation for one life and, according to their actions and their thinking in that one life so will be their eternal future. It endows man with no past, only an important present and an endless future—a future dependent upon the decisions of one life. What governs God's decisions as to a man's place and background and equipment remains unknown. There seems no reason for what He does under this 'one creation' plan. I had worried so over the apparent unfairness of God. Why should I have been born in such good circumstances with money, good looks, opportunity, and all the many interesting experiences which life had brought me? Why should there have been people like that wretched little soldier ... who was born with no equipment, with obviously no background, with no money and with no capacity in this life for success of any kind? I knew now why I could leave him to God; that both he and I in our separate places would go on climbing the ladder of evolution, life after life, until some day for each of us it would be equally true, 'As He is, so are we in this world.'

"It seemed reasonable to me that, 'As a man soweth so shall he also reap,' and it was a joy to me to discover that I could call in St. Paul and Christ, Himself, to substantiate these teachings. Clear light was being thrown on the old theology. I was discovering that the only thing that was wrong was man-made interpretations of the truth and it dawned on me how silly it was just because some learned preacher or scholar said that God meant this or that that we should accept it. He might be right and if so, intuitively one would know it; but the intuition does not work unless the mind is developed and that has been a lot of the trouble. The mass of people do not think and the orthodox theologian, no matter what he says, can always get a following. With the best intentions in the world he exploits the unthinking. It dawned on me, too, that there was really no reason because a priest or teacher six hundred years ago interpreted the Bible in one way (probably suitable for his time and age) that it should be acceptable now in a different time and age, under a different civilisation and with widely different problems. If God's truth is truth then it will be expansive and inclusive, and not reactionary and exclusive. If God is God, then His divinity will adapt itself to the emerging divinity of the sons of God, and a son of God today may be a very different expression of divinity from a son of God five thousand years ago."[14]

---

[14]IBID pp. 139-142

Towards the end of 1917, she moved to Hollywood California to be near the headquarters of the Theosophical Society, at Krotona, and settled into a cottage on Beechwood Drive. Here she went to work in the Society's vegetarian cafeteria and learned to manage it after starting in at the bottom scrubbing garbage pails.

In 1919, her divorce was finalized from Walter Evans and Alice met her future husband, Foster Bailey, who had been a lawyer, but who now had devoted his life to the Ancient Wisdom. Her three daughters adored Foster Bailey and Alice Bailey pointed out "what a marvelous stepfather he was to the children. He never allowed them whilst they were children to realize they were not his own and their indebtedness to him is very great."

They married in New York in 1920. But the year before, her real work, the work for which she had prepared herself for thirty-five years, the work alluded to by her Master Koot Hoomi, began:

"It was in November 1919 that I made my first contact with The Tibetan. I had sent the children off to school and thought I would snatch a few minutes to myself and went out on to the hill close to the house. I sat down and began thinking and then suddenly I sat startled and attentive. I heard what I thought was a clear note of music which sounded from the sky, through the hill and in me. Then I heard a voice which said, 'There are some books which it is desired should be written for the public. You can write them. Will you do so?' Without a moment's notice I said, 'Certainly not. I'm not a darned psychic and I don't want to be drawn into anything like that.' I was startled to hear myself speaking out loud. The voice went on to say that wise people did not make snap judgements, that I had a peculiar gift for the higher telepathy and that what I was being asked to do embodied no aspect of the lower psychism. I replied that I didn't care, that I wasn't interested in any work of a psychic nature at all. The unseen person who was speaking so clearly and directly to me then said that he would give me time for consideration; that he would not take my answer then and that he would come back in three weeks' time exactly, to find out what I intended to do.

"I then shook myself as if I was awakening from a dream and went home and entirely forgot all about the matter. I never gave it another thought and did not even tell Foster about it. During the interval I never remembered it but, sure enough, at the end of three weeks I was spoken to again one evening as I sat in my sitting-room after the children had gone to bed. Again I refused, but the speaker begged me to reconsider and for a couple of weeks, at least, see what I could do. By this time I was getting curious but not in the least convinced. I would try for a couple of weeks or a month and then decide what I felt about it. It was during these few weeks that I got the first chapters of Initiation, Human and Solar.

"I would like to make it quite clear that the work I do is in no way related to automatic writing. Automatic writing, except in the rarest cases (and, unfortunately, most people think their case is the rare exception) is very dangerous. The aspirant or disciple is never supposed to be an automaton. He is never supposed to let any part of his equipment out of his conscious control. When he does, he enters into a state of dangerous negativity. The material normally then received is mediocre. There is nothing new in it, and it frequently deteriorates as time goes on. Many a time, the subject's negativity permits the entrance of a second force which, for some peculiar reason, is never of as high a standard as the first. Then there comes danger of obsession. We have had to handle many cases of obsession as the result of automatic writing.

"In the work that I do there is no negativity but I assume an attitude of intense, positive attention. I remain in full control of all my senses or perception and there is nothing automatic in what I do. I simply listen and take down the words that I hear and register the thoughts which are dropped one by one into my brain. I make no changes in what I give out to the public from that which has been given to me except that I will smooth the English or replace an unusual word with one that is clearer, taking care, always, to preserve the sense as given. I have never changed anything that the Tibetan has ever given me. If once I did so He would never dictate to me again. I want to make that entirely clear. I do not always understand what is given. I do not always agree. But I record it all honestly and then discover it does make sense and evokes intuitive response.

"This work of the Tibetan has greatly intrigued people and psychologists everywhere. They dispute as to what is the cause of the phenomenon, and argue that what I write probably comes from my subconscious. I have been told that Jung takes the position that the Tibetan is my personified higher self and Alice A. Bailey is the lower self. Some of these days (if I ever have the pleasure of meeting him) I will ask how my personified higher self can send me parcels all the way from India, for that is what He has done.

"A few years ago a very dear friend and a man who had stood very closely with Foster and me since the inception of our work—Mr. Henry Carpenter—went out to India to try and reach the Masters at Shigatze, a small, native town in the Himalayas, just over the Tibetan frontier. He made this effort three times in spite of my telling him that he could find the Master right here in New York if he took the proper steps and the time was ripe. He felt he would like to tell the Masters, much to my amusement, that I was having too tough a time and that They had better do something about it. As he was a personal friend of Lord Reading, once Viceroy of India, he was given every facility to reach his destination but the Dalai Lama refused permission for him to cross the frontier. During his second trip to India when at Gyantse (the furthest point he could reach near the frontier) he heard a great hubbub in the compound of the dak bungalow. He went to find out what it was and found a lama, seated on a donkey, just entering the compound. He was attended by four lamas and all the natives in the compound were surrounding them and bowing. Through his interpreter, Mr. Carpenter made inquiries and was told that the lama was the abbot of a monastery across the Tibetan frontier and that he had come down especially to speak to Mr. Carpenter.

"The abbot told him that he was interested in the work that we were doing and asked after me. He inquired about the Arcane School and gave him two large bundles of incense for me. Later, Mr. Carpenter saw General Laden Lha at Darjeeling. The General is a Tibetan, educated in Great Britain at public school and university and was in charge of the secret service on the Tibetan frontier. He is now dead but was a great and good man. Mr. Carpenter told him of his experience with this lama and told him that he was the abbot of a certain lamaserie. The General flatly denied the possibility of this. He said the abbot was a very great and holy man and that he had never been known to come down across the frontier or visit an Occidental. When, however, Mr. Carpenter returned the following year, General Laden Lha admitted that he had made a mistake; that the abbot had been down to see him.

"After writing for the Tibetan for nearly a month I got completely scared and absolutely refused to do any more work. I told the Tibetan that the three little girls had only me to look to, that if I were ill or went crazy (as so many psychics seemed to do) they would be all alone and that I did not dare take the chance. He accepted my decision but told me to try to get in touch with my Master, K.H., and talk the matter over with Him. After thinking it over for a week or so I decided to get in touch with K.H. and proceeded to do so, following the very definite technique He had taught me. When I got my opportunity for an interview with K.H. we talked the whole thing through. He assured me that I was in no danger, either physically or mentally, and that I had the opportunity of doing a really valuable piece of work. He told me that it was He, Himself, Who had suggested that I help the Tibetan; that He was not transferring me into the Tibetan's ashram (or spiritual group) but that He wished me still to work in His. I therefore complied with the wish of K.H. and told the Tibetan that I would work for Him. I have been strictly his amanuensis and secretary and am not a member of His group. He has never interfered with my personal work or training. In the spring of 1920 I entered into a very happy time of collaboration with Him, while working as a senior disciple in the ashram of my own Master.

"I've written many books since then for the Tibetan. Shortly after finishing the first few chapters of 'Initiation, Human and Solar' I showed the manuscript to B. P. Wadia. He got very excited and told me that he would publish anything that 'came from that source' and printed the first few chapters in 'The Theosophist', published in Adyar, India.

"...The Tibetan's style has improved over the years. He dictated a cumbersome, poor English in the beginning, but between us we have managed to work out a style and presentation which is suited to the great truths which it is His function to reveal, and mine and my husband's to bring to the attention of the public.

"In the early days of writing for the Tibetan, I had to write at regular hours and it was clear, concise, definite dictation. It was given word for word, in such a manner that I might claim that I definitely heard a voice. Therefore it might be said that I started with a clairaudient technique, but I very soon found, as our minds got attuned, that this was unnecessary and that if I concentrated enough and my attention was adequately focussed I could register and write down the thoughts of the Tibetan (His carefully formulated and expressed ideas) as He dropped them into my mind. This involves the attaining and preservation of an intense, focussed point of attention. It is almost like the ability which the advanced student of meditation can demonstrate to hold one's achieved point of spiritual attention at the very highest possible point. This can be fatiguing in the earlier stages, when one is probably trying too hard to make good, but later, it is effortless and the results are clarity of thought and a stimulation which has a definitely good physical effect.

"Today, as the result of twenty-seven years work with the Tibetan I can snap into telepathic relation with Him without the slightest trouble. I can and do preserve my own mental integrity all the time and I can always argue with Him if it seems to me, at times, that—as an Occidental—I may know better than He does as regards points of presentation. When we have an argument along any line I invariably write as He wants the text written, though He is apt to modify His presentation after discussion with me. If He does not change His wording and point of view, I do not change what He has said in any way.

"After all, the books are His, not mine, and basically the responsibility is His. He does not permit me to make mistakes and watches over the final draft with great care. It is not just a question of taking His dictation and then submitting it, after I have typed it out, to Him. It is a question of His careful supervision of the final draft. I am mentioning this quite deliberately as quite a few people, when the Tibetan says something with which they do not personally agree, are apt to regard the point of disagreement as having been interpolated by me. This has never happened, even if I do not always agree or understand and I want to reiterate—I have published exactly what the Tibetan has said. On that one point I emphatically take my stand.

"Some students, also, when they personally do not understand what the Tibetan means say that His ambiguities, so called, are due to my having wrongly brought through what He was saying. Where there are ambiguities, and there are quite a number in His books, they are due to the fact that He is quite unable to be clearer, owing to the limitations of his readers, and the difficulty of finding words which can express newer truths and those intuitive perceptions which are still only hovering on the borders of man's developing consciousness.

"The books that the Tibetan has written are regarded of importance by the Teachers responsible for the giving out of the new truths which humanity needs. New teaching, along the line of spiritual training and the preparation of aspirants for discipleship has also been given. Great changes are being made in methods and techniques and because of this the Tibetan has been peculiarly careful to see that I do not make mistakes.

"At the time of the second phase of the World War, which started in 1939, many pacifists and well meaning, though unthinking, people among the students of the Arcane School and the general public, which we could succeed in reaching, took the position that I had written the pamphlets and papers endorsing the United Nations and the need to defeat the Axis Powers, and that the Tibetan was not responsible for the anti-Nazi point of view of these articles. This, again, was not true. The pacifists took the orthodox and idealistic point of view that because God is love it would be impossible for Him to be anti-German or anti-Japanese. Because God is love, He had no alternative, or the Hierarchy either, working under the Christ, to do anything else but stand firmly on the side of those who were seeking to free humanity from slavery, evil, agression and corruption. The words of the Christ have never been more true, 'He that is not with Me is against Me.' The Tibetan in His writings at that time took a firm and unshakable stand, and today (1945) in view of the unspeakable atrocities, cruelties and enslavement policies of the Axis nations, His position has been justified...

"The disciples of all the masters are everywhere in the world, working along the many different lines to bring humanity into the light and to materialise the kingdom of God on earth...

"Let there be no mistake, the movement indicated by Helena Petrovna Blavatsky was an integral part of a Hierarchical plan. There have always been theosophical societies down the ages—the name of the movement is not new—but H.P.B. gave it a light and a publicity that set a new note and that brought a neglected and hitherto somewhat secret group out into the open and made it possible for the public everywhere to respond to this very ancient teaching."[15]

In 1921, in New York, she started a Secret Doctrine class. There she was given the photographic plates of the Masters' pictures by a student of Helena Blavatsky and Col. Olcott and some documents of Blavatsky's which said that she would like to call her esoteric section the Arcane School. This had never been done, so when Alice Bailey began her school in April, 1923, she called it The Arcane School in honor of Blavatsky.

The Arcane School is a correspondence school and today has pupils in nearly every country in the world. Over one million people have studied the Ageless Wisdom through its auspices; Its teaching is based on the books dictated to Alice Bailey by the Tibetan Master, Djwahl Khul.

Her Unfinished Autobiography stops at the year 1934, although she passed away on December 15, 1949.

During the years 1919 to 1949 she received nineteen books from the Tibetan Master and wrote four others herself; in addition to her autobiography. These latter five show her to be a very intelligent, compassionate person and are quite different in tone and style from the books she received by telepathic dictation.

---

[15] IBID pp. 162-172

The four books which are entirely her own production are: *The Consciousness of the Atom, The Soul and Its Mechanism, From Intellect to Intuition*, and *From Bethlehem to Calvary* . All are well worth reading and studying. One of the books from the Tibetan Master, *The Light of The Soul*, is paraphrased into English by Him while the commentary is by Alice Bailey who referred to Him occasionally for reassurance as to meaning. The other books, all dictated to her telepathically by the Tibetan Master, Djwahl Khul, are: *Initiation, Human and Solar, Letters on Occult Meditation, A Treatise on Cosmic Fire , A Treatise on White Magic, Discipleship in the New Age, Vol. I , Discipleship in the New Age, Vol. II, Problems of Humanity, The Reappearance of the Christ, The Destiny of the Nations, Glamour: A World Problem , Telepathy and the Etheric Vehicle, Education In the New Age, The Externalization of the Hierarchy*, and the five volumes comprising a treatise on the Seven Rays: Vol. I—*Esoteric Psychology Vol. I*, Vol. II—*Esoteric Psychology Vol. II*, Vol. III—*Esoteric Astrology*, Vol. IV—*Esoteric Healing*, and Vol. V—*The Rays and the Initiations*.

The above books by Alice Bailey, including the ones dictated to her by Master Djwahl Khul, are all available from the Lucis Publishing Company, 866 United Nations Plaza, suite 566-7, New York, New York 10017.

Chapter 7

Quotations from Alice A. Bailey

The Purification of the Vehicles

The need arises these days for tested instruments. When Those Who guide human evolution at this period cast Their eyes over the race in the search for such instruments They see few as yet ready for the service required. But likewise They see some who, with a certain amount of training, will fill the need fairly adequately.

As evolution proceeds the polarisation of the race changes. Men are polarised now principally in their emotional bodies—the feelings, desires, the concerns of the personality sway them. The emotional body is the focal point for the personality. It acts as the clearing house for all that concerns it, and as the junction of the lower and the higher. It is like a busy railroad terminus, that receives cargo from all directions and empties it into the great city of the personal physical plane life. Then, as progress is made, the scene shifts higher, and the mental body becomes the focal point. Later the causal body becomes the important unit, and later still comes the ultimate sacrifice of even that, until the man stands bereft of all that vibrates to the three worlds, and all is over as regards the personal life—nought remains but the life of the Spirit, and the voluntary giving of that life for the helping of the world.

In the speeding up of evolution, certain things have to be brought about before the man can be used as a reliable instrument, true as tempered steel, for the helping of his race. Forget not that, as a rule, a man (when tested and tried) forms the best tool, because he comprehends utterly the race consciousness, and because he enters into the problems of the day in a manner more thorough than an Ego from an earlier period. Hence the Masters desire to use those of you who live now to heal the wounds of the present suffering generation.

What then has to be done? The matter I now give contains nothing very unusual, but it does hold thought for consideration by any who may desire to help.......In preparing a soul for service the Guides of the race have to deal with each of the bodies:

The training of the Physical Body.

This involves certain definite requirements:

The building in of matter of the higher subplanes and the elimination of the lower and coarser matter. This is needed because it is impossible for those with coarse bodies to contact high vibration. It is impossible for the Ego to transmit the higher knowledge and guidance through a coarse physical body. It is impossible for the loftier currents of thought to impact the little evolved physical brain. Hence the refinement of the physical body is an essential. It is effected in various ways, all of them reasonable and utilitarian.

By pure food. This involves a vegetarian diet, chosen with wise discrimination; it requires the eating of only those vegetables and fruits that vitalise. Careful judgment shown in the choice of food, wise refraining from too heavy eating, and a little pure good food perfectly assimilated are all that a disciple requires. You ask what foods? Milk, honey, whole wheat bread, all the vegetables that contact the sun, oranges (above all, oranges), bananas, raisins, nuts, some potatoes, unpolished rice, and may I again reiterate, just as much of all the above as to insure activity.

By cleanliness. Much use of water, externally and internally, is vitally required.

By sleep. This should be always between the hours of ten in the evening and five in the morning and as much as possible out of doors.

By sunshine. Contact with the sun should be much sought after, and the vitalisation that comes through its rays. The sun kills all germs and frees from disease.

When these four requirements are attended to adequately a definite process of elimination proceeds, and in the course of a few years the whole physical body shifts its polarisation gradually up until ultimately you will have a body composed of atomic subplane matter...... This may take several incarnations, but it should be borne in mind that at each fresh incarnation a body is taken of the exact quality (if I may so put it) as the one previously discarded at death. Hence time is never lost in building. Eventually two other methods will be available by which more rapid refining may be effected:

> *The use of coloured lights.* These lights are played on the body of the disciple and effect a shaking-out process and a simultaneous stimulation of the atoms. This cannot be done till further information is given anent the Rays; when a man's ray is known, stimulation will come from the use of his own colour, a building-in will be brought about by the use of his complementary colour, and disintegration of unwanted matter will be brought about by the use of an antagonistic colour. This knowledge will later on be communicated to the great bodies that hold custody of the Mysteries, the Church and the Masons. Wait, for the time is not yet. When the Mysteries are restored some of this information will be in the hands of the two bodies I refer to.

> *The stimulation of music.* Certain sounds shatter and break. Certain other sounds stimulate and attract. When the key of a man's life is known, when the sound he responds to is recognised, then comes the possibility of the utilisation of sound in refinement. All that is at present possible for those of you who seek to serve is to attend to the above essentials and to seek contact with high vibration.

One more point I would like to give, and that is, that in the manipulation of electricity lies hid much that concerns the vivification of the bodies, especially just now of the etheric. The principal use the sun has is the vitalising of the etheric. The heat of the sun is electrical force adapted to the need of the great average majority in all the kingdoms of nature. As progress is made an intensification of this force will be possible in individual cases. Herein lies one of the secrets of initiation. In the old days the Rod of Initiation acted actually as a conductor of this force to the centres of the initiate; it was so constructed that it answered this purpose. Now, on a higher turn of the spiral, just the same need and purpose are served, though the method of application necessarily differs, owing to the change in the polarisation of the race. The polarisation is now no longer physical, but is either emotional or mental. The method of application differs in all three, and hence the safeguarding of the secret. It holds the mystery hid.

The refining of the etheric.

This coincides with that of the physical body. The method consists principally of living in the sunlight, in protection from cold, and in the assimilation of certain definite combinations of vitamins which before long will be given to the race. A combination of these vitamins will be formulated and made into tabloid form, with direct effect upon the etheric body. This will not be until that etheric vehicle is recognised by science, and definitely included in the training offered by the faculty of medicine. The study of etheric diseases—congestion and atrophy—will ere long be a recognised study, and will lead to definite treatments and formulas. As before said, all that you can now do in sensitising the dual physical is to attend to the above rules, and allow time to bring about the remainder of the work.

The refining of the emotional body.

Here the method of procedure is different. The emotional body is simply a great reflector. It takes colour and movement from its surroundings. It receives the impress of every passing desire. It contacts every whim and fancy in its environment; every current sets it in motion; every sound causes it to vibrate unless the aspirant inhibits such a state of affairs and trains it to receive and register only those impressions which come from the intuitional level via the Higher Self, and therefore via the atomic subplane. The aim of the aspirant should be to so train the emotional body that it will become still and clear as a mirror, so that it may reflect perfectly. His aim should be to make it reflect only the causal body, to take on colour only in line with the great Law, and to move under definite direction and not just as blow the winds of thought, or rise the tides of desire. What words should describe the emotional body? The words: still, serene, unruffled, quiet, at rest, limpid and clear, of a quality mirror like, of surface even, a limpid reflector—one that accurately transmits the wishes, the desires, the aspirations of the Ego and not of the personality. How should this be accomplished? In several ways, some at the direction of the aspirant, and some at the direction of the Master.

a. By the constant watching of all desires, motives and wishes that cross the horizon daily, and by the subsequent emphasising of all those that are of a high order, and by the inhibition of the lower.

b. By a constant daily attempt to contact the Higher Self, and to reflect His wishes in the life. At first mistakes will be made, but little by little the building-in process proceeds, and the polarisation in the emotional body gradually shifts up each subplane until the atomic is reached.

c. By definite periods daily directed to the stilling of the emotional body. So much emphasis is laid in meditation on the stilling of the mind, but it should be remembered that the stilling of the emotional nature is a step preliminary to the quieting of the mental; one succeeds the other and it is wise to begin at the bottom of the ladder. Each aspirant must discover for himself wherein he yields most easily to violent vibrations, such as fear, worry, personality desire of any kind, personality love of anything or anyone, discouragement, over-sensitiveness to public opinion; then he must overcome that vibration, by imposing on it a new rhythm, definitely eliminating and constructing.

d. By work done on the emotional body at night under the direction of more advanced egos, working under the guidance of a Master. Stimulation of vibration or the deadening of vibration follows on the application of certain colours and sounds. At this particular time two colours are being applied to many people for the specific purpose of keying up the throat and foremost head centre, namely, violet and gold.

Remember that the work is gradual, and as the polarisation shifts up, the moment of transition from one subplane to another is marked by certain tests applied at night, what one might term a series of small initiations that eventually will be consummated in the second great initiation, that marks the perfection of the control of the body of the emotions.

Four small initiations find their culmination in the initiation proper. These are the initiations on the emotional plane, called respectively the initiations of earth, fire, water and air, culminating in initiation the second. The first initiation marks the same point of attainment on the physical plane. Each initiation marks the attainment of a certain proportion of atomic matter in the bodies. The four initiations, prior to that of the Adept, mark respectively the attainment of a proportionate amount, as for instance: At the first initiation one-fourth atomic matter, at the second one-half atomic matter, and so on to the consummation. The intuition (or buddhi) being the unifying principle and thus welding all, at the fourth initiation the lower vehicles go, and the adept stands in his intuitional body, and creates from thence his body of manifestation.

The refinement of the mental body.

This is the result of hard work and discrimination. It necessitates three things before the plane of the mental unit is achieved, and before the causal consciousness (the full consciousness of the higher Self) is reached:

Clear thinking, not just on subjects wherein interest is aroused, but on all matters affecting the race. It involves the formulation of thought matter, and the capacity to define. It means the ability to make thought forms out of thought matter, and to utilise those thought forms for the helping of the public. He who does not think clearly, and who has an inchoate mental body, lives in a fog, and a man in a fog is but a blind leader of the blind.

The ability to still the mental body so that thoughts from abstract levels and from the intuitional planes can find a receptive sheet whereon they may inscribe themselves. This thought has been made clear in many books on concentration and meditation, and needs not my elucidation. It is the result of hard practice carried over many years.

A definite process brought about by the Master with the acquiescence of the disciple which welds into a permanent shape the hard won efforts and results of many years. At each initiation, the electrical or magnetic force applied has a stabilising effect. It renders durable the results achieved by the disciple. Like as a potter moulds and shapes the clay and then applies the fire that solidifies, so the aspirant shapes and moulds and builds, and prepares for the solidifying fire. Initiation marks a permanent attainment and the beginning of a new cycle of endeavour.

Above all two things should be emphasised:

1. A steady, unshaken perseverance, that recks not of time nor hindrance, but goes on. This capacity to persevere explains why the non-spectacular man so frequently attains initiation before the genius, and before the man who attracts more notice. The capacity to plod is much to be desired.

2. A progress that is made without undue self-analysis. Pull not yourselves up by the roots to see if there is growth. It takes precious time. Forget your own progress in conforming to the rules and in the helping of others. When this is so, sudden illumination may come, and the realisation break upon you that the point has been reached when the Hierophant can demand your presence and bestow initiation upon you. You have, by hard work and sheer endeavour to conform to the Law and to love all, built into your bodies the material that makes it possible for you to stand in His Presence. The great Law of Attraction draws you to Him and nought can withstand the Law.[1]

---

[1] Letters on Occult Meditation, pp. 333-341

We stand today on the verge of great things. Humanity is on its way with renewed impetus. It stands no longer at the crossroads, but irrevocable decisions have been made, and the race is moving forward along a path which will lead it eventually into light and peace. It will find its way into "the peace which passeth understanding" because it will be a peace which is independent of outer conditions and which is not based upon what present humanity defines as peace. The peace which lies ahead of the race is the peace of serenity and of joy—a serenity, based upon spiritual understanding; and a joy which is untouched by circumstance. This joy and serenity is not an astral condition but a soul reaction. These qualities are not achieved as the result of disciplining the emotional nature, but demonstrate as a natural, automatic reaction of the soul. This is the reward of a definitely achieved alignment. These two qualities of the soul—serenity and joy—are the indications that the soul, the ego, the One Who stands alone, is controlling or dominating the personality, circumstance, and all environing conditions of life in the three worlds.

The Five Groups of Souls

1. Lemurian Egos................. our true Earth Humanity.
2. Egos which came in...........on Atlantis.
3. Moon chain Egos..............from the moon.
4. Egos............................ from other planets.
5. Rare and advanced Egos..... awaiting incarnation.[2]

The soul is light *essentially*, both *literally* from the vibratory angle, and *philosophically* from the angle of constituting the true medium of knowledge. The soul is light *symbolically*, for it is like the rays of the sun, which pour out into the darkness; the soul, through the medium of the brain, causes revelation. It throws its light into the brain, and thus the way of the human being becomes increasingly illumined. The brain is like the eye

---

[2] Esoteric Psychology vol. II, pp. 200-201

of the soul, looking out into the physical world; in the same sense the soul is the eye of the Monad, and in a curious and occult sense, the fourth kingdom in nature constitutes on our planet the eye of the planetary Diety. The brain is responsive to the seven senses:

1. Hearing	5. Smell
2. Touch	6. The mind, the common-sense
3. Sight	7. The intuition or the synthetic sense.
4. Taste	

Through these seven senses contact with the world of matter and of spirit becomes possible. The seven senses are, in a peculiar way, the physical plane correspondences of the seven rays, and are closely related to and governed by them all. The following tabulation will be found suggestive. That is all that it is intended to be:

1. Hearing.......7th Ray...Magic..........The Word of Power.
2. Touch.........1st Ray...Destroyer......The Finger of God.
3. Sight..........3rd Ray...Vision.........The Eye of God.
4. Taste..........6th Ray...Idealism.......The Desire of Nations.
5. Smell.........4th Ray...Art.............The Beauty of Revelation.
6. The Intellect..5th Ray...Mind..........The Knowledge of God.
7. The Intuition. 2nd Ray.. Love-Wisdom.Understanding of God.

Through the Words of Power the worlds came into ordered being, and the Lord of the Ray of Ceremonial Magic brings about the organisation of the divine organism.

Through the application of the Finger of God in its directing and forceful work, we have the cyclic destruction of forms, so that the manifestation of Deity may grow in power and beauty. Thus the Lord of Power or Will performs the task of destruction, thereby bringing beauty into being and the revelation of God's will and His beneficent purpose.

By means of the Eye of God light shines forth upon the way of the sun, the path of the planets, and the path of man. The Lord of Adaptability and the Intellect brings into expression and

into objectivity the intelligent working out of the divine idea and
Plan.

Ten Basic Propositions

One: There is one Life, which expresses Itself primarily
through seven basic qualities or aspects, and secondarily
through the myriad diversity of forms.

Two: These seven radiant qualities are the seven Rays, the
seven Lives, who give Their life to the forms, and give the form
world its meaning, its laws, and its urge to evolution.

Three: Life, quality and appearance, or spirit, soul and body
constitute all that exists. They are existence itself, with its
capacity for growth, for activity, for manifestation of beauty,
and for full conformity to the Plan. This Plan is rooted in the
consciousness of the seven ray Lives.

Four: These seven Lives, Whose nature is consciousness
and Whose expression is sentiency and specific quality, produce
cyclically the manifested world; They work together in the
closest union and harmony, and cooperate intelligently with the
Plan of which They are the custodians. They are the seven
Builders, Who produce the radiant temple of the Lord, under the
guidance of the Mind of the Great Architect of the Universe.

Five: Each ray Life is predominantly expressing Itself
through one of the seven sacred planets, but the life of all the
seven flows through every planet, including the Earth, and thus
qualifies every form. On each planet is a small replica of the
general scheme, and every planet conforms to the intent and
purpose of the whole.

Six: Humanity, with which this treatise deals, is an
expression of the life of God, and every human being has come
forth along one line or other of the seven ray forces. The nature
of his soul is qualified or determined by the ray Life which
breathed him forth, and his form nature is coloured by the ray
Life which—in its cyclic appearance on the physical plane at any
particular time—sets the quality of the race life and of the forms
in the kingdoms of nature. The soul nature or quality remains

the same throughout a world period; its form life and nature change from life to life, according to its cyclic need and the environing group condition. This latter is determined by the ray or rays in incarnation at the time.

Seven: The Monad is the Life, lived in unison with the seven ray Lives. One Monad, seven rays and myriads of forms—this is the structure behind the manifested worlds.

Eight: The Laws which govern the emergence of the quality or soul, through the medium of forms, are simply the mental purpose and life direction of the ray Lords, Whose purpose is immutable, Whose vision is perfect, and Whose justice is supreme.

Nine: The mode or method of development for humanity is self-expression and self-realisation. When this process is consummated the self expressed is the One Self or the ray Life, and the realisation achieved is the revelation of God as the quality of the manifested world and as the Life behind appearance and quality. The seven ray Lives, or the seven soul types, are seen as the expression of one Life, and diversity is lost in the vision of the One and in identification with the One.

Ten: The method employed to bring about this realisation is experience, beginning with individualisation and ending with initiation, thus producing the perfect blending and expression of life-quality-appearance.

This is a brief statement of the Plan. Of this the Hierarchy of Masters in Its seven divisions (the correspondences of the seven rays) is the custodian, and with Them lies the responsibility in any century of carrying out the next stage of that Plan.[3]

Some day the appearances which were called personalities, that mask or veil reality, will fully reveal the qualities of Deity. When that time comes, the purpose for which all creation waits will burst upon the awakened vision, and we shall know the true

---

[3] IBID vol. I, pp. 132-143

meaning of bliss, and why the morning stars sang together. Joy is the strong basic note of one particular solar system.

One of the foundational septenate of rays embodies in itself the principle of harmony, and this fourth Ray of Harmony gives to all forms that which produces beauty and works towards the harmonising of all effects emanating from the world of causes, which is the world of the three major rays. The ray of beauty, of art and harmony is the producer of the quality of *organisation through form.* it is in the last analysis the ray of mathematical exactitude and is not the ray of the artist, as so many seem to think. The artist is found on all rays, just as is the engineer or the physician, the home-maker or the musician. I want to make this clear, for there is much misunderstanding on this matter.

Each of the great rays has a form of teaching truth to humanity which is its unique contribution, and in this way develops man by a system or technique which is qualified by the ray quality and is therefore specific and unique. Let me point out to you the modes of this group teaching:

Ray I....Higher Expression: The science of statesmanship, of government.
Lower Expression: Modern diplomacy and politics.
Ray II....Higher Expression: The process of initiation as taught by the hierarchy of adepts.
Lower Expression: Religion.
Ray III...Higher Expression: Means of communication or inter-action. The radio, telephone, telegraph and the power to travel.
Lower Expression: The use and spread of money and gold.
Ray IV...Higher Expression: The Masonic work, based on the formation of the hierarchy, and related to the second ray.
Lower Expression: Architectural construction. Modern city planning.
Ray V....Higher Expression: The science of the soul. Esoteric psychology.
Lower Expression: Modern educational systems and mental science.

Ray VI..Higher Expression: Christianity and diversified reli-
gions. (Notice here relation to
Ray II.)
Lower Expression: Churches and organised religions.
Ray VII..Higher Expression: All forms of white magic.
Lower Expression: Spiritualism of "phenomena".

The fourth ray is essentially the refiner, the producer of
perfection within the form, and the prime manipulator of the
energies of God in such a way that the Temple of the Lord is
indeed known in its true nature as that which "houses" the Light.
Thus the Shekinah will shine forth within the secret place of the
Temple in its full glory. Such is the work of the seven Builders.
This ray is expressive primarily on the first of the formless
planes, counting from below upwards, and its true purpose
cannot emerge until the soul is awakened and consciousness is
adequately recording the known. The planes or manifested
spheres of expression are influenced in manifestation in a
numerical order:

Ray I......... Will or Power............Plane of divinity.
Ray II........Love-Wisdom............Plane of the monad.
Ray III.......Active Intelligence.......Plane of spirit, atma.
Ray IV.......Harmony..................Plane of the intuition.
Ray V........Concrete Knowledge....Mental Plane.
Ray VI......Devotion, Idealism.......Astral Plane.
Ray VII......Ceremonial Order........Physical Plane.

The fifth ray therefore works actively on the plane of the
greatest moment to humanity, being, for man, the plane of the
soul, and of the higher and the lower mind. It embodies the
principle of knowledge, and because of its activity and its close
relation to the third Ray of Active Intelligence might be regarded
as a ray having a most vital relation to man at this time in
particular. It is the ray which—when active, as it was in
Lemurian times—produces individualisation, which is literally
the shifting of the evolving life of God into a new sphere of
awareness. This particular transference into higher forms of
awareness tends, at the beginning, to separativeness.

The fifth ray has produced what we call science. In science
we find a condition which is rare in the extreme. Science is

separative in its approach to the differing aspects of the divine manifestation which we call the world of natural phenomena, but it is non-separative in actuality, for there is little warring between the sciences and little competition between scientists. In this the workers in the scientific field differ profoundly from those of the religious. The reason for this is to be found in the fact that the true scientist, being a coordinated personality and working therefore on mental levels, works very close to the soul. The developed personality produces the clear distinctions of the dominant lower mind, but (if one may use such a symbolic way of expression) the close proximity of the soul negates a separative attitude. The religious man is pre-eminently astral or emotional and works in a more separative manner, particularly in this Piscean age which is passing away. When I say the religious man I refer to the mystic and to the man who *senses* the beatific vision. I refer not to disciples nor to those who are called initiates, for they add to the mystical vision a trained mental apprehension.

The sixth Ray of Devotion embodies the principle of recognition. By this I mean the capacity to see the ideal reality lying behind the form; this implies a one-pointed application of desire and of intelligence in order to produce an expression of that sensed idea. It is responsible for much of the formulation of the ideas which have led man on, and for much of the emphasis on the appearance which has veiled and hidden those ideals. It is on this ray primarily—as it cycles in and out of manifestation—that the work of distinguishing between appearance and quality is carried forward, and this work has its field of activity upon the astral plane. The complexity of this subject and the acuteness of the feeling evolved becomes therefore apparent.

The seventh Ray of Ceremonial Order or Magic embodies a curious quality which is the outstanding characteristic of the particular Life which ensouls this ray. It is the quality or principle which is the coordinating factor unifying the inner quality and the outer tangible form or appearance. This work goes on primarily on etheric levels and involves physical energy. This is the true magical work. I should like to point out that when the fourth ray and the seventh ray come into incarnation together, we shall have a most peculiar period of revelation and of light-bringing. It is said of this time that then "the temple of the Lord will take on an added glory and the Builders will rejoice together." This will be the high moment of the Masonic work, spiritually understood. The Lost Word will then be recovered and uttered for all to hear, and the Master will arise and walk among His builders in the full light of the glory which shines from the east.

The spiritualising of forms might be regarded as the main work of the seventh ray, and it is this principle of fusion, of coordination and of blending which is active on etheric levels every time a soul comes into incarnation and a child is born on earth...[4]

We come at this time to consideration of the rays, which bring us immediately into the realm of psychology and of the various psychological influences. As we deal with the second of the ray manifestations, with the *Quality* aspect, we are dealing with those pre-determining factors which produce the myriad differentiations in the phenomenal world. The quality, the colouring, or the type nature of living energy (which is our inadequate definition of the word "life") settles or determines the aspect assumed and the characteristics expressed by all the forms in the four kingdoms of nature; the individual form emanations are settled thereby, and under the modifying influence of the contact of the living quality with the substance affected and with the kingdom which is the focus of attention, there is consequently produced the characteristic appearance, the specialised activity and the intrinsic emanation of any form in any kingdom. In my earlier books, I divided the rays into two groups:

Group I......Rays of Aspect, the three major rays.
Group II.....Rays of Attribute, the four minor rays.

The three great rays, which constitute the sum total of the divine manifestation, are aspect rays, and this for two reasons:

---

[4]IBID vol. I, pp. 49-52

First, they are, in their totality, the manifested Deity, the *Word* in incarnation. They are the expression of the creative purpose, and the synthesis of life, quality and appearance.

Secondly, they are active in every form in every kingdom, and they determine the broad general characteristics which govern the energy, the quality and the kingdom in question; through them the differentiated forms come into being, the specialised lives express themselves, and the diversity of divine agents fulfill their destiny in the plane of existence allocated to them.

Along these three streams of qualified life-force the creative agencies of God make their presence powerfully felt, and through their activity every form is imbued with that inner evolutionary attribute which must eventually sweep it into line with divine purpose, inevitably produce that type of consciousness which will enable the phenomenal unit to react to its surroundings and thus fulfill its destiny as a corporate part of the whole. Thus intrinsic quality and specific type radiation become possible. The interplay of these three rays determines the outer phenomenal appearance, attracts the unity of life into one or other of the kingdoms in nature, and into one or other of the myriad divisions within that kingdom; the selective and discriminating process is repeated until we have the many ramifications within the four kingdoms, the divisions, groups within a division, families and branches. Thus the creative process, in its wondrous beauty, sequence and unfoldment, stands forth to our awakening consciousness, and we are left awestruck and bewildered at the creative facility of the Great Architect of the Universe.

Looking at all this beauty from a symbolic angle, and thereby simplifying the concept (which is ever the work of the worker in symbols), we might say that Ray I embodies the dynamic idea of God, and thus the Most High starts the work of creation.

Ray II is occupied with the first formulations of the plan upon which the form must be constructed and the idea materialised, and (through the agencies of this great second emanation) the blue prints come into being with their mathematical accuracy, their structural unity and their geometrical perfection. The Grand Geometrician comes thus to the forefront and makes the work of the Builders possible. Upon figure and form, number and sequences will the Temple be built, and so embrace and express the glory of the Lord. The second ray is the ray of the Master Builder.

Ray III constitutes the aggregate of the active building forces, and the Great Architect, with His Builders, organises the material, starts the work of construction, and eventually (as the evolutionary cycle proceeds upon its way) materialises the idea and purpose of God the Father, under the guidance of God the Son. Yet these three are as much a unity as is a human being who conceives an idea, uses his mind and brain to bring his idea into manifestation, and employs his hands and all his natural forces to perfect his concept. The division of aspects and forces is unreal, except for the purpose of intelligent understanding.

The readers of this treatise who really want to profit by this teaching must train themselves ever to think in terms of the whole. The arbitrary tabulations, the divisions into triplicities and septenates, and the diversified enumeration of forces which are seen as emanating from the seven constellations, the ten planets, and the twelve mansions of the zodiac, are but intended to give the student an idea of a world of energies in which he has to play his part. From the standpoint of esoteric psychology, it should be noted that all the schools of psychology go astray in their handling of the human unit, for just this reason; they do not judge a man as a synthetic whole, and—owing to the lack of knowledge, and to the failure, as yet, of the intuitive faculty—the average psychologist seldom enters into the realms of true quality and of the life aspects; the man under investigation is considered more or less objectively, and the true sources of the phenomenal nature are seldom touched. The determining aspects of the personality ray which produce the sum total of the physical, emotional and mental qualities is in process of tabulation and research and much has been done of a valuable nature. A man's physical reactions, his emotional habits, and his mental processes—normal and abnormal—are far better understood than they were twenty-five years ago. Nevertheless, until there is a more adequate knowledge of ray qualities, and until a man's soul ray is determined and the effect of that ray upon the personality ray is charted and known, the true nature of his temperament and the real subjective cause of his varied reactions, his complexes and inhibitions will remain a problem most difficult to handle. When, for instance, psychologists realise that it is the play of soul quality and energy which determines whether a man in any particular life will function as an introvert or an extrovert, then they will work to produce that balancing of the ray forces which will make the man able to express himself in such a way that the path to the outer world is left open, and that to the inner world is also cleared of obstacles.

What is the real nature of a true mystic or introvert? He is one whose soul force, ray or quality is too strong for the personality to handle. The man then finds that the path to the inner worlds of desire-emotion, of mind and of spiritual vision are, for him, the line of least resistance, and the physical plane integration and expression suffer as a consequence. The "pull" of the soul offsets the outer "pull," and the man becomes a visionary mystic. I refer not to the practical mystic who is on the way to becoming a white occultist. The reverse condition can also be true, and then you have the pure extrovert. The personality ray focuses itself upon the physical plane, and the inner lure of the soul is temporarily offset, sometimes for several lives. Where this outer condition and "pull" is over-strong, and when all the personality ray qualities are focussed to a point, you will have either a display of exhibitionism, as it is called, or a constructive high grade personality, expressing genius and the creative possibilities of a coordinated physical, emotional and mental expression. The manifestation of this coordination will be outward into the world of doing, and not inward into the world of being or of the soul. Both these conditions indicate the "genius towards perfection;" where the equipment is mediocre, you have a thwarted or frustrated complex and a strong sense of inferiority which may diverge towards an abnormal exhibitionism. Where the equipment is fine and trained, you will have a brilliant worker in the varying fields of human endeavour. When, as is occasionally the case, you have added to the above a tendency to introvert, with the consequences of soul knowledge and of intuitional development, you then have a leader of men, a teacher from the gods, and a spiritual power. Hence the value to psychologists in these modern days (temporarily at least) if they will interest themselves in the hypotheses of the school of esoteric psychology. They may gain thereby, and in any case they lose nothing.

The four rays of attribute which find their synthesis in the third ray of aspect, produce the varying qualities in greater detail than do the three rays of aspect. It might generally be stated, as we endeavour to clarify our problem, that the three rays of aspect find their main expression in relation to mankind through the medium of the three periodical vehicles:

Ray I...Power................Life..............Ideas....The Monad
Ray II..Love-Wisdom.......Consciousness.Ideals...The Soul
Ray III.Active Intelligence..Appearance.....Idols....Personality

They find their secondary expression in the three bodies which form the personality of man:

Ray I.....Power.........Ideas....Mental body.....Purpose. Life.
Ray II....Love...........Ideals...Astral body......Quality.
Ray III...Intelligence...Idols....Physical body...Form.

The rays of attribute, though expressing themselves equally on all the planes and through the periodical vehicles and the three aspects of the personality, find their main expression through one or other of the four kingdoms in nature:

Ray IV...Harmony, Conflict.....4th kingdom.....Human. The
                                                                      Balance.
Ray V....Concrete Knowledge..3rd kingdom.....Animal.
Ray VI...Devotion................2nd kingdom.....Vegetable.
Ray VII..Ceremonial Ritual......1st kingdom.....Mineral.

These are their main fields of influence in the three worlds, and upon this we shall later enlarge.

In relation to mankind, these four rays of attribute find a wide expression in connection with the four aspects of the personality, or with the quaternary. The relationship is as follows:

Ray IV........Harmony through Conflict......the Physical body.
Ray V.........Concrete Knowledge............the Etheric body.
Ray VI........Devotion.........................the Astral body.
Ray VII.......Organisation.....................the Mental body.

But again remember that the interrelation and interplay is synthetic on all planes, on the formless levels and also on the planes of form, and in this connection, with all states of consciousness and throughout the created universe.

The Seven Rays

We are told that seven great rays exist in the cosmos. In our solar system only one of these seven great rays is in operation.[5] The seven sub-divisions constitute the "seven rays" which, wielded by our solar Logos, form the basis of endless variations in His system of worlds. These seven rays may be described as the seven channels through which all being in His solar system flows, the seven predominant characteristics or modifications of life, for it is not to humanity only that these rays apply, but to the seven kingdoms as well. In fact there is nothing in the whole solar system, at whatever stage of evolution it may stand, which does not belong and has not always belonged to one or other of the seven rays.

The following table may explain the various characteristics of the seven rays:

Characteristics No.	Methods of development	Planet (according to Besant)	Colour
I.....Will or Power	Raja Yoga	Uranus representing Sun.	Flame.
II....Wisdom. Balance. Intuition.	Raja Yoga	Mercury	Yellow. Rose.

---

[5]The one great ray in operation in our solar system is the second ray of Love-Wisdom. Thus the seven rays present for us and discussed here are all sub-rays of this great second ray. —H.B.

III.. Higher Mind	Exactitude		
	in thought	Venus	Indigo.
	Higher Mathematics.		Blue.
	Philosophy.		Bronze.
IV...Conflict	Intensity		
	of struggle	Saturn	Green.
Birth of Horus	Hatha Yoga, the most dangerous method of psychic growth.		
V...Lower Mind	Exactitude		
	in action	The Moon	Violet.
	Practical Science.		
VI..Devotion	Bhakti Yoga	Mars	Rose.
	Necessity for an object.		Blue.
VII.Ceremonial Order	Ceremonial observances	Jupiter	Bright.
	Control over forces in nature.		Clear. Blue.

It will be clear that each of the kingdoms—elemental, mineral, vegetable, and animal as well as the human—is divided into seven primary types of rays, and as individualisation (i.e. the transition from the animal to the human kingdom) can take place at present only through association with man, it follows that there must stand at the head of the animal kingdom, on each ray, some species of animal susceptible to human influence through which such individualisation can take place. The elephant is said to stand at the head of the second ray type of animal, while the cat and dog occupy a similar position on the fourth and sixth rays respectively. We have had no information as to the others, with this exception, that the animals of the first ray are no longer in existence on earth.[6]

There is a vast fund of interesting knowledge as to the action and results of the ray activity in the lower kingdoms of nature,

[6]Esoteric Psychology vol. I, pp. 157-164

but on this point no details can be given; and the following summary of what we have been told is necessarily imperfect and admits of endless amplification.

First Ray of Will or Power

Special Virtues:

Strength, courage, steadfastness, truthfulness arising from absolute fearlessness, power of ruling, capacity to grasp great questions in a large-minded way, and of handling men and measures.

Vices of Ray:

Pride, ambition, wilfulness, hardness, arrogance, desire to control others, obstinacy, anger.

Virtues to be acquired:

Tenderness, humility, sympathy, tolerance, patience.

This has been spoken of as the ray of power, and is correctly so called, but if it were power alone, without wisdom and love, a destructive and disintegrating force would result. When however the three characteristics are united, it becomes a creative and governing ray. Those on this ray have strong will power, for either good or evil, for the former when the will is directed by wisdom and made selfless by love. The first ray man will always "come to the front" in his own line. He may be the burglar or the judge who condemns him, but in either case he will be at the head of his profession. He is the born leader in any and every public career, one to trust and lean on, one to defend the weak and put down oppression, fearless of consequences and utterly indifferent to comment. On the other hand, an unmodified first ray can produce a man of unrelenting cruelty and hardness of nature.

The first ray man often has strong feeling and affection, but he does not readily express it; he will love strong contrasts and masses of colour, but will rarely be an artist; he will delight in great orchestral effects and crashing choruses, and if modified by the fourth, sixth or seventh rays, may be a great composer, but not otherwise; and there is a type of this ray which is tone-deaf, and another which is colour-blind to the more delicate colours. Such a man will distinguish red and yellow, but will hopelessly confuse blue, green, and violet.

The literary work of a first ray man will be strong and trenchant, but he will care little for style or finish in his writings. Perhaps examples of this type would be Luther, Carlyle, and Walt Whitman. It is said that in attempting the cure of disease the best method for the first ray man would be to draw health and strength from the great fount of universal life by his will power, and then pour it through the patient. This, of course, presupposes knowledge on his part of occult methods.

The characteristic method of approaching the great Quest on this ray would be by sheer force of will. Such a man would, as it were, take the kingdom of heaven "by violence." We have seen that the born leader belongs to this ray, wholly or in part. It makes the able commander-in-chief, such as Napoleon or Kitchener. Napoleon was first and fourth rays, and Kitchener was first and seventh, the seventh ray giving him his remarkable power of organisation.

The Second Ray of Love-Wisdom

Special Virtues:

Calm, strength, patience and endurance, love of truth, faithfulness, intuition, clear intelligence, and serene temper.

Vices of Ray:

Over-absorption in study, coldness, indifference to others, contempt of mental limitations in others.

Virtues to be acquired:

Love, compassion, unselfishness, energy.

This is called the ray of wisdom from its characteristic desire for pure knowledge and for absolute truth—cold and selfish, if without love, and inactive without power. When both power and love are present, then you have the ray of the Buddhas and of all great teachers of humanity—those who, having attained wisdom for the sake of others, spend themselves in giving it forth. The student on this ray is ever unsatisfied with his highest attainments; no matter how great his knowledge, his mind is still fixed on the unknown, the beyond, and on the heights as yet unscaled.

The second ray man will have tact and foresight; he will make an excellent ambassador, and a first-rate teacher or head of a college; as a man of affairs, he will have clear intelligence and wisdom in dealing with matters which come before him, and he will have the capacity of impressing true views of things on others and of making them see things as he does. He will make a good business man, if modified by the fourth, fifth and seventh rays. The soldier on this ray would plan wisely and forsee possibilities; he would have an intuition as to the best course to pursue, and he would never lead his men into danger through rashness. He might be deficient in rapidity of action and energy. The artist on this ray would always seek to teach through his art, and his pictures would have a meaning. His literary work would always be instructive.

The method of healing, for the second ray man, would be to learn thoroughly the temperament of the patient as well as to be thoroughly conversant with the nature of the disease, so as to use his will power on the case to the best advantage.

The characteristic method of approaching the Path would be by close and earnest study of the teachings til they become so much a part of man's consciousness as no longer to be merely intellectual knowledge, but a spiritual rule of living, thus bringing in intuition and true wisdom.

A bad type of the second ray would be bent on acquiring knowledge for himself alone, absolutely indifferent to the human needs of others. The foresight of such a man would degenerate into suspicion, his calmness into coldness and hardness of nature.

The Third Ray of Higher Mind

Special Virtues:

Wide views on all abstract questions, sincerity of purpose, clear intellect, capacity for concentration on philosophic studies, patience, caution, absence of the tendency to worry himself or others over trifles.

Vices of Ray:

Intellectual pride, coldness, isolation, inaccuracy in details, absent-mindedness, obstinacy, selfishness, overmuch criticism of others.

Virtues to be acquired:

Sympathy, tolerance, devotion, accuracy, energy and common-sense.

This is the ray of the abstract thinker, of the philosopher and the metaphysician, of the man who delights in the higher mathematics but who, unless modified by some practical ray, would hardly be troubled to keep his accounts accurately. His imaginative faculty will be highly developed, i.e., he can by the power of his imagination grasp the essence of a truth; his idealism will often be strong; he is a dreamer and a theorist, and from his wide views and great caution he sees every side of a question equally clearly. This sometimes paralyses his action. He will make a good business man; as a soldier he will work out a problem in tactics at his desk, but is seldom great in the field. As an artist his technique is not fine, but his subjects will be full of thought and interest. He will love music, but unless influenced by the fourth ray he will not produce it. In all walks of life he is full of ideas, but is too impractical to carry them out.

One type of this ray is unconventional to a degree, slovenly, unpunctual and idle, and regardless of appearances. If influenced by the fifth ray as the secondary ray, this character is entirely changed. The third and the fifth rays make the perfectly balanced historian who grasps his subject in a large way and verifies every detail with patient accuracy. Again the third and the fifth rays together make the truly great mathematician who soars into heights of abstract thought and calculation, and who can also bring his results down to practical scientific use. The literary style of the third ray man is too often vague and involved, but if influenced by the first, fourth, fifth or seventh rays, this is changed, and under the fifth he will be a master of the pen.

The curing of disease by the third ray man would be by the use of drugs made of herbs or minerals belonging to the same ray as the patient whom he desires to relieve.

The method of approaching the great Quest, for this ray type, is by deep thinking on philosophic or metaphysical lines till he is led to the realisation of the great Beyond and of the paramount importance of treading the Path that leads thither.

The Fourth Ray of Harmony through Conflict

Special Virtues:

Strong affections, sympathy, physical courage, generosity, devotion, quickness of intellect and perception.

Vices of Ray:

Self-centredness, worrying, inaccuracy, lack of moral courage, strong passions, indolence, extravagance.

Virtues to be acquired:

Serenity, confidence, self-control, purity, unselfishness, accuracy, mental and moral balance.

This has been called the "ray of struggle" for on this ray the qualities of rajas (activity) and tamas (inertia) are so strangely equal in proportion that the nature of the fourth ray man is torn with their combat, and the outcome, when satisfactory, is spoken of as the "Birth of Horus," of the Christ, born from the throes of constant pain and suffering.

Tamas induces love of ease and pleasure, a hatred of causing pain amounting to moral cowardice, indolence, procrastination, a desire to let things be, to rest, and to take no thought of the morrow. Rajas is fiery, impatient, ever urging to action. These contrasting forces in the nature make life one perpetual warfare and unrest for the fourth ray man; the friction and the experience gained thereby may produce very rapid evolution, but the man may as easily become a ne'er-do-well as a hero.

It is the ray of the dashing cavalry leader, reckless of risks to himself or his followers. It is the ray of the man who will lead a forlorn hope, for in moments of excitement the fourth ray man is entirely dominated by rajas; of the wild speculator and gambler, full of enthusiasm and plans, easily overwhelmed by sorrow or failure, but as quickly recovering from all reverses and misfortunes.

It is pre-eminently the ray of colour, of the artist whose colour is always great, though his drawing will often be defective. (Watts was fourth and second rays.) The fourth ray man always loves colour, and can generally produce it. If untrained as an artist, a colour sense is sure to appear in other ways, in choice of dress or decorations.

In music, fourth ray compositions are always full of melody, and the fourth ray man loves a tune. As a writer or poet, his work will often be brilliant and full of picturesque word-painting, but inaccurate, full of exaggerations, and often pessimistic. He will generally talk well and have a sense of humour, but he varies between brilliant conversations and gloomy silences, according to his mood. He is a delightful and difficult person to live with.

In healing, the best fourth ray method is massage and magnetism, used with knowledge.

The method of approaching the Path will be by self-control, thus gaining equilibrium amongst the warring forces of the nature. The lower and extremely dangerous way is by Hatha Yoga.

The Fifth Ray of Lower Mind

Special Virtues:

Strictly accurate statements, justice (without mercy), perseverance, common-sense, uprightness, independence, keen intellect.

Vices of Ray:

Harsh criticism, narrowness, arrogance, unforgiving temper, lack of sympathy and reverence, prejudice.

Virtues to be acquired:

Reverence, devotion, sympathy, love, wide-mindedness.

This is the ray of science and of research. The man on this ray will possess keen intellect, great accuracy in detail, and will make unwearied efforts to trace the smallest fact to its source, and to verify every theory. He will generally be extremely truthful, full of lucid explanation of facts, though sometimes pedantic and wearisome from his insistence on trivial and unnecessary verbal minutiæ. He will be orderly, punctual, business-like, disliking to receive favours or flattery.

It is the ray of the great chemist, the practical electrician, the first-rate engineer, the great operating surgeon. As a statesman, the fifth ray man would be narrow in his views, but he would be an excellent head of some special technical department, though a disagreeable person under whom to work. As a soldier, he would turn most readily to artillery and engineering. The artist on this ray is very rare, unless the fourth or seventh be the influencing secondary ray; even then his colouring will be dull, his sculptures lifeless, and his music (if he composes) will be uninteresting, though technically correct in form. His style in writing or speaking will be clearness itself, but it will lack fire and point, and he will often be long-winded, from his desire to say all that can possibly be said on his subject.

In healing, he is the perfect surgeon, and his best cures will be through surgery and electricity.

For the fifth ray, the method of approaching the Path is by scientific research, pushed to ultimate conclusions, and by the acceptance of the inferences which follow these.

The Sixth Ray of Devotion

Special Virtues:

Devotion, single-mindedness, love, tenderness, intuition, loyalty, reverence.

Vices of Ray:

Selfish and jealous love, over-leaning on others, partiality, self-deception, sectarianism, superstition, prejudice, over-rapid conclusions, fiery anger.

Virtues to be acquired:

Strength, self-sacrifice, purity, truth, tolerance, serenity, balance and common sense.

This is called the ray of devotion. The man who is on this ray is full of religious instincts and impulses, and of intense personal feeling; nothing is taken equably. Everything, in his eyes, is either perfect or intolerable; his friends are angels, his enemies are very much the reverse; his view, in both cases is formed not on the intrinsic merits of either class, but on the way the persons appeal to him, or on the sympathy or lack of sympathy which they shew to his favourite idols, whether these be concrete or abstract, for he is full of devotion, it may be to a person, or it may be to a cause.

He must always have a "personal God," an incarnation of Deity to adore. The best type of this ray makes the saint, the worst type, the bigot or fanatic, the typical martyr or the typical inquisitor. All religious wars or crusades have originated from sixth ray fanaticism. The man on this ray is often of gentle nature, but he can always flame into fury and fiery wrath. He will lay down his life for the objects of his devotion or reverence, but he will not lift a finger to help those outside of his immediate sympathies. As a soldier, he hates fighting but often when aroused in battle fights like one possessed. He is never a great statesman nor a good business man, but he may be a great preacher or orator.

The sixth ray man will be the poet of the emotions (such as Tennyson) and the writer of religious books, either in poerty or prose. He is devoted to beauty and colour and all things lovely, but his productive skill is not great unless under the influence of one of the practically artistic rays, the fourth or seventh. His music will always be of a melodious order, and he will often be the composer of oratorios and of sacred music.

The method of healing for this ray would be by faith and prayer.

The way of approaching the Path would be by prayer and meditation, aiming at union with God.

The Seventh Ray of Ceremonial Order or Magic

Special virtues:

Strength, perseverance, courage, courtesy, extreme care in details, self-reliance.

Vices of Ray:

Formalism, bigotry, pride, narrowness, superficial judgments, self-opinion over-indulged.

Virtues to be acquired:

Realisation of unity, wide-mindedness, tolerance, humility, gentleness and love.

This is the ceremonial ray, the ray which makes a man delight in "all things done decently and in order," and according to rule and precedent. It is the ray of the high priest and the court chamberlain, of the solder who is a born genius in organisation, of the ideal commissary general who will dress and feed the troops in the best possible way. It is the ray of the perfect nurse for the sick, careful in the smallest detail, though sometimes too much inclined to disregard the patients' idiosyncrasies and to try and grind them in the iron mill of routine.

It is the ray of form, of the perfect sculptor, who sees and produces ideal beauty, of the designer of beautiful forms and patterns of any sort; but such a man would not be successful as a painter unless his influencing ray were the fourth. The combination of four with seven would make the very highest type of artist, form and colour being both *in excelsis*. The literary work of the seventh ray man would be remarkable for its ultra-polished style, and such a writer would think far more of the manner than of the matter in his work, but would always be fluent both in writing and speech. The seventh ray man will often be sectarian. He will delight in fixed ceremonials and observances, in great processions and shows, in reviews of troops and warships, in genealogical trees, and in rules of precedence.

The bad type of seventh ray man is superstitious, and such a man will take deep interest in omens, in dreams, in all occult practices, and in spiritualistic phenomena. The good type of the ray is absolutely determined to do the right thing and say the right word at the right moment; hence great social success.

In healing, the seventh ray man would rely on extreme exactness in carrying out orthodox treatment of disease. On him the practices of yoga would have no physical bad results.

He will approach the Path through observance of rules of practice and of ritual, and can easily evoke and control the elemental forces.

From many of the above remarks it may have been inferred that the characteristics of any given ray find closer correspondence with one of the other rays than with the rest. This is a fact. The only one which stands alone and has no close relationship with any of the others is the fourth. This brings to mind the unique position which the number four occupies in the evolutionary process. We have the fourth root race, the fourth planetary chain, the fourth planet in the chain, the fourth planetary manvantara, etc.

Between the third and the fifth rays there is a close relationship. In the search after knowledge, for example, the most laborious and minute study of detail is the path that will be followed, whether in philosophy, the higher mathematics or in the pursuit of practical science.

The correspondence between the second and the sixth rays shews itself in the intuitive grasp of synthesised knowledge, and in the common bond of faithfulness and loyalty.

Masterfulness, steadfastness, and perseverance are the corresponding characteristics of the first and the seventh rays.[7]

RAY I—The energy of Will or Power. This ray is outstandingly related to that aspect of will which conquers death. It is nevertheless the Ray of the Destroyer. In this connection, I would remind you that the human attitude that death is the destroyer presents a limited and erroneous point of view. The first ray destroys death because in reality there is no such thing; the concept is all part of the Great Illusion, is a limitation of the human consciousness, and is basically connected with the brain and not with the heart, strange as that may seem to you. It is in a very true sense "a figment of the imagination." Ponder on this. The abolition of death and of the destruction of form is a manifestation of Ray I, for it brings about in reality the death of negation and the inauguration of true activity. It is the energy which can be called "divine incentive"; it is the life in the seed which destroys successively all forms in order that realised fruition may eventuate. That is the clue to Ray I. It is the *Will which initiates.*

Today, as regards humanity, its highest realisation is initiation.

RAY II—The energy of Love-Wisdom. The basic energy is the will to unify, to synthesise, to produce coherence and mutual attraction and to establish relationships, but—remember this—relationships which are entirely apart from the

---

consciousness of relation or the realisation of unity. It is the fact of unification as seen from the beginning and as existing ever and forever in the Mind of God Whose will embraces past, present and future and Whose mind does not think in terms of evolution or of process. The process is inherent in the seed; the evolutionary urge is the inevitable accompaniment of life in manifestation. It is the *Will to unification.*

Today, as regards humanity, its highest expression is the mystical vision.

RAY III—The energy of Active Intelligence. This is the will of conditioned purpose. The factors which are working out through its medium are the forceful carrying forward of the recognised plan with a goal intelligently conceived and an active incentive which carries the process intelligently forward on the strength of its own momentum. Again I would remind you that I am dealing not with human consciousness but with the sumtotal of that undertaking which makes matter subservient to and adaptable to the basic idea in the mind of God. And no human being is as yet able to conceive of that idea. No one knows what is the will of God or what is the nature of His intelligent purpose. It is the *Will to evolution.*

Today, as regards humanity, its highest expression is education, or progressive development through experience.

RAY IV—The energy of Harmony through Conflict. This is fundamentally the will to destroy limitation. This is not the same thing as the will to destroy negation as in the case of Ray I, but is an allied aspect of that. I am not referring to the consciousness aspect which recognises and profits by such struggle. I am referring to the energy, inherent in all forms and peculiarly strong in humanity (because man is self-conscious), which produces inevitably and unavoidably the struggle between life and that which it has chosen as a limitation; this eventually shatters or breaks up that limitation the moment that a point of real harmony or at-one-ment has been reached. Esoterically it might be said that the moment that form (limitation) and life balance each other a rift immediately appears and through it flows a fresh outpouring of the will. Christ had to die because He had achieved harmony with the will of God and then "the veil of the Temple was rent in twain from the top to the bottom." The significance of this fresh inflow of the Will will now appear; the stage is set anew for a fresh and renewed activity of the living principle. As far as humanity is concerned the "seeds of death" emerge through the medium of this Ray and the Grim Reaper, Death, is but an aspect of this will, conditioned by the fourth ray and emerging from the fourth plane. Death is an act of the intuition, transmitted by the soul to the personality and then acted upon in conformity to the divine will by the individual will. This is the *Will to harmonisation.*

Today, its highest expression as regards humanity is the intuition, as it works out through group activity. Death always releases the individual into the group.

RAY V—The energy of Concrete Science or Knowledge. To understand this expression of the divine will, the student should bear in mind the occult aphorism that "matter is spirit at its lowest point of manifestation and spirit is matter at its highest." Basically this is the will which produces concretion and yet at the same time constitutes the point at which spirit and matter are balanced and co-equal. That is the reason why human perfection is carried forward consciously upon the mental plane, the fifth plane; this is brought about by the fifth ray and upon this plane liberation takes place at the time of the fifth initiation. This is the will which is inherent in substance and which actuates all atoms of which all forms are made. It is closely related to the first solar system even whilst liberating members of the human family who will constitute the nucleus around which the third solar system is constructed. The energy of this ray is intelligence; it is the seed of consciousness but not of consciousness as we understand it; it is the inherent life of matter and the will to work intelligently; it is that living something for which we have no name which was the product of the first solar system. It is one of the major assets of God, the Father and also of the human Monad. This is the *Will to Action*.

Today, as regards humanity, its highest expression is liberation—through death or initiation.

RAY VI—The energy of Devotion or of Idealism. This is the will which embodies God's idea. It provides the motive power behind the working out of whatever may be the purpose of creation. What that purpose is we have not as yet the faintest idea. An ideal is related to the consciousness aspect as far as human beings are concerned. An idea is related to the will aspect. This ray embodies a dominant potency. It expresses God's desire and is the basic energy emanating from the cosmic astral plane. It conceals the mystery which is to be found in the relationship of the will and desire. Desire is related to consciousness. Will is *not*. We are not, however, dealing with consciousness but with that impersonal force which drives forward through all the seven planes of our solar system and which makes the idea of God a consummated fact in the Eternal Now. Does that statement mean much to you? I would surmise that it means but little; it is a basic statement of occult fact anent energy as it expresses itself through humanity in a manner which is unique and peculiar. I would here remind you of a statement in *The Secret Doctrine* that "an Idea is a Being incorporeal which has no subsistence by itself but gives figure and form unto shapeless matter and becomes the cause of the manifestation." This statement takes you straight back to God the Father, to the Monad, to the One. It is related, consequently, to the Will and not to consciousness. Consciousness is per se the recognition of a progressive plan. The Will is the cause, the energising Principle, Life, Being. This is the *Will to Causation*.

Today, as regards humanity, its highest expression is idealism, the incentive and cause of human activity.

RAY VII—This is the energy of Ceremonial Order. It is an expression of the will which drives through into outer manifestation; it is that which embodies both the periphery and the point at the centre. It is the will to "ritualistic synthesis," if I might so word it. It is Necessity which is the prime conditioning factor of the divine nature—the necessity to express itself; the necessity to manifest in an orderly rhythmic manner; the necessity to embrace "that which is above and that which is below" and, through the medium of this activity, to produce beauty, order, perfect wholes and right relationships. It is the driving energy which Being emanates as It appears and takes form and lives. It is the *Will towards Expression.*

Today, as regards humanity, its highest expression is organisation.

In the above statements anent the rays, you can see that the full circle of their activity is complete from the angle of God the Father; the will to initiate manifestation and its attendant progressive expression meets the will towards full achievement and the energy of Being itself arrives—in time and space today (in the mind of God) at full consummation.[8]

1. Every human being, in or out of incarnation, is a "fragment of divinity," and an outpost of the divine consciousness, functioning in time and space for purposes of expression.

2. All these souls, selves, or human beings are found, as we have seen, on one or other of the seven emanations of spiritual energy, issuing forth from God at the beginning of an era of creative activity. They return to their emanating Source when that particular cycle is brought to a close.

3. In the interim between emanation and reabsorption, these souls pass through various experiences until such time as they can "shine forth in all their exactitude of truth."

---

[8]Esoteric Astrology, pp. 596-601

4. They are called, as has been stated, in *A Treatise on Cosmic Fire*, page 855,

    1. Lotuses of revelation.
    2. Lotuses with perfume.
    3. Radiant lotuses.
    4. Lotuses wherein the flower is on the point of opening.
    5. Lotuses of closed and sealed condition.
    6. The colourless lotuses.
    7. Lotuses in bud.

5. These souls, cycling through various forms of life in the long evolutionary process arrive eventually at full, self-conscious existence. By this we mean that they are self-determined, self-conditioned, and self-aware. They are also conscious of and responsive to their environment.

6. Once this conscious awareness is achieved, then progress becomes more rapid. It should be borne in mind that many human beings are not thus aware. The groupings which arise out of this awareness (limiting our ideas entirely to those within the radius of the human family) can be expressed as follows:

    1. The souls who live but whose consciousness sleeps. These are the dormant human beings whose intelligence is of such a low order, and their awareness of themselves and of life is so dim and nebulous, that only the lowest forms of human existence come into this category. Racially, nationally, and tribally they do not exist as pure types, but occasionally such a person emerges in the slums of our great cities. They are like a "throw back" and never appear among what are called the natural savages, or the peasantry.

    2. The souls who are simply aware of physical plane life and of sensation. These people are slow, inert, inarticulate, bewildered *by their environment*, but they are not bewildered, as are the more advanced and emotional types, *by events*. They have no sense of time or of purpose; they can seldom be trained along any mental line, and they very rarely exhibit

skill in any direction. They can dig and carry, under direction; they eat, sleep and procreate, following the natural instincts of the animal body. Emotionally, however, they are asleep, and mentally they are totally unawakened. These too are relatively rare, though several thousands of them can be found upon our planet. They can be recognised through their complete incapacity to respond to emotional and mental training and culture.

3. The souls who are beginning to integrate and who are emotionally and psychically alive. In them, of course, the animal nature is awake and the desire nature is becoming rampant. These people are to be found in all races to a small extent, and a number of them can be found among the negroes, which race contains a large number of those who are today relatively children. These are child souls, and though the mental equipment is there and some of them can be trained to use it, the preponderance of the life emphasis is entirely upon physical activity as it is motivated by the desire for satisfaction of some kind, and by a shallow "wish-life" or desire nature, almost entirely oriented towards the physical life. These souls are the modern correspondences to the old Lemurian cultures.

4. The souls who are primarily emotional. The mind nature is not functioning strongly, and only rarely does it swing into activity, and the physical body is slipping steadily into the realm of the unconscious. In every race and nation there are millions of such souls in existence. They may be regarded as the modern Atlanteans.

5. Those souls who can now be classed as intelligent human beings, capable of mental application, if trained, and showing that they can think when need arises. They are still, nevertheless, predominantly emotional. They constitute the bulk of modern humanity at this time. They are the average citizens of our modern world—good, well-intentioned,

capable of intense emotional activity, with the feeling nature almost over-developed, and oscillating between the life of the senses and that of the mind. They swing between the poles of experience. Their lives are spent in an astral turmoil, but they have steadily increasing interludes wherein the mind can momentarily make itself felt, and thus at need effect important decisions. These are the nice good people, who are, nevertheless, largely controlled by the mass consciousness, because they are relatively unthinking. They can be regimented and standardised with facility by orthodox religion and government, and are the "sheep" of the human family.

6. The souls who think, and who are minds. These are steadily increasing in number and gaining in power as our educational processes and our scientific discoveries bring results, and expand human awareness. They constitute the cream of the human family, and are the people who are achieving success in some department of human life. They are writers, artists, thinkers in various fields of human knowledge and aspiration, politicians, religious leaders, scientists, skilled workers and artisans, and all those who, though in the front rank, yet take ideas and propositions and work with them for the ultimate benefit of the human family. They are the world aspirants, and those who are beginning to get the ideal of service into their consciousness.

7. Those souls whose sense of awareness on the physical plane is now of such an order that they can pass on to the Probationary Path. They are the mystics, conscious of duality, torn between the pairs of opposites, but who are yet unable to rest until they are polarised in the soul. These are the sensitive, struggling people, who long for release from failure and from existence in the world today. Their mind natures are alive and active but they cannot yet control them as they should and the higher

illumination remains as yet a joyous hope and final possibility.

8. Souls whose intelligence and love nature is becoming so awakened and integrated that they can begin to tread the Path of Discipleship. They are the practical mystics, or the occultists, of modern times.

9. The souls who are initiate into the mysteries of the kingdom of God. These are souls who are not only conscious of their vehicles of expression, the integrated personality, and conscious also of themselves as souls, but they know, past all controversy, that there is no such thing as "my soul and your soul," but simply "the Soul". They know this is not only as a mental proposition, and as a sensed reality, but also as a fact in their own consciousness.

10. The souls who have achieved release from all the limitations of the form nature and who dwell eternally in the consciousness of the One Soul, withdrawn from identification with any aspiration of the form life, no matter how highly developed. They can and do use the form at will for the purposes of the general good. These are the Masters of Life, the perfected adepts.

Higher than this we need not go, except by inference. A detailed analysis is not, however, in order, owing to the limitations of men's minds. The above is only a wide generalisation, and the various groupings shade into each other in a bewildering way. The varieties of intermediate types are myriad, but this analysis will serve as a skeleton structure upon which to build.[9]

---

[9] Esoteric Psychology vol. II, pp. 202-207

The Great Approaches (The Coming New Religion)

The Soul of Humanity

It can be seen, therefore, that a very difficult interlude is now taking place in the world today. It is one wherein a process is being undergone by humanity which is similar to that which takes place so frequently in the life of an individual. The soul of the world is taking cognizance of outer affairs, preparatory to taking hold of the world situation. In the life of an aspirant, such interludes frequently occur. The personality is aware of conditions of difficulty and of turmoil. It has, however, had in the past moments of high spiritual revelation and of divine impulsation. It has been sure of its goal temporarily and it has known that the soul is the directing factor; some dim idea of the goal and of the purposes underlying those impulses which have been granted to it by the soul have been vouchsafed. But, for the moment, all that lies in the past. It seems as if the soul has retreated; that the period of contact and of surety has ended; and that nothing remains except difficulty, a sense of futility, and an urge to be freed from conditions. This is frequently of such intensity that all other interests seem dwarfed.

But the soul has *not* retreated and inner spiritual conditions remain essentially unchanged. The divine impulses are still there and the soul is but gathering itself for a fresh effort and for a stronger and more determined preoccupation with the affairs of its shadow, its dim reflection, the personality.

What is true of the individual aspirant is equally true of humanity, the world aspirant. In May, 1936, a great forward moving effort of the world soul took place and definite and unchangeable progress was made. This had a three-fold effect:

1. The lives of all true aspirants and disciples were subjected to a stimulating process, with definite and specific results of the desired nature.

2. The stimulation of the masses of men also took place, so that they could be enabled to respond more easily and truly to the impact of ideas. This also was uniquely successful.

3. The Hierarchy of souls who have achieved freedom and whom you call the planetary Hierarchy were able to approach closer to humanity and to establish a more definite relationship and a closer contact than had been possible at any time since mid-Atlantean times. This result was more universal than had been anticipated. This was the third of the "Great Approaches" made by the Hierarchy towards humanity. The success of these aproaches is largely based on the intensity of the desire found in the world aspirants and among those who have, on their side, established also a "way of approach" through meditation and service. Their numbers being phenomenally greater than at any previous time, the year 1936 saw the Hierarchy make a step forward that was unprecedented (I had almost said, unexpected) in its experience. This was due to the world-wide activity of the New Group of World Servers.

I would like here to call your attention to the phrase I used above: "the Hierarchy of souls who have achieved freedom." I am not using that phrase in the ordinary sense. The aspirants and the disciples of the world employ it to signify the achieving of that liberty and that freedom which will release them from the three worlds of human endeavour and make them free citizens of the Kingdom of God. With that point of view you are quite familiar, and you will recognise that in it there lies a large measure of selfish purpose—inevitable and some day to be eliminated, but at this stage definitely present and perhaps desirable because it provides the adequate incentive towards the needed effort. The freedom, however, to which I refer, is the achieved success of the soul to move and act and manifest with freedom in the three worlds, as well as on its own high plane. This is a point seldom if ever emphasised. The soul itself, the Ego, has its own task to do, which might be expressed as being the reverse of that with which the personality is familiar. It has to learn to be at home and to function effectively in the world of human living and there to carry forward the plan. Such is the task of the Hierarchy and I felt that a statement of their peculiar problem and the difficulty of free activity which it necessarily involves, would prove both of interest and of enlightenment to those who read these papers.

From this highest standpoint, the Hierarchy was enabled to make a definite step forward in 1936 as the result of the work done in the last fifty years; having made it, it became necessary to stabilise the position and from the point then reached to lay plans for the next move to be taken on behalf of humanity.

Thus we find the interlude with which we have been almost distressingly familiar. You may have been led to expect some great onward sweep, some clear time of reaping, or some spectacular climax of happenings. When all that occurred was an interim of relative silence and a period wherein nothing seemed to occur, it was natural for the majority to experience a sense of disappointment, a reaction which was almost equivalent, in some cases, to loss of faith, and a feeling of emotional fatigue and mental futility which tried many to the utmost. It is wise to remember that these reactions do not affect the issue and in no way retard the event, though they may make the task of the approaching helpers more difficult and draw almost unnecessarily upon their spiritual resources.

These interludes of apparent silence, of inertia and of inactivity are part of the great preservative and constructive activity of the Hierarchy; they are both individual, group and planetary in nature. Aspirants must learn to work intelligently and understandingly with the law of cycles. They must not forget that they live in a world of seeming and have no real freedom in the world of reality.

In May, 1938, at the time of the full moon, the Council of the Hierarchy to which I have several times referred in the past, convened and the plans for the immediate future were laid down. I would remind you of something we are very apt to forget. The plans for humanity are not laid down, for humanity determines its own destiny. The plans to meet the immediate human emergency and the plans to make possible a closer relationship between humanity and the Hierarchy were established. The problem before the Hierarchy of Masters (speaking in a large and general sense) is to intensify the activity and the consequent potency of that hidden power. By thus bringing it to the fore in human lives, the needed changes in our civilisation can be produced. The average man works from the organisation angle and having visioned some illuminating idea, he begins to build the outer physical form which will house and express it. The planetary Hierarchy, working under the inspiration of the Divine vision as it is embodied in the Plan, seeks to evoke a response to that Plan in every human heart, and by fostering and fanning that response, to evoke not only a mental understanding but also an aspirational desire. These together will produce finally the emergence of the Plan upon the earth and thus express a conditioning factor in human affairs.

When there are a sufficient number of people who are in conscious touch with their souls, then the sheer weight of their numbers, plus the clarity of their intentions and their widespread distribution over the face of the earth, must necessarily become effective. These people will then bring about changes of such far-reaching importance that the culture of the future will be as far removed from ours today, as ours in its turn is removed from that of the red Indians who roamed for centuries over the American continent and of whose possessions the white race took charge.

This then is the task of the Workers in the field of human affairs: to awaken the soul ray to potency in the life of each human being, beginning with those whose mental equipment and achieved integration would warrant the belief that—once awakened—they would use the new forces at their disposal with a measure of wisdom and planned constructive intention.

The questions we shall first discuss are as follows: What are the psychological advantages of somewhat understanding the nature of the egoic ray? What intelligent use can be made by psychologists of the fact, if the soul ray is determined and recognised?

Early in this treatise we dealt with the general proposition of the value to psychology of a knowledge of the rays. We have considered the possibility of there being a scientific acceptance of the hypothesis of their existence, even if this recognition is only tendered provisionally. We must not forget that aspirants are increasing all over the world. Perhaps the simplest way to proceed is to state some of the developments which will manifest when the ray of the soul is admitted and recognised and developed. These will be:

1. *The solution of the present world conflict.* This conflict now amounts in the material sense almost to an impasse. The results of soul contacts on human beings and the effect to be seen in the personality life might be stated to be as follows:

   a. *Conflict,* turmoil, opposed loyalties, inner warfare and a collision of divergent views.

   b. *A sensitivity to ideas.* This amounts in the earlier stages to a flexibility of response, amounting almost to instability, and producing constant change of viewpoint. This leads eventually to a sensitivity to the intuition which will enable an individual to distinguish promptly between the unreal and the real.

   c. *A process of detachment.* This is the difficult and painful process of laying down the lines of demarcation between the soul and the personality. This inevitably produces at first separation and divided interests, leading later to a submergence of personality interests in those of the Plan, and the absorption of personal desire in the aspects of the soul.

   d. *A period of creativity,* due to the third aspect of the soul which is the creator aspect. This development will produce definite habit changes in the physical plane life of the aspirant. It will lead to the consecration of the disciple to certain types of endeavour summed up in the words "artistic career".

These four effects of soul activity, which are in reality only the pouring in of soul force, through the channel of contact which the man has opened, will give to psychology the four major causes of the present world difficulty. Each of these causes holds latent within itself its own solution. The present conflict, the widespread response to widely different ideologies, the economic pressure leading to material depredation, a most certain creativity of all the arts in the world today, and a new standard of values, are all problems confronting the trained thinker and psychologist. These conditioning effects are all of them to be seen among men today.

2. *The emergence of world government.* This emergence will be the result of these "five areas of difficulty", and the consequence of a more general understanding of:

   a. The causes of unrest.

   b. The point in evolution reached by humanity.

   c. The crises which must inevitably occur when man, the integrated human being, meets man, the spiritual reality.

   d. The moment of opportunity which is upon us. This is the result of certain astronomical happenings, such as the pouring in of energy from a new sign in the zodiac, and the shift of the earth's pole.

3. *The development of the new art .* This will be expressive of a sensitive response to ideas. The art of the past expressed largely man's understanding of the beauty of God's created world, whether it was the phenomenal wonder of nature or the beauty of the human form. The art of today is as yet almost a childish attempt to express the world of feeling and of inner moods and those emotionally psychological reactions which govern the bulk of the race. They are, however, to the world of feeling-expression what the drawings of the cave man are to the art of Leonardo da Vinci. It is in the realm of words today that this new art is most adequately expressing itself. The art of music will be the next approach nearer to the truth, and to the revelation of the emerging beauty; the art of the painter and of the sculptor will follow later. None of this is the art of expressing ideas creatively, which will be the glory of the Aquarian Age.

4. *The understanding of the diseases of mystics,* or the physical ills of the highly developed people of the world. These are predominantly psychological in character and may remain submerged in the realm of the mind and of sensitivity or they may work out as physiological effect with a definite psychological basis. These forms of physical disease are the most difficult to handle and are at present little understood. What do modern scientific investigators know of the distinction between those neurotic and psychological troubles which are based on personality integration, or on

excessive soul stimulation, and those which are the result of wrong polarisation? On these matters we may not here enlarge as the theme is too vast. It can, however, be noted that a recognition of the soul ray (as it makes its presence felt in the personality), will very frequently lead to definite psychological trouble. It might be well to add here a word of warning. We must be careful not to let our desire for soul contact fool us at this time into believing that our present physical difficulties (if there are any) are the result of this soul contact. It would be quite surprising if this were so. They are far more apt to be the result of astral polarisation, of physical unwisdom and experimentation, and perhaps of the too rapid integration of the three aspects of the personality.

In these four points there is probably indicated enough to make clear, or at least to suggest two important things. First, that much, if not all that can be seen going on in the world today, is caused by a greatly increased soul stimulation, to which the entire human family is reacting, even though, as individuals, they have not made a soul contact. This increased stimulation is due to two things:

1. A great many men, and the number is rapidly increasing, are making contact with their souls through an intense aspiration and—in many cases—very real desperation.

2. The Hierarchy of Masters is exceedingly active today, and this is due to two things:

   a. The demand on the part of humanity which has reached Their attention continuously for the past few decades, and which is calling out an inevitable response.

   b. A stimulation of the planetary Hierarchy itself. This leads many in the ranks of the Hierarchy to pass through one of the higher initiations. They therefore become much more potent and their influence is much more magnetic and radiating.

If we take the four points above enumerated and apply them both to the individual and to the race, we will find the answers to many questions, and the potency of the effects can be noted.[10]

The subject of egoic evolution cannot be fully comprehended until after initiation, but it is felt now by the Teachers on the inner side that the main principles had better be given out at once in view of the unexpected development (since the opening of this century) of two great sciences:

The Science of Electricity. The investigations of scientists have been greatly stimulated by the discovery of radium, which is an electrical phenomenon of a certain kind, and by the knowledge this discovery brought of the radioactive substances; the development of the many methods of utilising electricity has also greatly aided. This science has brought man to the threshold of a discovery which will revolutionise world thought on these matters, and which will eventually solve a great part of the economic problem, thus leaving many more persons free for mental growth and work. This expansion of knowledge can be looked for before one hundred and fifty years have transpired.

The Science of Psychology. The psycho-analytic theories which (though indicative of progress) are yet tending in a wrong direction, may prove disastrous to the higher development of the race unless the true nature of the "psyche" is elucidated. When the public mind has apprehended, even cursorily, the following briefly stated facts, the trend of popular education, the object of political science, and the goal of economic and social endeavour will take a new and better direction. These facts might be summed up in the following postulates:

[10]IBID vol. II, pp. 701-709

I. Man is *in essence* divine.[11] This has ever been enunciated throughout the ages, but remains as yet a beautiful theory or belief, and not a proven scientific fact, nor is it universally held.

II. Man is in fact a fragment of the Universal Mind, or world soul,[12] and as a fragment is thus partaker of the instincts and quality of that soul, as it manifests through the human family. Therefore, unity is only possible upon the plane of mind. This, if true, must lead to the tendency to develop within the physical brain a conscious realisation of group affiliations on the mental plane, a conscious recognition of group relationships, ideals and goal, and a conscious manifestation of that continuity of consciousness which is the object of evolution at this time. It will further produce the transference of the race consciousness from the physical plane to the mental, and a consequent solving through "knowledge, love, and sacrifice" of all present problems. This will bring about emancipation from the present physical plane disorder. It must lead to the education of the public as to the nature of man, and the development of the powers latent within him—powers which will set him free from his present limitations, and which will produce in the human family a collective repudiation of the present conditions. When men everywhere recognise themselves and each other, as divine self-conscious units, functioning primarily in the causal body but utilising the three lower vehicles only as a means of contact with the three lower planes, we will have

---

[11]Each human being is an incarnation of God. —S.D. III, p. 449. Compare: S.D. II, p. 541; S.D. III, p. 475; and the Biblical words: "I have said, Ye are Gods." "Know ye not that ye are the Temple of the Holy Spirit?"

No Being can become a God without passing through the human cycles. —S.D. II, p. 336.

Man therefore is like God in that he represents the pairs of opposites, good and evil, light and darkness, male and female, etc. He is a duality.

He represents also God in that He is a triplicity, being three in one, and one in three. —S.D. II, p. 553.

By man the divine Monad is meant. —S.D. II, p. 196.

[12]Secret Doctrine vol. I, Proem., pp. 42-44

government, politics, economics and the social order readjusted upon sound, sane and divine lines.

III. Man in his lower nature, and in his three vehicles, is an aggregate of lesser lives, dependent upon him for their group nature, for their type of activity, and collective response, and who—through the energy or activity of the solar Lord—will themselves later be raised, and developed to the human stage.

When these three facts are understood, then and only then will we have a right and just comprehension of the nature of man.

Again, this realisation will bring about three changes in the thought of the age:

(1)   *A readjustment of the medical knowledge of man*, resulting in a truer understanding of the physical body, of its treatment, and of its protection, and thus producing a juster apprehension of the laws of health. The aim of the physician will then be to find out what it is in a man's life which is preventing egoic energy from flooding every part of his being; to find out what lines of thought are being indulged in which are causing that inertia of the will aspect which is so conducive to wrong-doing; to ascertain what it is in the emotional body which is affecting the nervous system, and thus obstructing the flow of energy from the love petals of the egoic lotus (via the astral permanent atom) to the astral body, and from thence to the nervous system; to discover what is the hindrance in the etheric body which is preventing the right flow of prana, or of solar vitality to every part of the body.

It is essential that in days to come medical men should realise that disease in the physical body is incidental to wrong internal conditions. This is already being somewhat considered but the whole question will remain but a beautiful theory (even though an incontrovertible one in view of the achievements of mental scientists and of the various faith healers) until the true nature of the ego, its constitution, its powers, and its field of influence are duly apprehended.

This revelation will come when medical men accept this teaching as a working hypothesis, and then begin to note, for instance, the powers of endurance shown by the great souls of the earth, and their capacity to work at high pressure, and to remain practically immune from disease until (at the close of a long life of usefulness) the Ego deliberately chooses to "die-out" of physical existence. It will come when the medical profession concentrates upon the preventative action, substituting sunshine, a vegetarian diet, and the application of the laws of magnetic vibration and vitality for the present regimen of drugs and surgical operations. Then will come the time when finer and better human beings will manifest on earth. When also physicians learn the nature of the etheric body, and the work of the spleen as a focal point for the pranic emanations, then sound principles and methods will be introduced which will do away with such diseases as tuberculosis, debility, malnutrition, and the diseases of the blood and of the kidneys. When doctors comprehend the effect of the emotions upon the nervous system, they will turn their attention to the amelioration of environal conditions, and will study the effects of the emotional currents upon the fluids of the body, and primarily upon the great nerve centres, and the spinal column. When the connection between the dense physical and the subtler bodies is a fact established in medical circles, then will the right treatment of lunacy, of obsessions, and of wrong mental conditions be better comprehended, and the results more successful; finally, when the nature of egoic force, or of energy is studied, and the function of the physical brain as the transmitter of egoic intent is better comprehended, then the coördination of man's entire being will be studied, and illness, debility and disease, will be traced to their just cause, and will be treated through the cause and not just through the effect.

(2) *The entire social world of thought* will apply itself to the understanding of the emotional nature of humanity, to the group relationships involved, and to the interaction between individuals and other individuals, between groups and other groups. These relationships will be interpreted wisely and broadly and a man will be taught his responsibility to the lesser lives which he ensouls. This will produce a just direction of individual force, and its utilisation for the stabilisation, the development, and the

refining of the substance of the different vehicles. Men will also be taught their definite responsibility under law to their own individual families. This will bring about the protection of the family unit, and its scientific development; it will cause the elimination of marital troubles, and the abolition of abuses of different kinds, so prevalent now in many family circles.

Responsibility to the community in which a man is placed will likewise be emphasised. Men will be taught the true esoteric meaning of citizenship—a citizenship based upon egoic group relations, the law of rebirth, and the real meaning of the law of karma. They will be taught national responsibility, and the place of the community within the nation, and of the nation within the comity of nations. Men will finally be taught their responsibility to the animal kingdom. This will be brought about in three ways:

1. Man's truer understanding of his own animal nature.

2. A comprehension of the laws of individualisation, and the effect of the influence of the fourth, or human, kingdom upon the third, or animal, kingdom.

3. The work of an Avatar of a lesser order Who will come in the beginning of the next century to reveal to man his relationship to the third kingdom. His way is being prepared by the many who in these days are developing public interest through the various societies for the benefit and protection of animals, and through the many stories to be found in books and current periodicals.

We are told by H.P.B.[13] that the sense of responsibility is one of the first indications of egoic control, and as more and more of the human family come under egoic influence, conditions will be bettered slowly and steadily in every department of life.

(3) *In the educational world* an apprehension of man's true nature will bring about a fundamental change in the methods of teaching. The emphasis will be laid upon teaching people the *fact* of the Ego on its own plane, the nature of the lunar bodies, and the methods of aligning the lower bodies so that the Ego can

---

[13] IBID vol. III, p. 580

communicate direct with the physical brain, and thus control the lower nature and work out its purposes. Men will be taught how, through concentration and meditation, they can ascertain knowledge for themselves, can develop the intuition, and thus draw upon the resources of the Ego. Then will men be taught to *think*, to assume control of the mental body, and thus develop their latent powers.

In the above few remarks are indicated very briefly and inadequately the results which may be looked for from a true understanding of the essential nature of man. It has been written in view of the necessity these days of a statement as to the real or inner man, and as to the laws of the kingdom of God. That inner man has ever been known to be there, and the "kingdom within" has ever been proclaimed until H.P.B. came and gave out the same old truths from a new angle, giving an occult turn to mystic thought. Now comes the opportunity for man to realise the laws of his own being, and in that realisation those who stand on the verge of intuitional apprehension of knowledge and those of scientific bent who are willing to accept these truths as a working hypothesis to be utilised as a basis for experiment until proven false, will have the chance to solve the world problems from within. Thus will the Christ principle be manifested upon earth, and thus will the Christ nature be demonstrated to be a fact in nature itself.[14]

---

[14]<u>Cosmic Fire</u>, pp. 808-815

Some Tabulations on the Rays

The Rays In and Out of Manifestation

Ray I.....Not in manifestation.
Ray II....In manifestation since 1575 A.D.
Ray III...In manifestation since 1425 A.D.
Ray IV...To come slowly into manifestation around 2025 A.D.
Ray V....In manifestation since 1775 A.D.
Ray VI...Passing rapidly out of manifestation. Began to pass
out in 1625 A.D.
Ray VII..In manifestation since 1675 A.D.

Ray Methods of Teaching Truth

Ray I.....Higher expression: The science of statesmanship, and of government.
Lower expression: Modern diplomacy and politics.

Ray II....Higher expression: The process of initiation as taught by the Hierarchy of Masters.
Lower expression: Religion.

Ray III...Higher expression: Means of communication or interaction. Radio, telegraph, telephone and means of transportation.
Lower expression: The use and spread of money and gold.

Ray IV...Higher expression: The Masonic work, based on the formation of the Hierarchy and related to Ray II.
Lower expression: Architectural construction. Modern city planning.

Ray V....Higher expression: The science of the Soul. Esoteric psychology.
Lower expression: Modern educational systems.

Ray VI..Higher expression: Christianity and diversified religions. Note relation to Ray II.

Lower expression: Churches and religious organisations.

Ray VII..Higher expression: All forms of white magic.

Lower expression: Spiritualism in its lower aspects.

Discipleship and the Rays

1st Ray.. Force.........Energy........Action.......The Occultist
2nd Ray. Consciousness.Expansion...Initiation....The true Psychic
3rd Ray..Adaptation....Development..Evolution...The Magician
4th Ray..Vibration......Response.....Expression..The Artist
5th Ray..Mentation.....Knowledge...Science......The Scientist
6th Ray..Devotion......Abstraction...Idealism.....The Devotee
7th Ray..Incantation....Magic.........Ritual.......The Ritualist[15]

The Rays and the Four Kingdoms

Note: Much information and several interesting hints are scattered here and there in *A Treatise on Cosmic Fire* and in this series of Instructions. I have gathered some of it together and students would find it useful to familiarise themselves with the tabulations and points noted below. A.A.B.

The Numerical Influence of the Rays

The Mineral Kingdom................Rays 7 and 1.
The Vegetable Kingdom.............Rays 2, 4, and 6.
The Animal Kingdom................Rays 3 and 6.
The Human Kingdom................Rays 4 and 5.
The Soul Kingdom...................Rays 5 and 2.
The Planetary Kingdom.............Rays 6 and 3.
The Solar Kingdom..................Rays 1 and 7.

---

[15]Initiation, Human and Solar

The Expression of the Ray Influences

The Mineral Kingdom.......Ray 7......Radiation.
                                 Ray 1......Power.

The Vegetable Kingdom.....Ray 2......Magnetism.
                                 Ray 4......Harmony of colour.
                                 Ray 6......Growth towards light.

The Animal Kingdom........Ray 3......Instinct.
                                 Ray 6......Domesticity.

The Human Kingdom........Ray 4......Experience.
                                 Ray 5......Intellect.

The Kingdom of Souls......Ray 5......Personality.
                                 Ray 2......Intuition.

The Planetary Kingdom.....Ray 6......The Plan.
                                 Ray 3......Creative Work.

The Solar Kingdom..........Ray 1......Universal Mind Will.
                                 Ray 7......Synthetic Ritual.

Some Sets of Correspondences

I. Mineral.............Gonads...............Sacral Centre.
                                           Base of Spine.
    Vegetable..........Heart..................Heart.
                         Lungs.................Throat.
    Animal.............Stomach..............Solar Plexus.
                         Liver
    Human.............Brain..................The two Head
                                         Centres.
                    Vocal Organs

II. Mineral................Base of Spine................Adrenals.
    Vegetable..............Heart Centre...................Thymus.
    Animal.................Solar Plexus...................Pancreas.
    Human.................Sacral Centre.................Gonads.
    Egoic..................Throat Centre.................Thyroid.
    Planetary..............Ajna Centre...................Pituitary.
    Solar..................Head Centre...................Pineal.

III.

	Process	Secret	Purpose
Mineral	Condensation	Transmutation	Radiation.
Vegetable	Conformation	Transformation	Magnetisation.
Animal	Concretisation	Transfusion	Experimentation.
Human	Adaptation	Translation	Transfiguration.
Egoic	Externalisation	Manifestation	Realisation.

Some Notes on the Four Kingdoms

1. The Mineral Kingdom is divided into three main divisions:

    a. The base metals.
    b. The standard metals.
    c. The crystals and precious stones.[16]

Kingdoms

No.	Kingdom	Ray	Expression
1.	Mineral	7. Ceremonial Organisation.	Radio-Activity.
		1. Will or power	The basic reservoir of Power.
2.	Vegetable	2. Love-Wisdom	Magnetism.
		4. Beauty or Harmony.	Uniformity of colour.
		6. Idealistic Devotion.	Upward tendency.
3.	Animal	3. Adaptability	Instinct.
		6. Devotion	Domesticity.

---

[16] A Treatise on Cosmic Fire, p. 588

4. Human.........4. Harmony through...Experience. Growth. Conflict.
   5. Concrete Knowledge.Intellect.

5. Egoic or Soul..5. Concrete Knowledge.Personality.
   2. Love-Wisdom.......Intuition.

6. Planetary Lives.6. Devotion to ideas...The Plan.
   3. Active Intelligence..Creative Work.

7. Solar Lives.....1. Will or Power.......Universal Mind.
   7. Ceremonial Magic..Synthetic Ritual.

The Mineral Kingdom

Influence..............The seventh Ray of Organisation and the first Ray of Power are the dominant factors.

Results................The evolutionary results are radiation and potency, a static potency, underlying the rest of the natural scheme.

Process...............Condensation.

Secret.................Transmutation. *A Treatise on Cosmic Fire* defines this as follows: "Transmutation is the passage across from one state of being to another through the agency of fire."

Purpose...............To demonstrate the radio-activity of life.

Divisions.............Base metals, standard metals, precious stones.

Objective Agency...Fire. Fire is the initiating factor in this kingdom.

Subjective Agency...Sound.

Quality...............Extreme density. Inertia. Brilliance.

The Vegetable Kingdom

Influences.............The second Ray of Love-Wisdom, working out in a vastly increased sensibility.
The fourth Ray of Harmony and Beauty, working out in the general harmonisation

of this kingdom throughout the entire planet.

The sixth Ray of Devotion or (as it has been expressed symbolically in *The Ancient Wisdom*) the "urge to consecrate the life to the Sun, the giver of that life," or again, the "urge to turn the eye of the heart to the heart of the sun."

Results...............These work out in the second kingdom as magnetism, perfume, colour and growth towards the light. These words I commend to you for your earnest study, for it is in this kingdom that one first sees clearly the glory which lies ahead of humanity.

    a. Magnetic radiation. The blending of the mineral and vegetable goals.

    b. The perfume of perfection.

    c. The glory of the human aura. The radiant augoeides.

    d. Aspiration which leads to final inspiration.

Process...............Conformation, or the power to "conform" to the pattern set in the heavens, and to produce below that which is found above. This is done in this kingdom with greater pliability than in the mineral kingdom, where the process of condensation goes blindly forward.

Secret.................Transformation, those hidden alchemical processes which enable the vegetable growths in this kingdom to draw their sustenance from the sun and soil and "transform" it into form and colour.

Purpose...............Magnetism. That inner source of beauty, loveliness and attractive power which lures to it the higher forms to consume it for food, and the thinking entities to draw from it inspiration, comfort and satisfaction of a mental kind.

Divisions..............Trees and shrubs.
　　　　　　　　　　　The flowering plants.
　　　　　　　　　　　The grasses and lesser green things which
　　　　　　　　　　　　do not come under the other two
　　　　　　　　　　　　categories. A group of vegetable growths
　　　　　　　　　　　　which are found under the general
　　　　　　　　　　　　heading of "sea growths."
Objective Agency....Water.
Subjective Agency...Touch.
Quality................Rajas or activity.

Meditation and the Kingdoms

"One-pointed meditation upon the five forms which every element takes produces mastery over every element. These five forms are the gross nature, the elemental form, the quality, the pervasiveness and the basic purpose."

You have, therefore, an analogy for consideration:

1. The gross nature...................the mineral kingdom.
2. The elemental form................the vegetable kingdom.
3. The quality........................the animal kingdom.
4. The pervasiveness................the human kingdom.
5. The basic purpose................the kingdom of souls.

All of this is from the standpoint of consciousness.

Another Relationship

1. The body.......mineral kingdom...the dense prison of life

2. The akasha.....vegetable kingdom.the fluid conscious life

3. Ascension out
   of matter......animal kingdom...the evolutionary goal of
   　　　　　　　　　　　　　　　　　the relation between body
   　　　　　　　　　　　　　　　　　and akasha

4. Power to travel
   in space........human kingdom...the goal of the human con-
   　　　　　　　　　　　　　　　　　sciousness through the

realisation of the above three.

The Animal Kingdom

Influences............The third Ray of Active Intelligence or of Adaptability is potent in this kingdom and will express itself increasingly as time goes on, until it has produced in the animal world that reaction to life and to environment which can best be described as "animal one-pointedness." Then, at this point and cyclically, the sixth Ray of Devotion or Idealism can make its pressure felt as the urge towards a goal, and thus produce a relation to man which makes of him the desired goal. This is to be seen through the medium of the tamed, the trained and the domestic animals.

Results...............In the one case we find the third ray producing the emergence of instinct, which in its turn creates and uses that marvellous response apparatus we call the nervous system, the brain, and the five senses, which lie behind and which are responsible for them as a whole. It should be noted that, wide as we may regard the difference between man and the animals, there is really a much closer relation than that existing between the animal and the vegetable. In the case of the sixth ray, we have the appearance of the power to be domesticated and trained which is, in the last analysis, the power to love, to serve and to emerge from the herd into the group. Ponder on the words of this last paradoxical statement.

Process...............This is called concretisation. In this kingdom we have for the first time a true organisation of the etheric body into what are called "the true nerves and the sensory centres" by the esotericists. Plants also have nerves, but they have in them nothing of the same intricacy of relation and of plexus as we find in the human being and in the animal. Both kingdoms share the same general grouping of nerves, of force centres and channels, with a spinal column and a brain. This organisation of a sensitive response apparatus constitutes, in reality, the densification of the subtle etheric body.

Secret.................This is called transfusion, which is a very inadequate word to express the early blending in the animal of the psychological factors which lead to the process of individualisation. It is a process of life-giving, of intelligent integration and of psychological unfoldment to meet emergency.

Purpose...............This is called experimentation. Here we come to a great mystery and one that is peculiar to our planet. In many esoteric books it has been stated and hinted that there has been a mistake, or serious error, on the part of God Himself, of our planetary Logos, and that this mistake has involved our planet, and all that it contains, in the visible misery, chaos and suffering. Shall we say that there has been no mistake, but simply a great experiment, of the success or failure of which it is not yet possible to judge? The objective of the experiment might be stated as follows: It is the intent of the planetary Logos to bring about a psychological condition which can best be described as one of "divine lucidity."

The work of the psyche, and the goal of the true psychology is to see life clearly, as it is, and with all that is involved. This does not mean conditions and environment, but *Life*. This process was begun in the animal kingdom and will be consummated in the human. These are described in the *Old Commentary* as "the two eyes of Deity, both blind at first, but which later see, though the right eye sees more clearly than the left." The first dim indication of this tendency towards lucidity is seen in the faculty of the plant to turn towards the sun. It is practically non-existent in the mineral kingdom.

Divisions.............First, the higher animals and the domestic animals, such as the dog, the horse and the elephant.

Secondly, the so-called wild animals, such as the lion, the tiger and other carnivorous and dangerous wild beasts.

Thirdly, the mass of lesser animals that seem to meet no particular need nor to fill any special purpose, such as the harmless yet multitudinous lives found in our forests, our jungles and the fields of our planet. Instances of these in the West are the rabbits and other rodents. This is a wide and general specification of no scientific import at all; but it covers adequately the karmic divisions and the general conformation into which these groupings of lives fall in this kingdom.

Objective Agency....Fire and water—fierce desire and incipient mind. These are symbolised in the animal power to eat and drink.

Subjective Agency...Smell or scent—the instinctual discovery of that which is needed, from the activity of ranging forth for food, and the use of the power to scent that food, to the identification of the smell of a beloved master or friend.

Quality................Tamas or inertia—but in this case it is the tamasic nature of mind and not that of matter, as usually understood. The chitta or mind-stuff can be equally tamasic.

The Relation of the Rays to the Centres

1. Head Centre........Ray of Will or Power. First Ray.
2. The Ajna Centre...Ray of Concrete Knowledge. Fifth Ray.
3. The Throat Centre.Ray of Active Intelligence. Third Ray.
4. The Heart Centre..Ray of Love-Wisdom. Second Ray.
5. The Solar Plexus..Ray of Devotion. Sixth Ray.
6. The Sacral Centre. Ray of Ceremonial Magic. Seventh Ray.
7. Base of Spine......Ray of Harmony. Fourth Ray.

The Rays and the Planets

Each of the seven sacred planets (of which our Earth is not one) is an expression of one of the seven ray influences. The student however must remember three things:

1. That every planet is the incarnation of a Life, or an Entity or Being.

2. That every planet, like a human being, is the expression of two ray forces—the personality and the egoic.

3. That two rays are therefore in esoteric conflict in each planet.

The Rays and the Nations

Nation	Personality Ray	Egoic Ray	Motto
India..........4th ray of Art.........1st ray of.........Government			"I hide the Light."

China........3rd ray of Intellect...1st ray of........."I indicate
                                     Government   the Way."

Germany.....1st ray of Power.....4th ray of Art...."I preserve."

France........3rd ray of Intellect...5th ray of........."I release the
                                     Knowledge   Light."

Great Britain.1st ray of Power,....2nd ray of........"I Serve."
        of Government   Love

Italy..........4th ray of Art.........6th ray of........."I carve the
                                     Idealism   Paths."

U. S. A. .....6th ray of Idealism..2nd ray of Love."I light the
                                                    Way."

Russia........6th ray of Idealism...7th ray of Magic."I link two
                                     and Order   Ways."

Austria.......5th ray of Knowledge.4th ray of Art.."I serve the
                                                    Lighted
                                                    Way."

Spain.........7th ray of Order......6th ray of........."I disperse
                                     Idealism   the clouds."

Brazil.........2nd ray of Love......4th ray of Art...."I hide the
                                                    seed."[17]

    I challenge the thinkers of the world to drop their sectarianism, their nationalism, and their partisanships, and in the spirit of brotherhood to work in their particular nation, regarding it as an integral part of a great federation of nations—a federation that now exists on the inner side but waits for the activity of the world thinkers to bring it to materialisation on the outer side. I charge them to work in the cause of religion and in the field of that particular religion in which they, by an accident of birth or by choice, are interested, regarding each religion as part of the great world religion. They must look upon the activities of their group, society or organisation as demanding

---

[17]Esoteric Psychology vol. I, pp. 411-430

their help, just in so far, and only so far, as the principles upon which they are founded and the techniques which they employ serve the general good and develop the realisation of Brotherhood.

I ask you to drop your antagonisms and your antipathies, your hatreds and your racial differences, and attempt to think in terms of the one family, the one life, and the one humanity. I ask for no sentimental or devotional response, to this challenge. I would remind you that hatred and separateness have brought humanity to the present sad condition. I would add to that reminder, however, the fact that there is in the world today a large enough number of liberated men to produce a change in the attitudes of mankind and in public opinion, if they measure up by an act of the will to what they know and believe.

I challenge you also to make sacrifices; to give yourself and your time and your money and your interest to carry these ideas to those around you in your own environment and to the group in which you find yourself, thus awakening your associates. I call you to a united effort to inculate anew the ideas of brotherhood and of unity. I ask you to recognise your fellow workers in all the groups and to strengthen their hands. I ask you to seal your lips to words of hatred and of criticism, and to talk in terms of brotherhood and of group relationships. I beg of you to see to it that every day is for you a new day, in which you face new opportunity. Lose sight of your own affairs, your petty sorrows, worries and suspicions, in the urgency of the task to be done, and spread the cult of unity, of love and of harmlessness.

I ask you also to sever your connection with all groups which are seeking to destroy and to attack, no matter how sincere their motive. Range yourself on the side of the workers for constructive ends, who are fighting no other groups or organisations and who have eliminated the word "anti" out of their vocabulary. Stand on the side of those who are silently and steadily building for the new order—an order which is founded on love, which builds under the impulse of brotherhood, and which possesses a realisation of a brotherhood which is based on the knowledge that we are each and all, no matter what our race, the children of the One Father, and who have come to the realisation that the old ways of working must go and the newer methods must be given a chance.

If you cannot yourself teach or preach or write, give of your thought and of your money so that others can. Give of your hours and minutes of leisure so as to set others free to serve the Plan; give of your money so that the work of those associated with the New Group of World Servers may go forward with rapidity. Much time you waste on non-essentials. Many of you give little or nothing of time. The same is the case with money. Give as never before, and so make the physical aspects of the work possible. Some give of their very need, and the power they thereby release is great. Those on the inner side are grateful for the giving by those who can give only at great personal cost. Others give of what they can spare and only when it needs no sacrifice to give. Let that condition also end, and give to the limit, with justice and understanding, so that the age of love and light may be more rapidly ushered in. I care not where or to whom you give, only that you give—little if you have but little of time or money, much if you have much. Work and give, love and think, and aid those groups who are building and not destroying, loving and not attacking, lifting and not tearing down. Be not taken in by the specious argument that destruction is needed. It has been needed, no doubt; but the cycle of destruction is practically over, could you but realise it, and the builders must now get busy.

I challenge you above all to a deeper life, and I implore you for the sake of your fellow men to strengthen your contact with your own soul so that you will have done your share in making revelation possible; so that you will have served your part in bringing in the light, and will therefore be in a position to take advantage of that new light and new information, and so be better able to point the way and clear the path for the bewildered seeker at that time. Those who are not ready for the coming events will be blinded by the emerging light and bewildered by the revealing wonder; they will be swept by the living breath of God, and it is to you that we look to fit them for the event.[18]

---

[18]IBID vol. I, pp. 187-189